The 33rd

DREXEL UNIVERSITY
College of
Arts and Sciences

Managing Editor····················Sheila Sandapen

Director··························Kathleen Volk Miller
Drexel Publishing Group

Layout Editor·····················William Rees

Graphic Design···················Miles Waldron

Editorial Co-op···················Sharice Maxwell

Digital Communications Co-op······Caitlin McLaughlin

Student Interns···················Sara Aykit
Rachel Bomysoad
Victoria Daughen
Tori Rae Davis
Isabella Fidanza
Michelle Johnson
Katarina Kapetanakis
Lauren Lowe
Maryam Nasir
Koren O'Leary
Laura Somogie
Byshera Williams

Sponsors

Drexel University
The College of Arts and Sciences at Drexel University
The Department of English and Philosophy at Drexel University

Dr. Donna M. Murasko, College of Arts and Sciences,
Drexel University
Dr. Richard Astro, Interim Department Head, English and Philosophy,
Drexel University

The 33rd Volume 9
Drexel University
Department of English and Philosophy
3141 Chestnut Street
Philadelphia, PA 19104
www.5027mac.org

Cover photo by Laurel Gabel

The 33rd is published once a year.

Submissions are open in the spring and winter terms of each academic year. Manuscripts must be submitted as an e-mail attachment (MS Word). Look to www.5027mac.org for submission guidelines.

SBN 978-0-9820717-9-3

Deepest thanks to: Dr. Donna M. Murasko; Dr. Richard Astro; all the judges from the Drexel Publishing Group Essay Contest, the Week of Writing Contest, and the First-Year Writing Contest (Jan Armon, Joshua Benjamin, Ken Bingham, Valerie Booth, Judith Curlee, Ingrid Daemmrich, Albert DiBartolomeo, Anne Erickson, Lisa Farley, Robin Fradkin, Valerie Fox, Cassandra Hirsch, Henry Israeli, Jacqueline Landau, Deirdre McMahon, Karen Nulton, Margene Peterson, Gail Rosen, Fred Siegel, Errol Sull, Maria Volynsky, Marshall Warfield); Department of English and Philosophy, especially Mary Beth Beyer, Eileen Brennen, and Nicole Kline; contest participants; and Drexel Publishing Group staff.

The fonts used within this publication are Archer and Avenir.

XanEdu
Change the course.

Credits:

carrington, andré. "Afrofuturism, and *Fear of a Black Planet* at 25" was originally published in *Sounding Out!*, an online publication, November 9, 2015.

Fox, Valerie. "Insomnia" was previously published in the spring 2016 issue of SOUND:POETREE::Fanzine. "There Are Worms and There Are Butterflies," co-authored by Arlene Ang, was originally published in *Juked*, January 2016.

Israeli, Henry. "Blame the French" was originally published in published in *American Poetry Review* 44.3. March/April 2015.

Kaschock, Kirsten. "Theater in the Wake" was originally published in the online journal thINKing DANCE (www.thinkingdance.net), October 29, 2015.

Kotzin, Miriam. "Goldenrod," was originally published in *Shenandoah*, Spring 2016. "The Letter 'C'" was originally published in *Riverbabble*, Summer 2015. "Aviary" was originally published published in *Boulevard*, Fall 2015, reprinted in *Verse Daily*, Jan 5, 2016, to be included in anthology The Heart is Improvisational ed. Carol Lipsyck, Guernica 2017. All three will be in *Debris Field*, a collection of my poetry to be published in January 2017 by David Robert Books.

Knowles, Scott and Charles Strozier. "How to Honor the Dead We Cannot Name," was originally published online in *Slate*, May 12, 2014.

Levin, Lynn. "Spending Small Change" and "On Knowing One's Goblet at the Banquet Table" was originally published in *The Blue Lyra Review*, 2016. "Buying Produce from the Marked-Down Cart" was originally published in *Rattle*, 2015.

Millan, Harriet. "Axis Mundi," was originally published in The Academy of American Poets, Poem-A-Day. "Just Before" was originally published in *Apiary*. "The Road Between the Rims" was originally published in *Gulf Coast*.

Ottinger, Gwen. "Citizen Engineers at the Fenceline" was originally published in ISSUES IN SCIENCE AND TECHNOLOGY, Winter 2016, p. 72-78, by the University of Texas at Dallas, Richardson, TX.

Riggs, Don. "Alice in the 21st Century" is published in *The Smart Set*, Summer 2016.

Rosen, Gail. "Whedon's Women and the Law:Parallels from Slayers to S.H.I.E.L.D." was originally published in *The Comics of Joss Whedon: Critical Essays*, McFarland, Fall 2015.

Soble, Alan. A version of "The Love Call of F. Scott Fitzgerald" was originally published in *Per Contra*, Issue No. 37, Fall 2015.

Tapia, José. "Toward a New Global Recession? Economic Perspectives for 2016 and Beyond" was originally published in *The Brooklyn Rail*, February 2016.

Volk Miller, Kathleen. "Thanksgiving Tips For Parents of College Freshmen" was originally published in *Brain Child Magazine*, November, 2015.

Warfield, Marshall. "Grace" and "Just Drift" is published in *Paper Nautilus*, Summer 2016.

Warnock, Scott. "Driving Lesson" originally appeared on the website *When Falls the Coliseum*, September 24, 2015.

Welcome

The 33rd anthology is a visible expression of the College of Arts and Sciences' commitment to interdisciplinary scholarship and writing excellence. Within its pages is an eclectic mix of short stories, essays, and scientific articles written by students and faculty from fields across the University. This volume demonstrates the incredible diversity of Drexel scholarship: we are one institution composed of diverse perspectives. These unique perspectives enhance our community and have the power to inspire others to pursue new insights and innovations, whether that's writing the next best-selling novel or discovering a new molecule. But powerful stories and miraculous discoveries are nothing without the skills of communication. These skills allow us to share our ideas, our research, our vision, with the world.

Whether you dream of being an author, an architect, or an environmental scientist, your training starts here with the tools of communication.

Donna M. Murasko, Ph.D.
Dean
College of Arts and Sciences

From the Managing Editor:

Long before I became Managing Editor, I loved bringing *The 33rd* into the classroom to share with my students. It is remarkable to me that the Drexel Publishing Group puts together a collection of writing for students by students. Our students come to Drexel to be engineers, doctors, scientists, business moguls, dancers, designers, or lawyers. Very few come with the idea of being "writers." However, the campus is filled with examples of a viable writing culture: we have writing intensive classes across the disciplines, a thriving student literary magazine, a student newspaper, and several student online publications. Writing is part of this campus.

While the selections included in this anthology are edited for clarity and consistency, it is an editorial decision to leave the writing in their "natural" state. First-year students are taught writing is a process and this process is reflected in these collected works, which are on a trajectory from undergraduate first-year writers to upper class students and beyond. Thus, the writing will vary in theme, genre and perhaps the level of sophistication, but all are true, authentic and excellent representations of the writer's voice. *The 33rd* in bringing together work from current students, showcases a breadth and depth of what happens when students are given a chance to exercise their voices. This anthology also includes current published work from Faculty, which allows students to better understand some of the research and writing their professors are engaged in and to better understand audience and venue.

This collection of student and faculty writing is unique to Drexel and serves as a living document of the ways in which our students and faculty are using writing to think, inquire and start a conversation. Enjoy!

Sheila Sandapen, Ph.D.
Assistant Teaching Professor, College of Arts and Sciences
Managing Editor 2016

Table of Contents

Social Sciences

Zelda Provenzano Endowed STEM Writing Award

Fiction

Poetry

Creative Non-Fiction

Humor

Op-Ed

Faculty Writing

Contributors   221

Writings Arranged by Context

Persuasion

Poetry

First-Year
Writing

All incoming first-year students are expected to take a sequence of courses in writing, in which they explore narration, research, develop rhetorical skills and learn to practice writing as a discipline. The First-Year Writing courses also encourage students to use writing for inquiry, critical thinking and communication.

At the end of the Winter and Spring terms, writing teachers nominate up to 2 students per class for the First -Year Writing contest. The following pages include the winners.

First-Year Writing Merit Winners

Gage Agag
Ramsha Ahmad
Isabella Akhtarshenas
Kristofer Apellid
Sol Betesh
Audra Bishop
Lev Isaac Boonin
Neha Brahmbhatt
Michael Buss
Gowri Cheepurupalli
Kasey Chen
Natalie Christman
Michael Comunale
Chloe Corkery
Rachael Cortese
Alexandru Cristian
Kaleigh DeBowes
Rebecca DeCamp
Simone Dehel
Gabrielle Donatucci
Erin Drennen
Natalya Dyak
Dylan Farnsworth
Kassidy Ferrie
Shannon Frierson
Archer Gandley
Angie Giang
John Godfrey
Adam Grimes
Lauren Guild
Lilliana Guinto
Rob Hamersly
Tiffany Helfrich
Maggie Ho
Harrison Alen Huang
Garrett Hughes
Valerie Iovine
Meera Jain
Momana Jahan
Qiaoping Jiang
Jasmine Jones
Brian Jopling
Mary-Janat Kamagate

Alexander Kaplan
Megan Kebless
Lindsey Kerr
Pedram Keyvani
Ishani Khatiwala
Kaitlin J. Kirby
Sravya Koduri
Timothy Kutchner
Johnathan Lawless
Nick Maloney
Elizabeth McCluskey
Eva McGrath
Emma McTague
Sravani Meka
Rachel Molino
David William Nartey
Anna Nguyen
Eliza Nobles
Jack O'Brien
Virginia Penaloza-Jackson
Brandon Percia
Erika Pleskunas
Susan Reiff
Brooke Rysdon
Tejas Shah
Kateryna Shevchuk
Shayna Singh
Rachel Smith
Gi'Anna Sterling-Donaldson
Heather Tanner
Katherina Tanson
Bini Thankachan
Joshua Thompson
Kyle Tien
Erin Truesdell
Peter Vangelakos
Zoë Vella
Kyle Watson
Virginia Wardell
Erin Wiegman
Guna Yerrabolu
Xiaonan Zhang

Introduction

"Hi, how are you?"
"We have to get together"
"I'll text you"
"Friend me"

Words are complicated code systems. How can you tell when someone is being genuinely empathetic and not just repeating a platitude? The answer to *"How are you?"* is 99.9% of the time "Fine. You?" Some people don't always get this. Those are the people you may want to avoid asking because they will tell you in detail, and, if you don't want to know, it's best not to ask.

How many times do we casually say such phrases to people we encounter during our day? Why do we say it? To be polite? Because it is the norm? Words can become diluted if we throw them about freely and without care.

Words are powerful, that's why our entering First-Year students take a sequence of writing classes. For a ~~student~~ writer [read any writer] the skills of conveying the message, having a defined purpose and identifying a specific audience are skills that need to be practiced and honed. Writing teachers say this over and over in the classroom, in student conferences and in red ink on papers. If a writer cares about the writing, she will pay attention to the details. It is part of the rhetoric that says, I am actually being sincere, therefore, you should listen to me. I will not waste your time.

It is a small thing. But it is everything. Now turn the page and start reading.

Write about something that gives you a reason to write. What your writing will look like: You shall discover an organization that suits both your purpose for writing and the content of what you write.

— Dr. Jan Armon

Julian Whitehouse
Words for Myself

All names have been changed in this essay. — Editor's Note.

This...is not an easy story to tell.

It is a deeply personal story, something which exposes me wholly to the prying eyes of those who care enough to read it. Yet it is also a story I *must* tell, for both myself and for those daunted with similar troubles. I write to make sense of what is and isn't, I write to move on.

I went through several drafts trying to write this, but none of them felt right. The more I try to write my experience as a continuous storyline, the less genuine and the more distant it felt. As humans, we have a natural desire to search for a common thread in our own history, a thirst for a narrative to make sense of our lives. But real life is not coherent enough for the sort of narrative we want. Our lives are too rich, too complex to be neatly framed into dramatic structure with a beginning, climax, and end.

As such, it is better to tell my story in snippets, little glimpses of who I was before, during, and after I came out. Instead of retelling a drama, I instead will try to relay a picture of who I was, who I am, and who I want to be. Chronological order and narrative continuity will be thrown out the window for the sake of essence.

My name is Julian, and I am a transgender man. This is a fragmented soliloquy of why I am.

~

Instead of subscribing to the "dolls for girls, trucks for boys" theory of toy giving, my mother's degree in Education compelled her to theorize that all toys should serve as facets for a child's creative outlet. My childhood was consequently inundated with K'nex and LEGOs, Magnastix and DIY Toy Kits. I loved it, relished the process of creation like a child with an early blooming God Complex. Anton, on the other hand, insisted on acquiring toys of a more generic nature. On the occasions we were allowed to choose our own toys, both

[Handwritten marginal notes: "it's truth", "a story worth telling because of judgement to tell because its true"]

my little brother and I lined the shelves with plastic dinosaurs and off-brand transformers.

The Barbie dolls we did have were stored in a dusty box, all hand-me-downs from one cousin or another. They served their purpose well enough, usually brought out when our play-pretends needed a villain to lead a dark army with. Years later, a tween me would edgily yank the heads off those anorexic dolls in an ill-tempered fit called 'growing up.'

~

The others played, I read. When the teacher told us to write a paragraph about our friends, I began with "Books are my friends, they are always there for me." A Western teacher might have been concerned that a third grader's best friends were literally inanimate objects, but mine just praised me for my studiousness and gave me a big gold star.

It wasn't that I was purposefully anti-social at the tender age of five; boys wouldn't play with me because the skirted uniform I wore marked me as a bearer of cooties. Girls found me too rough and I didn't understand the utterly boring rules they played by; where were the ninjas, the armies? What's the point of pretending to be the father of a family if there weren't any robot swarms to defend my family from?

It was fine, anyway. The classroom library had a wealth of myths and folklore in its collections. Heracles and Odysseus were my playmates, I chased Sun Wukong between the yellowing pages and played hide and seek with Loki. My favorite hero, however, has always been Hua Mulan.

In the original text, no one ever found out what was beneath Mulan's uniform. Instead, she voluntarily returned to her comrades in a dress after the war ended; I could never understand that ending. The years she spent under her male alias felt magical to me. Why would Mulan ever give that up?

~

Puberty came late, but when it came the bastard did quite a number on me. The skinny, stick-like body I was fine with now metastasized in places I hated for growing. Mom bought me a training bra, and I cried because it felt disgusting, uncomfortable, wrong. While the girls in seventh grade displayed their budding bodies proudly in v-necks and skinny jeans, I opted to hide under baggy sweaters and cargo pants.

I grew used to seeing my reflection in the mirror as that of a stranger rather than my own. I frequently stared at 'her' with morbid, self-hating fascination, studying the alien curves and lines she...I had. I hated her for trapping me under her skin.

~

(The following is a short story I wrote in the December of 2014 and eventually published anonymously in the literary club.)

Molt

He flung the bedroom door open. Clumsy feet jammed in painful heels wobbled across the floor before kicking the torturous contraptions into a corner. The dress came next, shimmering silks shredded, vibrant velvets violently torn from his body. Pale white pearls cascaded across the room, the thread broken by a clenched fist and a hard pull.

'Such a pretty girl.'
Their sickly sweet whispers and compliments stuck to him like sticky tar, jamming his ears and clogging his mind until he wanted nothing but to scream and scream and claw off the disgusting layer of skin which belonged to her.

He stared into the wardrobe mirror, at the moonlit reflection of everything that wasn't. A face, weather-beaten from better days spent sparring, now hidden in an itching mask of powder and blush. Hair, that one part his family absolutely refused to let him have his way with, curled by the servants into lush brown ringlets slithering about his shoulders like oily snakes. Wrong, wrong, *wrong*.

His fingernails dug into the grain of the chestnut wardrobe as he fumbled with the roll of linen, wrapping layer upon desperate layer until a cloth viper coiled around his chest and every breath came out strangled. But it wasn't enough.

He couldn't look anymore. Glass shattered, forming jagged circles around the hand that smashed it.

~

"I'm fine with them, I just don't like how they're pushing their agenda on us." Dad commented casually over the dinner table. I chocked a little on my rice before looking up at him.

"What agenda are you even talking about?" an eyebrow raised in skepticism. Tricia joined in on my challenge. Anton nervously refrained from comment.

Dad just chuckled, "I don't care if they're gay or whatever, just don't try to call it marriage, you know? That's only between men and women."

"That's not the point, it's about equal *rights*." I argued, "Marriage gives you rights as partners that you wouldn't have as an unmarried couple."

"It's just not the same." Dad shook his head. "And at the very least they shouldn't spread their propaganda through our schools, don't try to tell my children that they can choose to be *gay*. Anyways, I don't really care what they do if they don't bother me," His expression turned several shades darker as he regarded each of his three children. "As long as none of *you* turn gay, got it? If any of my kids choose *that* lifestyle they won't be accepted as part of *this* family."

I had to hide my shaking hands under table before making an excuse about studying for finals and leaving the dinner table. My father's words terrified me and I could barely understand why. It wasn't like I was 'corrupted.' I was born into a female body, and I liked boys. That made me straight, right?

So why did it feel so wrong?

~

"Are you a lesbian?" Tricia asked out of the blue.

I dropped my pencil on the table and turned from my homework to look at my older sister with a skeptical brow. "Um...no?"

"Are you sure?" She was sprawled on my bed, lazily wasting her weekend off from work. "You cut your hair so *short*."

"That's a stereotype." I rolled my eyes.

"Well, yeah, but everyone's just going to assume you're a lesbian since you also dress like a butch."

"Just because I act a certain way doesn't mean I'm a lesbian."

"You can tell me, you know. I won't tell dad."

"I'm not a lesbian." I shifted uncomfortably. I didn't feel like a girl, that thought had finally wormed its way to my mind by then, but I wasn't sure *what* I was either. I certainly wasn't ready to share that detail while still living under my father's roof.

Either way, I liked boys. There was a period of time where I had questioned that; by stereotype lesbians got to wear boy's clothes and act *masculine*...and that appealed to me. It gave me thrills whenever a cashier or waiter looked at my jagged short hair and cargo pants and called me 'sir', but the 'liking girls' part never worked. So I settled for 'tomboy who is either mistaken for a lesbian or a twelve year old boy' instead, forced to be content as a nebulous question mark in between 'boy' and 'girl.'

~

"Have you ever had any thoughts of self-harm?" the doctor looked over his checklist.

"Sort of." I said flatly, staring down at the hospital sheets. I didn't need to be here, the school was over-reacting.

"Have you thought of how you are going to do it?"

"...yeah."

"Can you describe it for me?"

The ward didn't have any windows to look out of. I couldn't tell night from day, and they took my phone. The nurse even confiscated the plastic knife from my hospital lunch. I rubbed my eyes, feeling tired. "I don't know...every time I look into the mirror, I have this urge to smash it with my fist, I guess."

I didn't want to say more, and I never did. Not even to my parents, not even to the therapists who poked and prodded me for answers. Mother hugged me silently through the night while dad complained over the phone about hospital bills. I retreated further into silence.

I didn't voice the self-hatred I felt every time I looked at my reflection and instead spiraled deeper into depression. I didn't talk about how *wrong* it felt to be born the way I am, how I wished I was a boy instead of a girl.

I *couldn't* talk about it. Dictionaries failed me, I lacked words which described who I was, *what* I was. Other than 'freak of nature' and 'crazy,' I had no words for myself.

~

I came home on the first day of March 2014 and dad was simply...gone. Mom was sobbing alone in the bedroom, and my father's ever-looming presence departed our household for the last time. Everything else were just technicalities, a flurry of signed papers and stone-faced lawyers. He was more than willing to hand custody over to my mom; he had a new family waiting for him, and joint custody of two children would just be a burden.

My father was gone. He was the ticking bomb the entire family had to tiptoe around lest he exploded (and that was always just a matter of time). He was the patriarch who flung casual homophobia and racism around the room and constantly told me to 'be more girly' and 'act more feminine.' There was grief, there was anger, but most of all there was a near guilty sense of relief.

~

It was lunchtime, and for the hundredth time Gina was talking about how much she wished her chest was smaller so it wouldn't hurt her back so much. I replied — only half-jokingly and *also* for the hundredth time — about how much I hated my own chest and wished I could get rid of them entirely. This time around, Gina followed her laughter by a looked that was a little bit *too* concerned.

"Have you ever considered the possibility that, well..." She frowned thoughtfully. "That you're trans?"

I snickered through a mouth full of peanut butter and jelly. "Isn't that when dudes dress up like ladies or something?"

"No, that would be called drag." Gina shook her head in disapproval then went into her teaching mode. "Transgender means someone who is a boy but was born into a female body, or a girl who was born into a male body."

"I..." I was at a loss for words, my lips half-parted in surprise. I never knew there was a *word* for how I felt. The word promised a community, but it also promised *change*. Like all human beings I was afraid of change, instinctively tried to reject it. I pursed my lips and stared down into my PB&J. My voice was quiet. "...I don't know. I don't think so."

Gina gave me her mother-hen smile and patted me on the shoulder, knowing when to change the subject. Later on, I started a search into that term with the fervor of a madman. The more I learned, the more the term resonated with me. I could just...*be* a boy. There was nothing wrong with me simply *being* a boy, body be damned. I nearly cried while looking at medical terms, face dimly lit by a computer screen at midnight.

Yet the fear grew stronger too. If I was transgender...there was a figurative hell to go through to be who I am. Bigotry, discrimination, violence...it was a scary truth to be. For months I danced around the issue, not yet ready to call myself the boy I was.

~

The silence stretched like a rubber band, and never have I been so scared in my life. I loved my mother so much, I *needed* her to understand, *needed* her to accept me. Could she ever love me as a son?

The silence broke with a snap, releasing a flood of well-intentioned, misinformed words which hurt more than I could have imagined. I was just traumatized from the divorce. It was just a phase. I wore plenty of dresses as a child, I couldn't possibly be a man. I was so *feminine*.

"...I think you just need to find a man who will make you feel like a woman again."

"It's not like that, mom. Sexuality and gender are separate things. I'm a gay man. I don't *want* someone to love me as a woman, I want someone to love me as a *man*." But I was too crushed to explain properly, and she was too shocked to listen. It was too much. I made up the age-old excuse that I needed to finish homework and started my escape upstairs.

"Julia, wait." The birth name was simply adding salt to my wounds, but I turned around.

"No matter what happens, I'll always love you, okay?" Mom said. She pulled me into a hug, and I realized just how small she was, how much taller I have grown. I could barely see through the tears pooling up around my eyes.

"I love you too, mom." I said, and it felt like an acceptable time to start bawling like a toddler.

~

Hello Mr. _____!

This is "Julia" from your Robotics class. I apologize for disturbing you but I just wanted to inform you of a situation of mine. I am FTM transgender and recently came out in school, and I've begun to socially transition to my identified gender.

Transgender is the state in which one's gender identity or gender expression does not match one's assigned sex. Basically, transgender means the gender which I was assigned at birth does not match up with the gender identity inside my head, and the FTM part is short for "female-to-male." The simplest way to summarize this is that I am a boy who was born into a girl's body. I understand that this can be kind of confusing and I don't blame you if you do not completely understand.

Nonetheless, I refer to myself as "Julian" and use male pronouns when referring to myself. I feel that I would be more comfortable and that I would succeed the most in your class if you can call me by the name "Julian" instead of "Julia" from now on and refer to me with male pronouns such as "he" and "him." I would also be grateful if you can allot me one or two minutes at the beginning of class so I can explain to my classmates about my change of name and pronouns.

Thank you for your patience and understanding! If you have any questions or concerns, please feel free to email me back or stop me at the beginning or end of class to discuss it with me.

Sincerely,

Julian

I liked the ending up

Writing is much more than putting words on a paper. Explain a unique experience or attitude you have had with writing in the larger sense. What made it valuable for you? Why should your audience care about it? Wow us with smoothness and clarity.

— Professor Charles Haub

Russell H. Souders III

Healing Through Writing

On April 1st, 2011, I deployed to Kandahar, Afghanistan as a medic. Four months later I pronounced a child dead. Two months after that, I saw a twelve-year-old boy suffer a gunshot wound to the leg because he was simply in the wrong place at the wrong time. Every little detail has been etched into my mind, as permanently as an artist's ink on paper. In the few months after those experiences, my ability to tolerate these images within my brain was beginning to wane. It was an emotional struggle that I was beginning to lose.

How did I overcome it? I continue to ask myself. I can't say that I've completely won the war against post-traumatic stress, but I've definitely beaten back the tide of difficult emotions. I did many things to help calm my fears and doubts about what I had seen. I talked to my friends, who shared in the difficulty of these experiences with me. I talked to my superiors, who saw the same and worse, and they gave me their most sincere advice. The best thing I did, though, didn't involve talking to anybody about anything. Driven by emotional will and desperation, I wrote a story.

Using words and an emphasis on metaphor, I put onto paper all the emotional turmoil that I could. I used creative writing as an introspective means to deal with what I had seen. Was it effective? I cannot be sure of the specific outcome writing has had on my emotions, but I am sure that it had at least a minor role in improving my ability to cope with my memories.

However, is this true for everyone? Post-traumatic stress does not only affect soldiers, but is also associated with many other disturbing experiences, such as the sudden loss of a loved one, sexual assault, or a physically painful experience. For many, drinking and drug abuse seem the most effective in dealing with these issues. However, what if they had the same opportunity and mindset as I did... to project their emotions through writing? Does creative writing truly allow those suffering from post-traumatic stress to more easily recover?

According to some research, the answer may be a resounding "yes." Joshua Smyth, a researcher at Syracuse University, studied the effectiveness of expressive writing on the symptoms and moods of individuals suffering from PTSD, including military veterans. The experimental group, who wrote specifically about their traumatic experiences, showed "...significantly greater reductions in tension... anger... and depression..." than the control group upon follow-up (89). The results are similar to past experiments measuring writing's effect on mood, showing a correlation between expressive writing and long-term improvement (Smyth et al 91).

Emotional mood swings and angry outbursts have rarely been a problem for me following my writing experience. Although I've sometimes become extremely emotional reflecting on my traumatic experiences, I've been able to handle these situations fairly well. On the other hand, many soldiers I've talked to have suggested that their disturbing memories have led them to be easily aggravated, especially when reminded of the experience, or when their military service seemed undervalued. I've asked some of these soldiers, those who were my friends, if they had tried writing out their experiences in much the same way that I did. Only a very few had done so. However, those few authors have had fewer issues than those who did not put their thoughts onto paper.

So, writing has helped me and a few of my friends in dealing with our trauma, but why is writing such a good way to deal with stress? Geoff Lowe, a researcher at the University of Hull's Department of Clinical Psychology, reviewed multiple studies and clinical uses of writing as a psychological treatment. Overall, he saw trends that writing, when paired with other psychological therapeutic methods such as psychological counseling and discussion groups, improved the emotional and physiological states of individuals suffering from general stress (60). Lowe affirms that these expressive writing exercises "... can represent a direct line from feeling and thinking to healing..." and that as more research is conducted, more theories are being developed to explain the possible benefits of writing in psychologically-suffering patients (67).

If writing is such an effective way to deal with post-traumatic stress, why hasn't it been implemented in all psychological treatments for those suffering from its symptoms? I must admit, after I had written my short stories regarding my trauma, I was unable to read through the entirety of my story without emotionally breaking down. Even during the writing, I couldn't suppress the disturbing images brought on by remembering the very events I was describing. So, are there negative aspects of writing about post-traumatic stresses?

In Lowe's research of writing as a treatment for PTSD, many experiments showed very severe, intense effects that writing can have on individuals. One study showed that immediately following a writing exercise, patients reported worse mood states and even had worse symptoms. Without additional peer or psychological counseling, "Writing (privately) about intensely personal experiences does not allow for an objective outside opinion, support from others, or helpful coping information" (64). In Smyth's experiment, there was at least one individual studied who could not complete the writing task because the emotional feedback was too intense for him to continue (Smyth et al 91). These studies not only point to further acute mental distress due to writing, but that it may even be MORE stressful than other coping mechanisms. Despite the long-term benefits, writing therapy can sometimes be too intense to perform without some type of emotional peer counseling.

Thankfully, I had coupled my writing with much peer counseling. As I mentioned earlier, I talked on many occasions with my comrades to find other ways to deal with my emotional issues. Some said they prefer to exercise as a way to deal with their stress. Others suggested having a beer or two at the end of the day to calm my nerves. Despite combining their coping methods with my own, nothing has COMPLETELY eliminated all my symptoms of post-traumatic stress. Though rare, there are situations in which flashbacks and panic come unbidden into my mind. The severity of the emotional attack can vary, but it has been serious at times. Was my writing really effective, then, at treating my symptoms?

In Smyth's experiment, writing was shown to improve mood states in the long term. However, when it came to the frequency and intensity of PTSD symptoms, "Both [control and experimental] groups had (non-significant) decreases in re-experiencing, avoidance, and hyperarousal from baseline to follow-up" (89). In other words, even after writing about their experiences, individuals still experienced flashbacks, still avoided situations that may have triggered flashbacks, and still had intense physiological symptoms from these flashbacks. Smyth's experiment shows, like Lowe's research, that expressive writing alone does not alleviate symptoms of PTSD. No matter the benefits on mood in patients, the actual psychological symptoms of post-traumatic stress cannot be treated with writing alone.

As I look at this research and think on my own experiences, I have to ask myself, "Did writing about my traumatic experiences truly help me cope with what I had seen?" My generally pleasant mood is at least partially the result of my writing. As an introspective method of self-reflection, writing has allowed me to address issues privately on a level unavailable with peer counseling. On the other hand, the actual writing was very stressful and ultimately did not eliminate all my post-traumatic stress symptoms. It appears, however, that as an adjunct to professional and personal counseling, writing can be a very effective supplement to the recovery experience. In the end, I may never forget the faces of the injured I've treated overseas. I'll always be affected by the things I've experienced. However, by writing about these unforgettable moments, I may have at least saved myself from a lifetime of depression and anger. If writing can do that for me, perhaps it can work for others, too.

Works Cited

Lowe, Geoff. "Health-Related Effects of Creative and Expressive Writing." *Health Education* 106.1 (2006): 60-70. Web.

Smyth, JM, JR Hockerneyer, and H. Tulloch. "Expressive Writing and Post-Traumatic Stress Disorder: Effects on Trauma Symptoms, Mood States, and Cortisol Reactivity." *British Journal Of Health Psychology* 13.1 (2008): 85-93. Web.

For this project you will be teaming up in groups of two and exploring the pivotal concepts of happiness, success, purpose or meaning in human life. Your project will argue in support of a specific hypothesis, using high-quality research to support your views. The paper should also analyze philosophical or cultural ideas that have influenced your views about these concepts.

-Professor Bob Finegan

John Buccieri and Haley McMenamin

Losing Our Minds

On January 17, 2014, the lives of Jim and Stacy Holleran, parents of 19 year old Madison Holleran, would be changed forever. The Holleran parents had every reason to be proud of their daughter. She was a well-known track star at the prestigious University of Pennsylvania, considered "popular, attractive, and talented" amongst her peers, and her Instagram flourished and shined with pictures that showed her "smiling, dappled in sunshine or kicking back at a party" (Scelfo). Through the scope of social media, everything seemed to be going right for Madison Holleran. Her life seemed to be the epitome of happiness. Yet, no one knew the internal struggles going on inside her, constantly battling with anxiety, depression, and thoughts of suicide. Through the scope of her own eyes, Madison looked at her life as inferior to others, not seeing any true purpose to her own. These feelings culminated on that fateful day of January 17, 2014, when an hour before ascending a Penn parking garage, Madison Holleran posted "a dreamy final photo of white holiday lights twinkling in the trees of Rittenhouse Square," and scribbled down her last words on a note, detailing gifts she was leaving to family (Scelfo). Atop the parking garage, Madison Holleran took her final breath as she stepped off the roof of the parking garage, falling to her death. Not too long after her death, Kathryn Dewitt, another student at the University of Pennsylvania, also suffering from depression, posted a response on her blog, "What the hell, girl?! I was supposed to be the one who went first! You had so much to live for!"

Madison Holleran was not the first Penn student to take her own life that year. She was the third of six students at Penn to commit suicide in a span of thirteen months. Other universities also experienced suicide clusters similar to the University of Pennsylvania. In the 2014 school year, Tulane University lost four students to suicide, and in the 2009-10 academic year, Cornell University lost six of its own students (Scelfo). The patterns of these suicide clusters are not randomly happening from year to year. They are part of a trend in suicide rates among people ages 15 to 24 years old that has been growing steadily from 2007: from 9.6 deaths per 100,000 to 11.2 deaths per 100,000 as of 2013 (Center for Disease Control and Prevention). Moreover, this trend is not the only one to show an increase over recent years. It is only one of many increases in mental health diseases taking part in an epidemic that is beginning to sweep through the minds of today's youth.

The rise of depression and anxiety in adolescents and young adults has also had significant correlations with the steady rise of suicide rates in the same demographic. A study lead by Jean Twenge, a professor of psychology at San Diego State University, found that rates of depression and anxiety have been increasing in adolescents and young adults for over the last five to seven decades (Gray). Along with this rise, as of 2013, suicide hit a new apex, becoming the fourth leading cause of death of people from ages 10 to 14, and the second leading cause of death of people ages 15 to 34 (Center for Disease Control and Prevention). Likewise, anxiety and depression are now the two most commonly diagnosed mental health diseases diagnosed among college students (Center of Collegiate Mental Health at Penn State). Young adults, ages 18 to 25, make up the highest percentage of 15.7 million adults who suffer from depression in the United States, and 10.7% of the adolescent population, ages 12 to 17, of the United States suffer from depression yearly. (National Institute of Mental Health). The trends are telling of something very disastrous that is happening to the youth of today's world; their general happiness is decreasing. Yet, no explanation exists to explain why these rates are on rise. The most puzzling reality of it all is that mental health disorders in humans are increasing in an environment that is much more benign than the times of 20th century. More people are living longer today, are generally making more money, and are capable of providing for their families. Yet, anxiety and depression rates now are greater now than they were during times like the Great Depression or World War II (Gray). These trends did not fluctuate drastically up or down during times of war or peace, economic turmoil or flourishment; instead they just kept steadily rising, slowly but surely, offering no correlation between the way the world changes. The data suggests that there is simply no relationship to suggest why these rates are on the rise in a world that is significantly more stable than it was one hundred years ago. The potential answer lies in a different place, not looking at how the surrounding environmental changes influence a person, but rather the way a person defines self-worth relative to happiness.

The idea of self-worth as a human characteristic has been around since the earliest times of man. Self-worth is linked to a human's capability of being self-aware, because their history in the human psyche can be seen as linked. Humans evolved from beings that "lived in groups that rewarded members for living up the common values, norms, and ideals." The people that could "adjust their actions to meet those standards fared better" than those who were not capable (Baumeister and Tierney 114). Humans growing self-aware involved a process of comparing one's self to societal standard (Baumeister and Tierney 112). In order for a person to understand where a standard is in relation to where it should be requires some level of self-awareness. Along with the rise of self-awareness in order to examine what societal standards were came the rise of the ability for people to be able to measure how well they met those standards. This ability can be thought of as self-worth.

In the early development of self-worth, the standards that humans were comparing themselves with and trying to meet were relatively simple, and thus the psychological factors that governed it were also of the same simplicity. However, as humans' unique capability of higher thinking, and thus the possibility of more complex emotions, grew more prominent through evolution, complexities formed in the way people measure self-worth because societal standards became more involved (Rottenburg). What was once a societal standard to eat to survive turned into formations of gathered meals which in turn formed proper etiquette for meal times. What was once an easy task for the brain to handle began to grow more demanding of the mind. As complexities in the way people measured self-worth enumerated, so did the number of things that could go wrong. Depression, anxiety, and suicide are three very common manifestations of the way the use of self-worth can maliciously affect the human mind.

One of the main symptoms of depression is "low self-esteem and the constant feeling of hopelessness," and the highest mental disease coupled with it is anxiety (Clinicalkey Journal). The American Psychologist Association defines depression as experiencing prolonged feelings of "self-worthlessness." Emile Durkheim, famous 19th century sociologist, argued in his 1897 theory titled "Le Suicide" that "suicidal feelings occur in response to a person's relationship with society," that is, people feel as if they are no longer connected to society (Tingley). When people feel disconnected from society since they are not meeting the standards of societal culture, their self-worth is diminished. When there is failure for this self-worth to be brought back up to societal standards, the process repeats, lowering a person into depressive habits, anxious routines, and, ultimately, suicidal tendencies. The repeated diminishing of a person's self-worth causes a feeling of shame, which serves as a societal byproduct of the realization that societal norms are not being met. Cognitively, the feeling of shame serves as a way for the mind to know if an action is morally acceptable based on social standards (Holloway). Shame is most prevalent in young adolescents, when the mind is still developing and malleable, since it helps for youth to learn what is socially acceptable and what is not (Holloway). However, there is a limit to how much shame can be psychologically beneficial. In today's world, where standards are becoming more and more complex, it is much easier for a person to fall into the cycle of being shamed by society. It is within the concept of shame that an answer to the steady rise of depression, anxiety, and suicide in adolescents and young adults can be found.

Fyodor Dostoyevsky, the 19th century Russian novelist and philosopher, captures the idea of shame in the human mind in a quote from his novel Notes From The Underground:

> "Every man has reminiscences which he would not tell to everyone, but only to his friends. He has other matters in his mind which he would not reveal even to his friends, but only to himself, and that in secret. But there are other things which a man is afraid to tell even to himself, and every decent man has a number of such things stored away in his mind" (qtd. in Holloway 242).

Dostoyevsky highlights the fact that the idea of shame leads people to form masks that make society think they're meeting up with cultural norms set in place. People are reluctant to bring forth their true personalities because they lack what society deems as the right thing to be. They are afraid of what others think, sometimes they are afraid even to accept truths about themselves. Today's culture, not only in the United States, but in all of world, supports an environment where shame is prevalent. Societal standards no longer support the same purpose they did when self-awareness and self-worth were developing. Instead of allowing people to keep in check with societal standards as to remain a part of the community, today's societal standards support a social isolation instead. Harry Holloway, a professor of psychiatry, in his commentaries on Thomas Scheff's "Shame and Community: Social Components of Depression" highlights how extreme shameful behavior – as deemed by society – promotes social isolation. There are three main cases of social isolation: self-initiated, initiated by others, or both (Holloway). Holloway uses the example that if someone receiving psychiatric care for an anxiety disorder or depression were to openly identify as psychiatrically ill, then shame from society would immediately follow. Likewise, in society, homosexuality tends to be kept secret, while heterosexual encounters are often put on display in public (Holloway). In each case, some form of social isolation is occurring because societal standards do not agree with the behavior these people are displaying. Therefore, the people displaying these behaviors isolate that portion of their personality that harbors the tendency to go away from societal norm. In short, they create a mask.

This type of thinking is causing the adolescents and young adults of today's society, who are dealing with more complex societal standards, to alter the ways they think in order to be what society calls right. Before, societal standards were used in order to achieve survival, as Baumeister and Tierney suggest. Today, societal standards are instead being used to achieve a much more complex emotion, happiness. People today are using their self-worth in society to measure their happiness, when in reality, happiness has a plethora of dimensions beyond self-worth. In looking at Holloway's examples, the only reason those people were isolated in the first place was because society said their actions were wrong. What does being gay have to do with self-worth? How does suffering from a mental illness reduce a person's value? The answer is absolutely nothing. Yet, people are being distorted into thinking that their happiness is solely based off the way they fit into societal norms, but this notion is completely wrong. In the environment people are in, they are defining self-worth as happiness. They only are seeing things from a very narrow scope, in which the societal standards are the center point. The shame society brings for not meeting these standards causes for reality to become distorted, and when this happens, happiness can also become skewed.

Tim Urban, writer for the website "Wait But Why," came up with an equation that can easily generalize a measurement of someone's happiness:

The relationship is simple: if the reality of someone's world turns out to be greater than their expectations, then the expression on the right will turn out positive, resulting in happiness. However, if expectations are greater, the expression on the right will end up being negative, resulting in sadness. A problem arises, however, when one of the terms in the expression is erroneously represented. Since the reality of the youth's world is being skewed by societal standards, the reality variable can never come out to be positive, because people who live in a reality governed by societal standards they can never achieve will always have a negative outlook on the reality they are set in.

Doctor Peter Gray, a research professor of psychology at Boston College, notes the distortion of today's youth's reality in the way today's generation focuses more on extrinsic goals, or goals with material rewards, than intrinsic goals, or goals with rewards in the person's development or philosophy of life, which were more prevalent in the 1970s and 1980s. Gray relates this shift towards a shift in adolescents and young adults believing more in an external locus of control (control by circumstances outside the person), than an internal locus of control (control by the person) as proven by an experiment conducted by Jean Twenge. The experiment was conducted on people from ages 9-14 and college students, and used a test developed by Julien Rotter measured on the Rotter's scale (the actual experiment used a scale that was similar to the Rotter's scale, but designed for children). The test consisted of 23 questions that could be answered with the following choices:

(a) I have found that what is going to happen will happen.

(b) Trusting to fate has never turned out as well for me as making a decision to take a   definite course of action.

Choice A corresponds with external locus of control and choice B corresponds with internal locus of control. Thus, it makes sense with the results of the experiment showing a shift towards an external locus to believe that there is some correlation between the youth of today being more oriented on extrinsic goals. Extrinsic goals are not controlled nearly as much by the person as they are by circumstances outside of the person with that goal. It takes much more personal control over one's mind to obtain a positive philosophy on life than earning positive judgement from others. The idea of having to meet societal standards follows a path that is more focused on outside control, being told what to do. Both Twenge and Gray agree that the rise of these extrinsic goals is related to the materialistic values held in today's society. The youth of today have society pressuring everything they should do, implying materialistic values like "happiness depends on good looks, popularity, and material goods", all things pushed by an external locus (Gray). In agreement with Twenge and Gray on this idea is Doctor Jonathan Rottenberg.

Jonathan Rottenberg, professor of psychology at the University of South Florida, recently examined two studies lead by Iris Mauss. Each study found that people who valued more happiness were actually less likely to achieve their goals becoming happy. In the first study, people who valued happiness were more likely to identify with statements such as "If I don't feel happy, maybe there is something wrong with me," and "To have a meaningful life, I need to feel happy most of the time" (Rottenburg). The second experiment reached the same conclusion, that "paradoxically, valuing happiness more may lead people to be less happy, especially when happiness is within reach" (Rottenburg). Rottenburg associates this counterintuitive trend much to the similar reason that Gray and Twenge associate the rise of extrinsic goal thinking with the way society externally controls the thoughts of people, specifically youth. He evaluated the way that the "current cultural ethos is that achieving happiness is like achieving other goals." Those goals are the materialistic societal standards set in place for the minds of the youth to absorb. Rottenburg takes this a step further, associating this trend with the idea of low mood thinking, a cognitive process in which humans attempt to analyze a low mood being experienced in order to understand why they are feeling that emotion (Rottenberg). Rottenberg summarizes this process well, stating "If I understand why I feel bad, then I know how to fix." This notion is not completely wrong, but can lead to humans developing depressive and anxious tendencies.

Rising happiness standards widen the gap between what humans want to feel and what humans actually feel (Rottenburg). This widening gap presents dangers to this going through the process of low mood thinking. During low mood thinking, when a standard cannot be reached, the shame felt will cause a person to enter a low mood. In this low mood, that person begins to examine the current emotions in order find what onset those emotions. Now, however, the person realizes that the problem lies inside him or herself. Due to the extrinsic values that today's youth are thinking with, they do not think their problem lies within corrupted societal standards, but rather themselves. The cause of the low mood shifts "its focus from a problematic environment to a problematic self" (Rottenburg).

For example, imagine the current environment that teenagers and adolescents have to grow up in. Despite the world being an overall more benign place physically, the surroundings of a teenager or young adult are much more hostile mentally. Judgement is always peering around a corner. Picture a boy, 16 years of age, growing up in that world where his reality is distorted into thinking that his fate is controlled by something outside of his control. This teenager is slightly overweight with acne, socially awkward, and not the most athletic or intelligent person. Picture a girl, of the same age, who is smart, intelligent, and beautiful, going through the tough transitional period of adolescence, where she is pressured by the promiscuity of society. Each sees the advertisements on TV promoting the image of perfection, each sees the posts on social media from their peers promoting image of friendship, each feels the harassment of peers at school promoting the image of a problematic self. They feel socially isolated because they are not meeting today's societal standards. They feel their self-worth lower from onset shame, and they mask their true personalities. They try to conform, but it takes its toll on their minds. Despite conforming, they still feel no happiness. In their low moods, each equates their self-worth to the way they match societal standards, and, in their skewed realities, realize that they are to blame for not meeting the extrinsic value of society, seeing no intrinsic value in themselves. They feel no control over their minds or their lives. Each contemplates what the world would be without them, seeing no benefits, no worth of them being locked in it. Each writes their respective suicide notes, one who by society was in error, the other, who on the surface, by society, had everything. Each kills themselves, and society praises them as heroes.

It is no wonder why the rates of depression, anxiety, and suicide in adolescents and young adults is increasing. Today's society nurtures a breeding ground much more potent for mental illnesses than the society of one hundred years ago did. Modern culture fosters an environment where an external locus of control is favored by the youth, and it was proven in Twenge's experiment that those who identified closer with an external locus of control became depressed (Gray). Extrinsic goals are becoming more popular because materialistic values are becoming more accepted. There is no longer any sense of control over a person's fate. Intrinsic goals are becoming a thing of the past. Instead of striving to become a better person based on internal values, people are seeking acceptance from others. There is this perception that "nobody wants to be the one who is struggling while everyone else is doing great" (Scelfo). If a person so much as falters, social shame is right there to take away any idea of self-worth. That person then falls into the same cyclical pattern of low mood thinking many depressed people go through every day. They come to the conclusion that they are to blame, because society forced them to value self-worth in incorrect philosophy. Adolescents and young adults no longer have full control over their being, because societal standards play too much of a role in measuring happiness. They are, quite literally, losing their minds.

The night Madison Holleran decided to commit suicide, she took some time in her final hour to write a suicide note that cryptically warns about the constant pressure to meet all social standards. The note reads:

> "I thought how unpleasant it is to be locked out, and
> I thought how it is worse perhaps to be locked in. For
> you mom... the necklaces... For you, Nana & Papa...
> GingerSnaps (always reminds me of you)... For you
> Ingrid... The Happiness Project. And Dad... the Godiva
> chocolate truffles. I love you all... I'm sorry. I love you."

Her first lines express the same thought processes that so many people going through depression feel. Madison Holleran was a person who, on the surface level, across all kinds of social media, seemed to have it all. Yet, she felt locked out from society, experiencing the disconnect Durkheim talks about, because she could not obtain the high standards of happiness. The gap between what humans feel and want to feel was too wide for Madison. It was too hard to maintain that societal picture of happiness that everyone thought she had. So she released herself from being locked in, using the only answer she though viable: suicide. Madison was one of the many victims to be claimed by the way society dictates a person's view on happiness. There is an obvious epidemic sweeping through the adolescents and young adults, and it's causing them to lose their minds. The first step to a cure is simple: stop defining happiness solely based on social standards.

Work Cited

Baumeister, Roy F, and John Tierney. *Willpower: Rediscovering the Greatest Human Strength*. New York: Penguin Books, 2012. Print.

Center for Disease Control and Prevention as cited in Scelfo, Julie. "Suicide on Campus and the Pressure of Perfection." *The New York Times*. The New York Times, 01 Aug. 2015. Web. 25 Oct. 2015.

Center for Collegiate Mental Health as cited in Scelfo, Julie. "Suicide on Campus and the Pressure of Perfection." *The New York Times*. The New York Times, 01 Aug. 2015. Web. 25 Oct. 2015.

Dewitt as cited in Scelfo, Julie. "Suicide on Campus and the Pressure of Perfection." *The New York Times*. The New York Times, 01 Aug. 2015. Web. 25 Oct. 2015.

Durkheim as cited in Tingley, Kim. "The Suicide Detective." *The New York Times*. The New York Times, 29 June 2013. Web. 5 Nov. 2015.

Gray S, Pete. "The Decline of Play and Rise in Children's Mental Disorders." *Psychology Today*. Sussex Publishers, 26 Jan. 2010. Web. 25 Oct. 2015.

Goldman, Stuart J. "Depression in Children and Adolescents." *ClinicalKey*. Elsevier Inc., 14 Mar. 2014. Web. 25 Oct. 2015.

Holloway, Harry C. "Commentary on "Shame and Community: Social Components in Depression": Shame, Loss of Face, and Other Complexities: Which is Cause, which is Effect, and how does it Work?" *Psychiatry* 64.3 (2001): 242-7. *ProQuest*. Web. 12 Nov. 2015.

Mauss as cited in Rottenburg, Jonathan. "You're Making Your Depression Worse: Self-help Is Bringing Us down." *Saloncom RSS*. N.p., 16 Feb. 2014. Web. 29 Oct. 2015.

National Institute of Mental Health. "Major Depression Among Adolescents." *NIMH RSS*. National Institute of Health, 2013. Web. 23 Oct. 2015.

National Institute of Mental Health. "Major Depression Among Adults." *NIMH RSS*. National Institute of Health, 2013. Web. 23 Oct. 2015.

Rottenburg, Jonathan. "You're Making Your Depression Worse: Self-help Is Bringing Us down." *Saloncom* RSS. N.p., 16 Feb. 2014. Web. 29 Oct. 2015.

Scelfo, Julie. "Suicide on Campus and the Pressure of Perfection." *The New York Times*. The New York Times, 01 Aug. 2015. Web. 25 Oct. 2015.

Tingley, Kim. "The Suicide Detective." *The New York Times*. The New York Times, 29 June 2013. Web. 5 Nov. 2015.

Twenge as cited in Gray S, Pete. "The Decline of Play and Rise in Children's Mental Disorders." *Psychology Today*. Sussex Publishers, 26 Jan. 2010. Web. 25 Oct. 2015.

This project's broad focus is education in general. Your challenge is to identify a relatively narrow topic within that broad focus that you're curious about and to which you have some personal connection. As we work through the readings and videos during the first half of the term, reflect on your own experiences in school and how they have shaped you, for better or for worse. Identify a subtopic related to education that intrigues you enough to sustain you through a process of investigation. From your personal POV, what's right and what's wrong about our educational system?

-Dr. Donna Rondolone

Sean Kirker

Art & Education in America

Art isn't being taken seriously in this country. We are falling behind as a country, our test scores are lower than other countries, we are dropping in the rankings as a superpower, and these huge achievement gaps are just the tip of the iceberg that is the failing American academic system. Taking time out of the day to have a class dedicated to art is now considered a "waste." We are focusing all of our time, energies, and efforts into S.T.E.M (Science Technology Engineering Math) majors, basically industrializing the education process, leaving the arts in the dust. Art degrees are laughed at, and kids who indicate a desire to go to an art school or a major in an art discipline are told that they are "wasting their money." Because of this stigma attached to the arts that has formed over recent decades, schools are pulling away from the arts programs in their schools. This same pull away from the arts has coincided with America's decline in ranking. Is there a relationship here? Do the arts, in particular, visual arts, have any academic benefits? Is this why the American school system is failing?

Visual arts stimulate areas of the brain not otherwise stimulated throughout a typical school day. The United Nations Educational, Scientific and Cultural Organization (and published in Anne Bradford's "The WOW Factor: Global research compendium on the impact of the arts in education") conducted multiple studies on arts integration all over the world, focusing on different topics in different regions, all stemming from the central theme of results from reintegrating art into everyday curriculum. Teachers who incorporated art into their everyday curriculum spoke of how "the increased engagement students evidenced in arts units seemed to help them remember more" (Bamford). The students' minds had a different way of approaching the information being presented to them. When arts are incorporated into the curriculum/ atmosphere, it inspires the student to use different pathways and avenues not typically explored, which makes "more analytical and more oriented towards conceptual understanding than factual recollection. Further, their affective connections with the content they studied were generally deeper and vastly more positive and personal in their arts units than in the non- arts units" (Bamford). This only proves the fact that art plays an essential role in creating a learning culture in which actual connections to the material are made, instead of the passive, unmotivated learning that occurs otherwise. When children have arts in their environment, they tend to think a bit more in the abstract, and are better able to understand concepts instead of strict memorization, which rarely leads to mastery of a subject. Sandra Ruppert makes the case for arts benefiting academic achievement, stating, "researchers from the University of California at Los Angeles found students with high arts involvement performed better on standardized achievement tests than students with low arts involvement. Moreover, the high arts-involved students also watched fewer hours of TV, participated in more community service and reported less boredom in school." (Ruppert) This bit displays the evidence that there is, in fact, a link proven many times again by science that there are clear and distinct benefits to learning art, both in and out of the classroom.

Art isn't held in the same high regard as other disciplines such as math, reading, science, social studies, even though according to current federal law, the arts are considered a "core academic subject." This should mean that the arts should be appropriated the same funding and resources as the other "core subjects," but this is simply not the case. Following the recession of 2008 and the subsequent budget cuts for an estimated 80% of schools nationally, many schools sought to cut their arts programs funding to remedy their financial struggles. In 1990-2000, the number of public elementary schools offering visual arts programs was 87%, but in a 2009-2010 poll the number had dropped to 83%. Similarly, 20% of schools offered dance and theatre classes in 1990-2000, but dropped to 3% in 2009-2010 (Parsad and Spiegelman). As you can see, arts were one of the first things to be dropped. Even though, according to federal law, the arts are considered "core subjects," when times got hard funding for the arts programs got the axe as was clearly displayed in the aforementioned statistics. Arts simply aren't held in the same esteem math and science are. The current academic system is built upon creating science, technology, math and engineering (S.T.E.M) oriented students who are well equipped for "industry" jobs. The arts are often pushed aside and labeled as "hobbies," thus sidelined and put to the back of students' minds when considering a career. Those who choose a major in the arts are often negatively labeled, and arts degrees are often stigmatized and told they aren't "applicable" or they are equivalent to throwing your money away. This is certainly not the way science or engineering degrees are treated. Only around 3.9% of degrees awarded are visual and performing arts degrees as compared to the 34.9% devoted to science and engineering (Siebens and Ryan). This may stem from the No Child Left Behind Act, signed into law by George W. Bush in 2002, which stated the "term core academic subjects' means English, reading or language arts, mathematics, science, foreign languages, civics and government, economics, arts, history, and geography" (*The No Child Left Behind Act of 2001*). As you can see, visual arts, dance and theater seem to have been lost from this mix, even though they have a definitive impact on academic performance. Because of laws and practices like this, the stigmatization of arts education perpetuates, and soon enough they will be erased from education entirely.

Art not only benefits students in academic capacities, but can provide a channel for energies that are otherwise labeled as "ADHD," "ADD" or other related hyperkinetic disorders. David Henley conducted research for the *American Journal of Art Therapy* on using art as a form of treatment for ADHD students, instead of turning to medication instantly, which is a disturbingly all too true trend in the United States. Henley took a group of ADHD kids and introduced them to a program focused on expressive therapies (behavioral, cognitive, psychodynamic and medical). There were weekly two-hour sessions divided into three stages: free play, group discussion, and an expressive arts category. The report specifically narrows in on eleven-year-old Tim, suffering from ADHD, who benefited most from this art therapy approach to tackling the disorder. In the beginning of the study, Tim was very hyperactive, basically whirl winding around the classroom disrupting the other children, impulsively and aimlessly taunting the playtime. After being steered toward the art table and directing his energies towards a clay project, "Tim's ADHD symptoms dramatically fell away." (Henley). The art-psychotherapy is specifically designed to provide a "therapeutic vehicle for exploring and addressing a range of emotional, cognitive, and perceptual problems" (Henley). This was an especially powerful tool for helping the students express themselves adequately, who are often struggling to properly convey their emotions, feelings, and thoughts. "Drawing about a behavior helps fix an incident in time and space, and, by making it concrete, the problem can be objectively examined" (Henley). This is also a particularly useful tool in the classroom setting, where drawing out concepts and ideas can help give the student something "solid" to work with, and mold to complete understanding. Also, frustration is a common tendency among ADHD students as they feel distracted easily, thus never feeling like they are fully grasping the material. Art media uses "psychic-energy," while displacing overwhelming feelings of anxiety, aggression and attachment through this fine motor process which helps direct these destructive feelings into something constructive, creative and positive. In the case of Tim, when using clay, he displayed great social functionality as opposed to him simply running wild during free play. Not only does this kinetic interaction enhance social function, it may "enhance the cognitive domain as it encourages the child to solve problems, an undertaking which requires planning, experimentation, and communication of personally relevant subject matter" (Henley). Another study published by Valerie Smitheman-Brown and Robin R. Church corroborated these results with their similar study of ADHD children using mandala coloring exercises, and their preliminary findings indicated their exercises had "the effect of increasing attentional abilities and decreasing impulsive behaviors over time, allowing for better decision making, completion of task, general growth in developmental level, and an interest in personal aesthetics." (Smitheman-Brown and Church). These findings are in alignment with the work done by Henley, thus providing evidence that there are some benefits to using art as a tool to focus children with ADHD which could, in turn, improve academic performance.

Not only can art provide means for positive student achievements, it also helps to develop competency skills needed for functioning in this modern world we live in. The arts are important because they are "intrinsic components of human culture, heritage, creativity, and are ways of knowing, representing, presenting, interpreting and symbolizing human experience." (Bamford). They provide a medium for expression, perception, achievement, judgment, organization, and creativity- all of which are integral to the classroom (and beyond). Interaction with the arts helps to open the mind, form connections, question and challenge what is in front of you, explore ideas in a safe space, and critically analyze the world around you. A study done by researchers at the University of New Mexico explored students' cognitive processes whilst engaged in "arts-integrated instruction"(Bamford). For this study, thirty students were selected randomly across ten classes from three learning levels (high, medium and low achievers), and their academic gains from art-integration were recorded versus "traditional" learning. The results differed dramatically, and the scientists concluded that an arts-centric education had numerous benefits including, "more independent and intrinsically motivated investments in learning," (Bamford) basically motivating students to genuinely understand the concepts behind the material, as opposed to strict memorization without thinking about what is truly going on. In doing so, a new work ethic is created, one that transforms students' view of problems as definitive barriers into "challenges to be solved." This genuine passion and zeal for learning all was spurred from incorporating arts into everyday education, and valuing the arts for the critical role that they do in fact play. Arts education is accessible for all, and can be incorporated into existing curricula. For example, two researchers, Nick Rabkin and Robin Redmond, state that "Arts-integrated programs are associated with academic gains across the curriculum as reflected in standardized test scores, and they appear to have more powerful effects on the achievement of struggling students than more conventional arts education programs do"(Rabkin and Redmond). This is yet another piece corroborating the research previously done stating the correlation between arts integration and academic gains. With all this evidence and research backing this claim, it truly is hard to ignore this connection, which is why it is so frustrating that art is seen as a "waste."

I was curious as to whether or not political leaning or age had any effect on whether or not people valued arts, and arts education, so I surveyed my friends and family to gather data on just that. I sent a simple survey with six questions asking their age, political leaning, whether they took art classes in high school, whether they wished they had more arts options in high school, whether or not they thought arts were taken seriously in their high school, and if art was an integral part of their life. My initial hypothesis about this was that people with more liberal tendencies would put a higher value on arts and the humanities, as artists usually are left leaning. I also imagined that younger people would put more of an emphasis on art in their life. After putting my survey out there, and receiving 105 responses, I disaggregated my data into two cross sections-age and political leaning on one side, and the arts questions on the other. I did this to analyze the relationships between arts value and age/political leaning. Here are the results:

		What is your age group?				What is your political leaning?			
		>18	18-30	30+	Total	Republican	Democrat	Independent	Total
Did you take art classes in high school?	Yes	1	37	10	48	16	21	10	47
	No	10	39	8	57	13	34	10	57
	Total	11	76	18	105	29	55	20	104
Do you wish you had more arts options in high school?	Yes	4	46	11	61	13	36	11	60
	No	7	30	7	44	16	19	9	44
	Total	11	76	18	105	29	55	20	104
Do you think that arts were taken seriously?	Yes	4	29	5	38	9	21	7	37
	No	7	47	13	67	20	34	13	67
	Total	11	76	18	105	29	55	20	104
Is art an intergral part of your life?	Yes	6	44	10	60	13	33	13	59
	No	5	32	8	45	16	22	7	45
	Total	11	76	18	105	29	55	20	104

What I was initially not so surprised to find is that less and less kids are taking arts classes in high school. In the 30+ category, over 55% of the respondents took art classes, whereas only 48% of 18-30-year-old took art classes, and a shocking 9% of kids below 18 took art classes in high school ("Art & Education"). Art used to be valued as one of the core disciplines, but it simply has fallen out of favor and replaced by the STEM surge. Because of this, I wasn't surprised that the overall percentage of people who took arts in high school was less than that of people who did. I was, however, surprised that a higher percentage of those who identified as Republicans (55%) took art classes than those who identified as Democrats (38%). This is a shock because according to an article published in the Public Administration Review about artists and their political leaning, "relative to the general population, artists, donors, and patrons are (1) less religious, (2) more socially liberal, (3) more likely to favor individual freedom over traditional morality, and (4) more opposed to traditional sex roles." (Lewis and Brooks). I just assumed that more Democrats, being liberal, would have pounced on the opportunity to delve into their creative side. On this same vein of liberals being more artsy, my survey corroborated this fact by showing that higher percentages of Democrats (60%) considered art an integral part of their life, as opposed to Republicans who had just 44% agreeing. As far as independents go on this survey, I initially didn't include them in the options because they don't fit on either end of the spectrum, but in this case they seemed to swing more on the liberal side. Overall, I am not too surprised with the results, as they mostly fit with the predictions I had made.

Some are pushing to eradicate teaching the arts in schools with the logic that we are falling behind in other countries S.T.E.M wise, so we should have a push to expand upon those classes, instead of wasting our time with arts. Other critics say art isn't a useful skill to have in life, and that if kids feel the need to express themselves they should do so at home or in an extracurricular activity. This sort of mentality keeps driving the arts farther toward the brink of extinction in elementary schools and beyond. Bringing back the value and emphasis of arts in education could have a huge impact on bringing the United States of America back into the competition with the other highly evolved nations. As Barack Obama once said, "to remain competitive in the global economy, America needs to reinvigorate the kind of creativity and innovation that has made this country great. To do so, we must nourish our children's creative skills. In addition to giving our children the science and math skills they need to compete in the new global context, we should also encourage the ability to think creatively that comes from a meaningful arts education" (Dwyer, Knight Foundation, and United States President's Committee on the Arts and the Humanities.). This, I think, truly sums up the entirety of my argument. Many other countries have come to this realization, "For example, Austria noted that the social component of working in a process-oriented basis and in groups as occurs in quality arts education influences and improves the level of educational realization."(Bamford). We must revive the arts in education so that kids grow up thinking outside the box, using different approaches to common problems in any field they decide to go into. This is imperative.

Works Cited

Bamford, Anne. *The wow factor: Global research compendium on the impact of the arts in education.* Waxmann Verlag, 2006.

Dwyer, M. Christine, Knight Foundation, and United States. President's Committee on the Arts and the Humanities. *Reinvesting in Arts Education: Winning America's Future through Creative Schools*. Washington, D.C: President's Committee on the Arts and the Humanities, 2011. Web.

Henley, David. "Art Therapy in a Socialization Program for Children with Attention Deficit Hyperactivity Disorder." *American Journal of Art Therapy* 37.1 (1998): 2. ProQuest. Web. 22 Feb. 2016.

Kirker, Sean. "Art & Education." Survey. *Qualtrics*. Qualtrics, 14 February 2016. Accessed Online, 22 February 2016.

Lewis, Gregory B., and Arthur C. Brooks. "A question of morality: Artists' values and public funding for the arts." *Public Administration Review* 65.1 (2005): 8-17.

Parsad, Basmat, and Maura Spiegelman. "Arts Education in Public Elementary and Secondary Schools: 1999-2000 and 2009-10. NCES 2012-014." *National Center for Education Statistics* (2012).

Rabkin, Nick, and Robin Redmond. "The arts make a difference." *The Journal of Arts Management, Law, and Society* 36.1 (2006): 25-32.

Ruppert, Sandra S. Critical Evidence: *How the Arts Benefit Student Achievement*. National Assembly of State Arts Agencies. 1029 Vermont Avenue NW, Washington, DC 20005, 2006.

Siebens, Julie, and Camille L. Ryan. "Field of Bachelor's Degree in the United States: 2009. American Community Survey Reports. ACS-18." *US Census Bureau* (2012).

Smitheman-Brown, Valerie, and Robin R. Church. "Mandala drawing: Facilitating creative growth in children with ADD or ADHD." *Art Therapy* 13.4 (1996): 252-260.

U.S. House. 107th Congress, 1st Session. H.R. 1, *The No Child Left Behind Act of 2001*. Act. Washington: Government Printing Office, 2002.

For this project you will be teaming up in groups of two and exploring the pivotal concepts of happiness, success, purpose or meaning in human life. Your project will argue in support of a specific hypothesis, using high-quality research to support your views. The paper should also analyze philosophical or cultural ideas that have influenced your views about these concepts.

-Professor Bob Finegan

Denica-Lynyl Santos & Codi Leager

North Korean Citizens Can Justifiably Claim Their Happiness

Imagine surfing the internet, scrolling through your Facebook feed or checking the latest Tweets, and coming across an article titled "North Korea's Happiness Index Rank: China top, US Bottom." What would you think? Many of us might think that it is typical clickbait and either click the link or scroll past it. Those of us who fall for clickbait skim the article and read that according to a survey conducted in North Korea in 2011, North Korea is the second happiest country on earth ("North Korea's Happiness Index Rank"). Some of us shake our heads, wondering how it is possible that others actually believe that people who live under such an oppressive government are amongst the happiest; but, we have to remember: the survey was conducted by and in North Korea. This has several implications regarding the data collected and released. One possibility is that the North Korean government may have manipulated that data in its favor, but what about the idea that North Koreans genuinely believe that they have the second happiest population in the world? The latter seems like a bizarre conclusion on the surface; however, after thorough examination of a few factors, specifically the way that different customs, adaptations and lifestyles influence perception of happiness and well-being, it is also plausible.

One thing to consider is the fact that the information that enters and exits North Korea is highly controlled. The government determines what can be accessed on the Internet, restricts foreign material such as books and television shows, and even requires permission from people to travel even within the country's borders (Ford and Kwon 80).We have already encountered a problem because of said fact: we cannot trust the survey results that North Korea released. But nonetheless, the results open doors for us to investigate the possibility that North Koreans really think that they live the happiest lives under such an oppressive government. The information that the government chooses to provide and withhold affects North Korean citizens' way of thinking and perceiving many things, including their level of happiness and well-being.

There is little that North Koreans know about what truly lies outside of North Korea's borders. According to Andrei Lankov, Russian professor of Kookmin University in Seoul and a specialist in Korean studies, shares a story about his conversation with a man who helps North Korean officials travel to a tiny town in Manchuria. The man recalls that, typically, the officials "are so shocked and overwhelmed by the prosperity of the place" (Lankov 102). One thing to keep in mind, which Lankov also points out, is that to someone reading this paper, like you, would say that the town is not of high quality at all. Lankov says that "the present writer" would say that the Chinese town "looked more like an abandoned steel mill" (Lankov 102). Many of us would have this reaction because we are accustomed to seeing or experiencing much more lavish and lively places such as New York City, Paris, or Hong Kong. The small town in Manchuria would be next to nothing compared to what we are used to seeing or experiencing. This puts into perspective how little even some North Korean officials know about the prosperity, and life in general, about the rest of the world.

Government monopoly of information means that the general North Korean public mostly only know what leaders want and choose to expose and express about the outside world. Some South Koreans go as far to say that North Koreans are "completely brainwashed" ("North Korea's Happiness Index Rank"). A radio broadcast aired in January 2009 and directed to the public emphasized the message that "the general's health and well-being are [their] happiness and joy" and are responsible for the country's future prosperity and success ("North Korea's "Happiness" Lies in Kim Jong Il's 'Health and Wellbeing'"). From the point of view of an outsider, it may very well look like the government brainwashes its people through messages such as the one presented in the radio broadcast; however, for the average North Korean, hearing such proclamations is customary. According to the Federal Research Division of the Library of Congress, "the Dear General" "dominates every aspect of North Korean Life" (Worden 74) and people "strong[ly] believe in the rightness of their cause and their faith...[and] can see through the difficulties that nonbelievers might not weather as well" (Worden 77). In North Korea Kim Jong Il and Kim Jong Un are seen as demigods and are prevalent in almost all areas of people's daily lives. They are present both physically and mentally for they are on people's minds in their thoughts, on pictures in their homes, on posters in public facilities (Worden 75). This is the type of lifestyle that North Koreans have grown accustomed to and, according to the Federal Research Division of the Library of Congress, lived since childhood, when they are disciplined to have faith, loyalty, and love for the state at the youngest age possible (Worden 112). To many who observe North Korea through the lenses of the outside world, it is outrageous and irrational for people to be so invested in a country that is totalitarian; however, many North Koreans do not have the knowledge to put their situation into the context of the rest of the world. Based on the teachings and standards that are introduced to North Koreans at a very young age, they deduce that they live a normal life. This way of teaching children the conventional North Korean way of life at a very young age, paired with the information that is exposed to them as they grow older, makes for a North Korean population that is under the impression that they are living decent, if not the best, quality lives.

Individuals, however, cannot be absolutely controlled. This is displayed by the way that North Koreans defy the government. Some North Koreans find ways to illegally smuggle goods and people in and out of the country (Lankov 102-103). Similarly, information will enter and leave in ways that cannot be totally prevented. For instance, refugees who return home, whether it be on their own accord or through repatriation by authorities, will return with and share stories of the outside world (Lankov 102-103). Consequently, there is some knowledge about the prosperity of South Korea circulating in North Korea. This has hurt North Korea's legitimacy because North Korean ideology states that it can provide its people with the best economic and political standing (Lankov 215); but, North Korean government has failed to do so, as evident through South Korea's prosperity.

Since the beginning of the 21st century though, North Korea has used propaganda to demonstrate that, although it is true that South Korea is wealthier, they have corrupted their national identity by working with Americans, who are seen as egocentric imperialists. North Korean media portrays South Korea as a discontent state that does not suffer from hunger, but rather humiliation (Lankov 105). In this way, the North Koreans demonstrate national identity constitutes what makes a better life more than opulence does. This introduces the idea that because of different standards and customs, various factors are valued and weighed differently when analyzing happiness and well-being. Because North Koreans lead different lifestyles with distinct conventions and standards from the rest of the world, they may authentically be happy despite what others think. North Koreans are able to live happily despite the poverty and oppression that they are faced with on a day to day basis. This idea is explored by Carol Graham, who is a Leo Pasvolsky Senior Fellow at the Brookings Institution and has conducted projects on well-being based on factors such as poverty, inequality, and health in developing countries and Latin America.

Graham's findings have been published in her book *Pursuit of Happiness: An Economy of Well-Being*. Based on her research, she concludes that "people seem to have different norms regarding what is tolerable or intolerable" in many areas of life, such as economic stability, personal well-being, and freedom and that these norms appear to "mediate the effects that those particular phenomena have on well-being" (Graham 82). The data from her study in Afghanistan in particular help support this notion. The results show that Afghans have relatively high happiness ratings for a population that faces many difficulties on a daily basis and also knows about the possibilities of better lives in the rest of the world. According to Graham's data, Afghanistan has a happiness rating of 4.67 while the world rating is 5.42 (Graham 75). In Afghanistan, incidents involving crime and corruption are typical and so Afghans have learned to adapt to the environment and society in which they live. Although misdemeanors lead to a population that is generally less happy, the negative effects coupled with them do not necessarily make people unhappy either because they are common occurrences. From this, Graham concludes that the "difference in norms and tolerance for adversity means that people can report being happy in conditions that are intolerable by standards of most other people" (Graham 105). This conclusion offers a reason why North Koreans can claim that they are happy despite what other people perceive.

Many North Koreans may have adapted to and accepted their lives under the rule of an extremely oppressive, authoritarian government in a similar way that Afghans adapted to the crime and corruption in their country. One interesting thing that Graham also found was that in areas in Afghanistan where Taliban influence was prevalent, people were happier with less crime and corruption and people who suffered as victims from such experiences were unhappier. The general public in areas influenced by Taliban teachings and beliefs opposed such offenses. As a result, they are more affected by it when they experience crime and corruption, such as theft (Graham 98). In contrast, Afghans in areas without Taliban influence were less affected by them. With these results, Graham surmises that corruption has less effect on people who live where corruption is typical because they acclimatized to it (Graham 94).

Graham's findings can also be applied to the different economic circumstances in North and South Korea. North Korean officials justify their ideology by using propaganda to portray the idea that that national identity is more valuable than economic status (Lankov 105). As a result, the general North Korean population begins to believe that even though it has a healthier economy, South Koreans are unhappier because of their corrupt identity due to American influence despite the fact that they enjoy more lavish foods and products. In the long run, this convinces many North Koreans that they are living the more fulfilling, higher quality lives. Graham's discoveries and reasoning can also explain why many North Koreans might believe they are happier than the rest of the world as well. People who live in other countries may believe it is outrageous and irrational that North Koreans can live happily because they are not used to living in such extreme, cruel conditions and experiencing such intense oppression. But, because many North Koreans are accustomed to restricted and controlled lives under their government, they may believe it is normal and are not necessarily unhappily living in such conditions; therefore, they are able to lead content lives.

From Graham's studies, we can see the importance of different standards and adaptations have on the way that different contextual circumstances affect happiness and well-being. Graham puts her conclusions into a broader perspective in an example on page ninety-one of her book, where she describes the difference in the way that the rich and the poor value work and health versus friendships and family. According to Graham, work and health may be worth more to the rich because it allows them to achieve success in what they want to achieve, which makes them happier. On the other hand, friendships and family give the poor safety and comfort as opposed to wealth, and therefore constitute what make them happy (Graham 91). North Koreans present a similar case.

Chad O'Carroll, the founder of a website entitled North Korea News and a journalist who has been writing on North Korea since starting this website in 2009, reports that in spite of the painful memories that they experienced while living in North Korea, North Korean refugees actually miss some parts of their life in their homeland. In a refugee insight interview series that he conducted for his website, O'Carroll asked several North Koreans what they missed about their life in North Korea. Many refugees reported the same thing: they missed their friends and family the most. Nayoung Koh, a woman who left North Korea in 2009 and is currently a studying at a university in Seoul, compared her present life in South Korea with her life in North Korea and said, "although we were poor, we were all friends with neighbors and we all were very close in North Korea. Life in South Korea may be affluent and wealthy, but South Koreans aren't as innocent or sympathetic as North Koreans...Back in North Korea, people always shared with people" (O'Carroll). This displays one factor that brings North Koreans happiness within their country: close relationships with family and friends. This shows that it is possible for North Koreans to be really happy about something in their lives despite having an oppressive government or weak economy.

This is not to say that North Koreans are completely happy with their lives; in fact, there are several things that cause North Koreans great discontent. According to Marcus Noland, who has a Doctorate from John Hopkins University and has written extensively on the economies of several Asian countries, and his coauthor Stephen Haggard, a distinguished professor at the School of Global Policy and Strategy at the University of California, several North Koreans are discontent with their social status, which is called the *songbun* (Noland and Haggard 80-81). As described by Ahlam Lee, an assistant professor at Arkansas State University, *Songbun* is established by the background of an individual's ancestors and ultimately decides a person's fate: where one works and studies, if even allowed to, where someone lives, and even the amount of food an individual is provided by the state (Lee 31). This social system causes discontent at all levels of the social hierarchy as demonstrated by a North Korean defector of high status. According to Noland and Haggard, this particular defector had great privileges in life, for he had access to great schools, training, and international experience; however, he felt it was unfair that he felt like he had to serve underneath incompetent, unworthy people who escaped training and obtained their status thanks to their *songbun* (Noland and Haggard 81). Criticism sessions are also a source of discontent throughout North Korea. In one case, a student refused to speak to another student ever again after being criticized by him for skipping class (Worden 90). Some North Koreans have adapted to these criticism sessions in such a way so that they are less affected by them. Friends and families get together and decide who will be criticized a specific week so that the selected person will be prepared for the criticism and how to react to it (Worden 90). This is one particular example in North Korea that relates to Graham's findings about Afghans who have adapted to the crime and corruption in their country because the North Koreans have adapted to something that occurs in their daily life so that their happiness and well-being is barely affected, if at all.

As for things that are beyond the ordinary North Korean citizen's control, such as a life determined by *songbun*, people take matters into their own hands. Some manage to escape as refugees. Leaving the country is not something to be taken lightly, for North Koreans must face various challenges once escaping their homeland. They risk and fear punishment by both North Korean and Chinese authorities, abuse (especially in the case of women, who are caught up in sex trafficking in both China and South Korea), and unemployment because of lack of skills and abilities (Noland and Haggard 39). Furthermore, refugees also leave behind their families and friends in North Korea, which also causes great distress (Noland and Haggard 35), especially since relationships with friends and families is one major source of happiness in North Korea.

Interestingly enough, despite insecurities about a "successful" future and "preference for decent life in North Korea," North Korean refugees would rather test their luck and work to overcome the challenges that faced them (Noland and Haggard 19). In some cases, though, North Korean defectors returned home on their own accord to conduct illegal business or provide money and food to their families. Moreover, a few people found that opportunities in other areas, such as China, were bare (Noland and Haggard 35). The amount of refugees who returned to conduct business and because they believed China had little to offer is very small and, therefore, barely significant. According to Noland and Haggard's research, many North Koreans made the decision to stay out of North Korea because of their experiences prior to leaving the oppressive country. People disliked the unfairness of the distribution of food, death of loved ones, and the North Korean prison system (Noland and Haggard 44). This evidence suggests that, once North Koreans open their eyes and see what life is like beyond their county's borders, they also discover the possibilities of leading much better lives compared to the ones that they experienced in at home.

Nonetheless, although they may be unhappy with certain elements of their lives, it does not mean that North Koreans cannot be happy in their country. Of course, some influences on North Korean happiness levels include the values and information that they are taught by their government in combination with lifestyle adaptations and personal pleasures, such as spending time with family and friends; however, their sources of happiness does not mean that their happiness is unjustified. Therefore, it is plausible that North Koreans genuinely feel happy within the borders of their homeland. This conclusion can also be applied to people other than North Koreans. People can genuinely be happy despite living in conditions or areas that are different from the norm that others may accustomed to.

Works Cited

Ford, Glyn, and Kwon, Soyoung. *North Korea on the Brink: Struggle for Survival*. London, GBR: Pluto Press, 2007. Print.

Graham, Carol L. *Pursuit of Happiness: An Economy of Well-Being*. Washington, DC, USA: Brookings Institution Press, 2012. Print.

Lankov, Andrei. *The Real North Korea: Life and Politics in the Failed Stalin Utopia*. New York, NY: Oxford University Press, 2013. Print.

Lee, Ahlam. *North Korean Defectors in a New and Competitive Society: Issues and Challenges in Resettlement, Adjustment, and the Learning Process*. Lanham, MD: Lexington Books, 2016. Print.

Noland, Marcus, and Haggard, Stephan. *Witness to Transformation: Refugee Insights into North Korea*. Washington, DC, USA: Peterson Institute for International Economics, 2011. Print.

"North Korea's Happiness Index Rank: China top, US bottom." *International Business Times* [U.S. ed.] 27 May 2011. *Academic OneFile*. Web. 8 November 2015.

"North Korea's 'Happiness' Lies in Kim Jong-Il's 'Health and Wellbeing' - Radio." *BBC Monitoring Asia Pacific*. January 30 2009. ProQuest. Web. 8 November 2015.

O'Carroll, Chad. "Defectors: What We Miss the Most about Life in North Korea." *The Guardian*. North Korea Network., 6 May 2014. Web. 8 November 2015.

Worden, Robert L., ed. *North Korea: A Country Study*. Washington, DC, USA: Federal Research Division, Library of Congress. 2008. Print.

Choose one of the multi-faceted environmental issues we have been exploring in class, or another related to environmental justice, and do two things: 1. Describe, as objectively as possible, the various sides/thoughts/beliefs about the issue and 2. Analyze the rhetoric that each side employs to convince people that their side is the right one. If the issue doesn't have more than one side, you need to find a different issue.

-Professor Blythe Davenport

Chloé C. Segui

Toxic Waste, Toxic Class, Toxic Race

Americans are always working to come up with faster, more efficient, and useful ways to improve the economy. With newer technology comes more innovative ways to acquire natural resources. One of these new technologies is called fracking, or hydraulic fracturing. Yes, I know that these resources benefit the economy by producing more jobs and lowering gas prices, but the adverse effects that hydraulic systems cause such as water pollution, respiratory issues, and headaches are ruthless. There is more to fracking and coal-to-gas.

When taking a closer and more focused look into the topic of environmental justice, a deeper issue arises. The main areas in which the hydraulic systems are being used are underprivileged areas all over the US. This makes me wonder whether environmental justice has more to do with race and class as it does the environment itself. There have been many cases of environmental justice cases that have recently been tied to racial issues.

Javier Sierra, editor of Monthly magazine and author of "Racism is in the Air" reports "Researchers came to the conclusion that people of color breathe 46-percent more nitrogen dioxide (NO2) — a toxic compound resulting from the burning of coal and oil — than do non-Hispanic whites" (Sierra, 2014). The study, conducted by the University of Minnesota, proves that there is an underlying issue apparent when discussing environmental justice situations. All of these detrimental hydraulics are mostly being used in areas that are deprived and too weak to take any real action towards what is happening in their communities. Kim Wasserman-Nieto, an environmental justice hero, has noticed this underlying issue as well, "These are the realities of what our people are feeling on a day-to-day basis. Things are not getting any better. We are the ones producing the least amount of pollution and yet feeling the most impact" (Sierra, 2014). Evidently, the term 'environmental racism' is very prominent in this day and age.

The CDC has added credibility to the issue by stating, "According to a Center for Disease Control study, more than 5 million people of color live close to these highways, especially in Southern California" (Sierra, 2014). Of course, the highways being spoken of are the ones close to the lower income areas.

Professional organizations and researchers are not the only ones who notice this environmental racism. People living in these underrepresented areas are also very aware of what is going on around them. The United Church of Christ (UCC) released a pamphlet conveying the sentiments this community has towards environmental racism. They see it too and are addressing the issue to educate more individuals about it. "It wasn't until approximately two decades ago that a series of events was able to demonstrate the connection, in an explicit manner, of the issues of environmental contamination with the elements of race, color and socio-economic status" (Jaramillo, n.d). People are unhappy with the conditions they are being put in without a say. They are now coming to a realization and speaking up for themselves in hopes that this issue gets resolved.

Let's take a look at the rhetoric being employed by those speaking out against environmental racism. This first image is a great play on tugging at the hearts of those allowing environmental racism to go on. This image, although small, is composed of big rhetorical pathos. The fact that there are mainly young children in the picture is a way for the UCC to show people who is being hurt by the damages done from hydraulic systems. It is a convincing image for the UCC is place this picture on the cover of their pamphlet.

Another instance in which environmental racism is apparent is in the Flint, Michigan. Flint is an area populated mainly by minorities and is currently suffering lead contamination in their water supply. This is a recent case that came out in the New York Times and other mainstream news stations. It was discovered that this city's water was contaminated by lead due to a change in water supply and excess hazardous environmental work.

The citizens of Flint have reported many illnesses because of this tragedy. As one resident summed it up, "It doesn't take a scientist to tell us brown water is not good" (Davis, 2016). Residents of Flint were very much aware of what was happening to them and were able to speak up about issue. The New York Times article expresses how the town was compensated for their troubles, stating "The Michigan House on Wednesday approved Mr. Snyder's request for $28 million in help for Flint; the measure now moves to the Senate" (Davis, 2016). This is a good start in taking action towards the elimination and recognition of environmental racism, though there is much more to be done. No citizen, regardless of their economic status, should be treated with such disdain by their own government.

Even searching the keywords 'environmental justice' on Google directed me to environmental racism. The fact that it was that easy to find a website about 'environmental racism' when searching about 'environment justice' proves how real of a dispute this is. It is not hard to see the problem at hand. Those who are choosing to be oblivious to environmental racism are choosing to simply not care.

For example, the Environmental Protection Agency, also known as the EPA, states, "Environmental Justice is the fair treatment and meaningful involvement of all people regardless of race, color, national origin, or income with respect to the development, implementation, and enforcement of environmental laws, regulations, and policies" (Environmental Justice). It is disheartening that the previous quote is meant to embody what the EPA stands for, however, their standards, based off of their definition of what environmental justice is, are not being met. The EPA knows this too and has been trying to work towards making environmental racism disappear, "The EPA has this goal for all communities and persons across this nation" (Environmental Racism). Hopefully, with so much talk about environmental racism, something will be done to fix it.

Now that more and more people are becoming educated on environmental topics in depth due to the global warming scare, I hope they will start to take action and change things for the betterment of all people. Race or class should not be the determining factor of whether an individual gets to breathe fresh air or drink clean water. It should not be a determining factor of who gets to live in areas of high risk of illness that may arise from the damage being done to this earth. The earth is not only my home but it is our home.

Growing up, I have always been taught that we are all brothers and sisters. So why is it okay to mistreat some of our brothers and sisters by dumping the majority of this toxicity on them? Some people see environmental justice, or better yet, environmental injustices, as a one-sided topic that focuses only and primarily on the environmental issues. Although this should be the case, it is truly not when looking at specific demographic areas where these things are taking place. The second side of environmental justice lies at the heart of environmental racism.

Works Cited

"Environmental Justice | US EPA." Environmental Justice | US EPA. N.p., 16 Nov. 2015. Web. 20 Jan. 2016. <http://www3.epa.gov/environmentaljustice/>.

Davis, Julie H., and Richard Perez-Pena. "Obama Says If He Were a Flint Parent, He'd Be 'Beside Myself'." Editorial. The New York Times. The New York Times Company, 20 Jan. 2016. Web. 20 Jan. 2016.

Jaramillo, Linda M., Rev., and Carlos C. Bernier. "Almost Everything You Need To Know About Environmental Justice." United Church of Christ (n.d.): 1-15. Web. 20 Jan. 2016.

Sierra, Javier. "Racism's in the Air: Race Is the Determining Factor When It Comes to Who Breathes Bad Air." The Huffington Post. The Huffington Post, 05 May 2014. Web. 19 Jan. 2016.

Write about a person or group of people who has/have been important in your life and who has/have in some way influenced you. This could be in either a negative or positive fashion. Your purpose is to create a vivid portrait of the person so that readers will have a good idea of what the person or group of people is/are like. Your readers will want to be able to see the person or group of people, both through your descriptions and through anecdotes and/or habitual actions that say something about the person's or the group's character. Others in the class will also be interested in what you think or feel about this person or group of people, which might be another way of saying how this person influenced your life.

-Dr. Irvin Peckham

Kiera Townsend

 Mr. Sidoli

"Life is worth leaving!," Mr. Sidoli shouts, a huge grin plastered on his mouth and in his eyes, spit pooling at the corners of his lips. He is crazed, but this is normal. Before him we sit, a classroom full of groggy Calculus students, our amusement keeping us awake. He has gone off-topic again, as he does each class, and he is in his element. This time he is impersonating one of his favorite comedians. We are – as always - amazed and entertained at the energy of this 60-something-year-old man who had a heart attack a few years ago but continues to move and speak with the jauntiness of a 20-year-old. We chuckle as he fills the room with hundreds of ideas on topics ranging from the fractal nature of flowers to the merits of jumping off a bridge.

The man who stands before us has done something amazing: he has made Calculus class interesting for each student, even those who hate Calculus (like myself). He is huge, and not because of his stature. Sure, he has a stomach that hangs down over his belt and sagging khakis, a loose XL button-down that is covered in chalk and keeps coming untucked, and his six-foot-three frame and flailing arms seem a bit large for the tiny chalkboards provided by our school. But he is gigantic because of his mind. And because he is a rare breed of person and math teacher: one who does not shrink behind lesson plans and perfect calculations; rather, he has a dynamic stage presence, and he improvises.

Our laughter swells as his voice grows louder, continuing the joke as he pretends to stand at the edge of an imaginary bridge and consider jumping off. Wait - he abruptly remembers the curriculum he has to follow, and so his smile remains as he stops joking about suicide and resumes musing about math instead.

He bounds from one end of the chalkboard to the other, drawing a continuous line which he claims will approach infinity.

"So what does it mean to approach infinity?," he asks us.

Silence and quiet giggles at his expectant smile as it springs open further to reveal his silver tooth. He is not self-conscious. He is sweating, no one in the audience is responding, and the show must go on.

He swings the door open and grabs the first student he sees walking down the hall. He asks her what it means to approach infinity, as though she is supposed to know even though she is only a sophomore. He asks who her math teacher is and jokingly says he will yell at that teacher later.

I raise my hand with one of the curious questions I love to ask him. "Mr. Sidoli," I say in my typical uncertain tone, always a little bit afraid that he will grow tired of my questions (though he never does and never would show it if he were to) "Is it possible to approach infinity from the right-hand side, or can you only approach it from the left?"

He opens his eyes wide and raises his eyebrows, the deep creases in his bald head straightening out. "Kiera, are you talking about approaching infinity from the unknown side? Black holes, the event horizon? You're getting way, way out there now. Slow down! We're just talking lines here, and you're – man, you're hypothesizing about things that scientists can hardly imagine. You're way ahead of us, take it easy there."

He loves to make fun of me by pretending my questions are brilliant, looking at me like I'm about to discover the cure for cancer, even though he knows my poor work in his class. That's what makes it funny.

He poses his original question a second time and eventually forces Madison, one of the smartest students, to answer. She responds with the correct answer, and he tells her she has a powerful mind. I wish he would say that to me. But I guess Madison will actually discover a cure for cancer, and I will just keep asking stupid questions and laughing at my teacher's jokes while he laughs at my serious attempts at comprehension.

It is so natural for him to look at the world in sine and cosine waves, to see the way everything functions. He gives us tests, he grades them and hands them back the next day (refusing to use red pen, because of its damaging psychological effects). He has no time to finish the curriculum, he condenses it and holds extra help sessions and somehow we mostly all pass. The Smart Board will not work, he uses the chalkboard to teach. He knows how to solve each problem. No worries, man. And yet it is never boring to solve all these problems, as no solution process is ever really the same. He is a pro at saying, "Yes, and... ."

Ironically, he hates theatre. This will never make sense to me, but he does hate it. His wife is the one who loves theatre. Maybe he hates it on purpose in order to keep their passions separate. The couple met at a small liberal arts college, and she does theatre for a living. Her name is Elizabeth, and she reminds me of Meryl Streep. I meet her at one of my Shakespeare shows. I exit backstage after changing from my costume, and Mr. S. is there with his giant bear hug and wonderful toothy smile. I am glad he gets to see me in my element. I want him to know that I am capable of getting things right sometimes.

Anyway, his theatrical clown makeup melts away on certain days, at certain times. His forehead crinkles deepen, his crow's feet look like stress lines, his funny silver tooth hides and his smile flips upside down. This happens for a number of reasons.

One day, he speaks of a student he tutors outside of school, a boy whose father abuses him and calls him stupid because he has trouble understanding math. Mr. Sidoli despises the boy's father. He spends 30 minutes of class time spewing hatred toward the man, giving us a portrait of a terrible father. He is not funny now, he is making us depressed. He ends the 30 minutes with a profound conclusion, always. He gives a reflective closing statement about how life makes some people bitter and then those people make more people bitter and the cycle continues. It makes me angry that he always has to deliver a conclusion, because it seems forced sometimes. After detailing to us a tragic story of a broken family that is not his own, he tacks on a series of profound, conclusive statements. Nothing overconfident, just reflections. But still - some stories speak powerfully on their own, no ending needed. He simply cannot keep himself from trying to generate concise solutions from problems.

There is one day he cannot possibly generate a solution. It is a freezing January day, our first school day after a long series of lazy snow cancellations. The man who stands before us looks his 60-something years old, as though he could have a heart attack again at any moment. The room is dismal. He is sweating more profusely than is normal for him, wiping his forehead and smearing chalk everywhere he cannot see. His eyes do not focus on us or the board. His mind is distant. In the middle of class, an invisible rope pulls him toward the door without warning, and we hear only footsteps down the hall. He returns in 10 minutes with puffy eyes and no color in his face.

His mother has passed away, he says, and he continues to teach. At the end of class he says, "She had a great life. I'm blessed to have had her. I'll be out tomorrow and back the next day. Please do the assignment, don't give the substitute a hard time."

We slowly exit the classroom, each student lingering a bit to awkwardly whisper, "I'm sorry for your loss."

And we really were sorry.

When Mr. S. is laughing, so are we. And when he is sad and pensive, we all are, as well. He gives so much to us.

I see him in the hallway later that day, my binders and extracurricular flyers and tape spilling out of my arms and fingers as always, speed-walking to my next class after the bell has already rung. He is digging into the floor and storming forward with a furrowed brow. The uncertainty in our eyes line up. We are both a mess, figuring things out in our heads. He smiles and nods and says, "Hi, Kiera," like always. Things continue to function.

His father made him go to school for math when he was younger, because he had talent for the subject. Mr. Sidoli himself wished to become a classical pianist. He promises us all year long that he will play for us one day, and he finally does. We go to the music room in a long parade. He sits down and positions himself as we stare and wait for him to put on a show. He closes his eyes and plays, for 10 minutes, what feels like an entire lifetime's worth of the most beautiful live piano music I have ever experienced. And he is not performing. He is baring his soul to us. His face is different again, not a comedian or a sad clown but a man who is asleep and dreaming; he has no facial control, his mouth and nose twitching, eyes fluttering. He creates an entire world with his music, immerses us in the unconscious memories spilling from his fingers which once practiced for hours and now dance like butterflies across the keys.

This is only the beginning of the dreams he shares with us. He is building a house upstate for himself and his wife to escape to. He is sailing around the world sometime soon. He is retiring as early as possible so he can work more on his paintings and open a gallery. He knows we will all do great things, he tells us each day.

Drexel Publishing Group
Essays

The annual Drexel Publishing Group writing contest is open to all students engaged in thinking, researching and writing within their discipline. Winning entries are chosen based on how well students exemplify a firm grasp of subject matter and a facility of language. Submissions are open during the Winter and Spring terms.

Introduction

Researching, thinking, and writing are at the core of the College of Arts and Sciences. No matter what field students are in, they must be able to research, to find and evaluate the best evidence and information on topic and most of all keep an open mind. Research can be exhilarating when you are engaged in pursuing a thought and seeing it through to its natural conclusion. Sometimes the thought process is validated, other times not. Conducting research is not about proving but uncovering. Students must be able to think, to form original ideas, and takes a fresh approach to a problem or question. And, of course they must be able to write. It is a skill set employers continue to value.

The essays and articles in this section of *The 33rd* contribute to a range of disciplines in the arts and sciences and reflect work that strives to form original ideas and takes a fresh approach to the subject at hand.

The editors have decided to honor the stylistic requirements of each field and reproduced the essays and articles in their original forms.

Bhavya Sharma

Masking Evil Behind Another Personality: The Question of Dual Identity In Stevenson's *Dr. Jekyll and Mr. Hyde*

In his novel *The Strange Case of Dr. Jekyll and Mr. Hyde,* Robert Stevenson presents Dr. Jekyll as a victim to his transformation into Mr. Hyde. It is not clear whether Dr. Jekyll voluntarily becomes Mr. Hyde or if he enjoys adopting the latter's personality more than his own. While on one hand, Dr. Jekyll, in his narrative, writes that "[he] had not conquered [his] aversions to the dryness of a life of study" and that he indulged in "undignified pleasures," he also makes it seem like his transformation to Hyde was detestable to him to the extent that he commits suicide in the end (63). This paper will argue that Dr. Jekyll willingly transforms into Hyde to indulge in his "undignified pleasures" and that his narrative cannot be trusted completely. Jekyll, who acts as the censored ego (a Freudian concept which will be expanded upon in the paper), fulfills his repressed sexual desires through Hyde (his uncensored Id). Furthermore, Dr. Jekyll is trying to shift the blame of his wrongdoings by perpetuating the theory of the dual brain, but unlike real patients who do not control their transformations, Dr. Jekyll, by drinking his chemical potion, willingly transforms into Hyde.

In the first chapter of his book "Generation of Edward Hyde: The Animal Within," Jay Bland writes about how Stevenson might have been influenced by the Platonian idea of one's body reflecting the good or evil in one's soul, which explains why Dr. Jekyll physically changes after his transformation into the apish-looking Hyde, who is the evil part of his soul. Bland writes, "Hyde may be apish, but Stevenson's language consistently presents him as a Platonic expression of the evil element in Jekyll's soul" (Bland, 31). Bland argues that Hyde is another part of Jekyll's personality, and reading Jekyll and Hyde as two different personalities is an inherently flawed reading of the novella considering that Stevenson was influenced by Plato's idea of the body reflecting the soul, according to Bland. Dr. Jekyll's evil side manifests itself in the form of Hyde to fulfill his repressed pleasures.

To gain an understanding of the intentions motivating Dr. Jekyll's actions, it is important to cite examples of what the "undignified pleasures" that Jekyll refers to are to gain an understanding of why they are repressed and not acceptable by social norms. In the chapter "Frankenstein's Gate" in

Screams of Reason, David J. Skal points out that according to the literary critic Elaine Showalter, Stevenson's novella can be read as a "homosexual allegory" in which the homosexual male body is represented in a narrative inducing images of anal intercourse. Skal writes that "Hyde travels in the 'chocolate-brown fog' that beats about the 'back-end of the evening' while the streets he traverses are invariably 'muddy' and 'dark;' Jekyll's house with its two entrances, is the most vivid representation of the male body" since Hyde always enters it through the "blistered back door" (Skal, 70). Skal states that homosexuality was criminalized in the year that the novella came out. Jekyll, who can not fulfill his homosexual desires because of the criminalization of the act, has to repress his desires until he assumes another persona to indulge in them. However, unlike Freudian repression in which an individual is not fully conscious of his or her desires, Jekyll's repressed desires are not locked away in his subconscious – he is very much aware of them and willingly concocts a potion that would make him appear as Mr. Hyde.

Another example that points to why Dr. Jekyll willingly transforms into Hyde is presented by Shubh Singh and Subho Chakrabarti in their paper "A Study in Dualism: The Strange Case of Dr. Jekyll and Mr. Hyde." The authors state that behind Dr. Jekyll's intellectuality and dignified reputation resides an evil that is analogous to the Victorian London setting in which "dualism [is] present in every individual but also in society as a whole, where the aristocracy that superficially was genteel and refined, had dark secrets to hide behind the high walls of the mansions in which they lived" (4). The "dark secrets" that the authors refer to are Dr. Jekyll's violent and homosexual desires that he represses. Singh and Chakrabarti also note that "most significantly, Mr. Hyde enters and leaves Dr. Jekyll's house through the back door which seems a metaphor for the evil that lies behind the façade of civilization and refinement" (4). Dr. Jekyll's professional front is a façade for the evil that resides within him.

Since the basis of the above argument is about the "repressed" evil that lurks within Dr. Jekyll, it is important to take into account the Freudian concept of the psyche, which was concerned with repression and consequently, its expression in excess. Freud developed the theory of instincts according to which the "id" is the uncensored part of the psyche that acts upon violent and sexual desires, the "superego" comprises the broader social norms governing moral behavior, and the "ego" is the mediator between these two extremes. In their paper, Singh and Chakrabarti argue that instead of viewing Hyde as another personality, he can be viewed as a part of Dr. Jekyll's psyche, which would make him very much a part of Dr. Jekyll's personality. The authors write, "Mr. Hyde would seem easily recognizable as the id, seeking instant gratification, having an aggressive instinct, and having no moral or social mores that need be followed...Dr. Jekyll is then the ego; he is conscious and rational, and is dominated by social principles" (6). This line of argument proves that Dr. Jekyll does not have a "dual" personality, but he simply lets himself be governed by his "id" in the form of Hyde.

It is important to question why Dr. Jekyll decides to write a disclosure at the end that would reveal his intentions and point to the fact that he, at least in the beginning, wanted to transform into Hyde. Wouldn't Dr. Jekyll's statement criminalize himself? Nicola Lacey answers this question in her article "Psychologising Jekyll, Demonising Hyde: The Strange Case of Criminal Responsibility." She points out that in the eighteenth century, criminal law was more concerned with "external facts of conduct" rather than a perpetrator's "state of mind." By this, Lacey means that crime was attributed to "bad character," an external evaluation presented by the society, rather than to hidden intentions that would reflect the perpetrator's "state of mind" (117). Lacey calls this "manifest criminality" – the belief that "crime is readily recognizable by members of the community. It is therefore underpinned by a belief in a widely shared ability to make confident evaluations on the basis of appearances," much like how characters in Stevenson's novella insist that Hyde's appearance is evil-looking (Lacey, 118). The attribution of criminality to appearance meant that Dr. Jekyll could blame his conduct on the evil-looking Hyde, thereby victimizing and exonerating himself of the crimes that he committed. The Victorian society, which was more concerned with external conduct, believed Hyde to be the real villain and Dr. Jekyll to be subject to the former's whims.

Dr. Jekyll commits what can be recognized in psychology as an "attribution error" in which he tries to explain the cause of his behavior by wrongly attributing it to another personality, even though the behavior was very much a part of his psyche. He "diffuses" his responsibility, which means that by blaming his wrongdoings on Hyde, he has a "reduced sense of personal responsibility and individual accountability" (Colman, Oxford Dictionary of Psychology). By committing suicide at the end, Jekyll victimizes himself further by showing how he was being controlled by Hyde and how, in the end, Hyde's destructive personality took over his benign one.

Literary critics like Anne Stiles in "Robert Louis Stevenson's Jekyll and Hyde and the Double Brain" present the argument that Stevenson was influenced by the theory of the dual brain while writing his novella. By presenting the stories of Felida X. and by comparing the similarities of the dual personality disorder in Mr. Hyde and Felida X., Stiles argues that Stevenson's novella reflects how the "multiplex personality disorder" affects Dr. Jekyll. While Stevenson might have been influenced by case studies on dual personality disorder, Stiles' argument does not consider that Felida X.'s dual personality is not brought about by any external circumstances. Dr.

Jekyll's chemical potion brings about certain physical, if not psychological, changes within his body, and these changes are initiated by him. His narrative at the end also wrongly attributes his crimes on the chemical potion and its effects. While the potion could have brought about physical changes in Dr. Jekyll's body (making him hairier and apish), the above-mentioned examples of motivations behind his crimes prove that his adoption of Hyde as another personality was to mask his crimes behind another persona. When Dr. Jekyll becomes aware of the gravity of his crimes such as the murder of Sir Carew, he realizes that if he is incriminated, he would either be condemned to death or he would be institutionalized. Stiles, in her article, points out the condition of mental institutions in eighteenth century in which the patient was considered subpar to the doctor, whose case study on the patient would be "dry, emotional and detached from the patient's suffering" (Stiles, 891). According to Stiles, Stevenson in his novella points out the "limitations in the ways in which clinicians constructed their 'case'" (897). Considering that as someone in the medical field, Dr. Jekyll was aware of the treatment of mental patients, it would be fair to assume that his suicide in the end was the better alternative for him than being subjected to the treatment of mental institutions.

The reading of *The Strange Case of Dr. Jekyll and Mr. Hyde* as the battle between two personalities representing good and evil respectively is inherently flawed. The argument does not take into account Dr. Jekyll's willing transformation, his hidden instinctual desires that he represses, and his fulfillment of his desires through Hyde. Rather, the novella is about the lack of criminal accountability in which Dr. Jekyll is exonerated of his crimes by blaming it on "another personality." While the multiple personality disorder has been recognized as a real psychological affliction, the above examples prove that in the case of Dr. Jekyll, this "disorder," or a similar condition, was self-induced by Jekyll to diffuse criminal responsibility for his actions.

Works Cited

Bland, Jay. "Part One - Body and Soul. Sin and Deformity." *Generation of Edward Hyde: The Animal within, from Plato to Darwin to Robert Louis Stevenson*. Bruxelles, BEL: Peter Lang AG, 2010. ProQuest ebrary. Web. 26 February 2016.

Colman, Andrew M. "diffusion of responsibility." A Dictionary of Psychology. : Oxford University Press, 2015. Oxford Reference. 2015. Date Accessed 14 Mar. 2016.

Lacey, Nicola. "Psychologising Jekyll, Demonising Hyde: The Strange Case of Criminal Responsibility." *Criminal Law and Philosophy* 4.2 (2010): 109-33. Springer Link. Web. 18 Feb. 2016.

Singh, Shubh M., and Subho Chakrabarti. "A Study in Dualism: The Strange Case of Dr. Jekyll and Mr. Hyde." *Indian Journal of Psychiatry* 50.3 (2008): 221–223. PMC. Web. 26 Feb. 2016.

Skal, David J. "Chapter One: Frankenstein's Gate." *Screams of Reason: Mad Science and Modern Culture*. New York: W.W. Norton, 1998. Print.

Stiles, Anne. "Robert Louis Stevenson's Jekyll and Hyde and the DoublemBrain." *Studies in English Literature*, 1500-190046.4 (2006): 879-1081.

Chloe Hriso

The Ethics of UN Peacekeeping

In the founding charter signed in 1945, the United Nations assumes the duty of maintaining international security and peace via attempts towards international cooperation, development, and the upholding of non-discriminatory human rights and international law. The UN is the symbol of a "centre for harmonizing the actions of nations," meaning that the UN facilitates these nations working together in order to improve certain conditions.[1] In today's globalized world, global governance such as that of the UN, fosters a platform from which collective action may be taken to address some of the world's most pressing issues. A central function of the United Nations is spearheading complex humanitarian operations amidst conflict and disorder towards peace. This usually takes on the form of *peacekeeping*. The UN's peacekeeping force is one of its most important tools used to pave paths towards peace in such circumstances. However, past peacekeeping failures have put into question both the credibility and the ethical standing of UN peacekeeping and its true efficacy when intervening on such intra-state situations.[2]

The notion of peacekeeping long existed before the birth of the United Nations, however, it was the United Nations that formalized it. According to the UN, the overarching purpose of its peacekeeping force is to create the conditions in conflict-torn countries necessary for the development of peace.[3] It thus allows for a more *active* intervention to ensure globally collective security.[4] They do so by providing security and support from peacebuilding and political agents.

Its guiding principles involve consent from the parties involved, impartiality, and not using force unless in cases of self-defense or in defense of a mandate. Peacekeeping in of itself is multidimensional in the sense that it is flexible and relative to the context it is operating within. Its goals not only consist of maintaining peace and security but also attempting to mediate and prevent conflict as well as facilitating political processes, protecting innocent civilians in the line of conflict, assisting in disarmament, and demobilizing as well as reintegrating those who were once combatants. They may also aid in the support of election processes. Peacekeepers aim to both promote and protect human rights through these actions and assist in reestablishing law and order so that peace may be lasting long after they leave. However, the

UN acknowledges that its peacekeeping does not guarantee success every time, especially considering that they typically operate within politically and physically complex environments.[5]

UN peacekeeping first began in 1948, just a few years after the United Nations was founded.[6] On one of the first missions, UN military observers were deployed on an operation set forth by the Security Council to oversee the Armistice Agreement settled between Israel and its surrounding Arab neighbors. This first peacekeeping operation is known as the "United Nations Truce Supervision Organization", or UNTSO[7] which still continues to monitor armistice agreements, ceasefires, prevent conflict, and aid other UN peacekeeping processes in the Middle East today.[8] UN peacekeeping continued to evolve throughout the Cold War era, a time when tense rivalries around the world were constantly undermining the implementation of peacekeeping measures by the Security Council. During this time, the notion of peacekeeping was chiefly limited to the maintenance of ceasefires and stabilization of situations in support of conflict-resolving political efforts. These actions led to an increase in trust in this global organization and a realization of its central role in global affairs.[9]

After the Cold War, the context in which UN peacekeeping strategy was developed quickly transformed over the years as the nature of the conflicts also changed. As the UN's centrality in the global community grew, it took on increasingly multifaceted tasks.[10] The post- Cold War Era was marked by two trends regarding global conflicts. First, there was a rise in internecine violent conflicts particularly involving civil wars and internal oppression typically resulting in civilians as victims. The second trend was a rise in global governance and security, with the UN leading the way. The result was an increase in the use of peacekeeping and peacebuilding as intervention strategies in societies overcome by the latter kind of conflict.[11] Therefore, the amount of UN peacekeeping operations increased significantly at the end of the Cold War up until the mid-1990s. There was a shift in intervention action upon inter-state conflicts between countries to intra-state conflicts between groups within an individual country. These actions went from the attempt to stabilize inter-governmental situations to stabilizing security within a country, reorganizing police and military, and electing new governments upon which to build democratic foundations.[12] Though the amount of civil wars increased dramatically during this period, intra-state conflict is not a new occurrence. However, its rise to the center of attention within the international community was considered a new phenomenon and can be attributed to the increase in UN peacekeeping missions. In this era, the UN's involvement in these conflict-torn societies was increasingly systematized as it sought to emphasize its self-determined *"raison d'être"* in world politics. [13] Peacekeeping is one of the only modes in which the UN renders itself visible in its capacity as an international actor.[14]

The purpose of the United Nations peacekeeping force was redefined: "UN peacekeeping is defined here in terms of UN-authorized deployment of multinational personnel in situations of potential or actual violent conflict with the express purpose of addressing such violence".[15] The UN military force remained as the backbone of many peacekeeping missions during this time, but now there are many more actors involved in these multifaceted situations including but not limited to: economists, administrators, legal experts, local enforcement officers, human rights monitors, specialists in civil affairs in governance, humanitarian aid workers, and communications experts.[16] Though, there are drawbacks. This type of closed-system intervention brings up many ethical concerns over how the objectives are carried out as well as the particular complications that may arise when an outsider such as the United Nations intervenes on such internally complex situations.

In the 1990s, Rwanda had a population of about seven million which included three ethnic groups –the Hutu, which made up about 85% of the population, the Tutsi which was 14% and the Twa which was 1% of the population. Extremists from the Hutu group that made up a portion of the political elite of Rwanda placed blamed on the minority Tutsi population for the increasing economic, social, and political pressures within the country and for supporting a rebel group that was dominated by the Tutsis. Insidious use of propaganda and political manipulation created an increased divide between the Hutu and the Tutsi by 1992 perpetuated by fear and resentment. Violence escalated in 1994 in which Hutu extremists propelled a genocidal plan to eliminate the Tutsi civilian population. It was estimated that around 200,000 people took part in perpetuating the Rwandan genocide. The Tutsi or anyone suspected of being a part of the minority were killed, either within their homes or as they tried to flee the country. Whole families were killed on the spot. Systematic rape was being used as a horrendous tool to forward the Hutu plan. This resulted in 800,000 deaths –men, women, and children alike, almost all of the Tutsi population.[17]

In the light of gross human rights violations in Rwanda, the United Nations became actively involved in 1993 under the international force known as UNAMIR, the United Nations Assistance Mission for Rwanda.[18] There was some deliberation that occurred before a peacekeeping operation could be deployed in Rwanda to determine if it such an operation could be possible in the first place and if the parties would consent. The primary objective was to create a level from which a democratic government can be transitioned into so conflict be laid to rest. However, much of those who investigated in Rwanda were strongly misled as they solely met with moderates and not a single extremist. This was coupled with a lack of a deeper understanding of the Rwandan conflict, making the deployment of a peacebuilding operation grounded in naivety.[19] Additionally, the operation received low economic and political backing from the international community and the UN Security Council. "UNAMIR was deployed naively and was undernourished, a deadly combination, a gift from member states who hoped for a quick victory and were willing to take shortcuts to get there".[20] The failure in the attempt to establish a transitional democratic government, as if it could magically correct the ramifications of the Rwandan genocide, in fact further contributed to the deteriorating security within the environment –this would ultimately backfire and make the establishment of such a government absolutely impossible.[21] And because UN armed peacekeeping forces are not allowed to inflict force in the administering of their mandate, it was not long before the eventual hasty retreat of UN peacekeeping forces, leaving Rwandan civilians to fend for themselves.

The UN peacekeeping operation in Rwanda clearly failed in the face of ethnic violence and civil conflict that was beyond their comprehension and control. In an independent inquiry commissioned by the Secretary General in 1999 regarding the Rwandan genocide, the United Nation's systematic failure to prevent and put an end to the genocide is acknowledged. Here it was noted the central failure was the lack of resources and political commitment from the international community backing the UN's presence.[22] There was also neglect to obtain a fuller understanding of the conflict that ultimately undermined the entire operation. The failure was indicative of the shortfalls of UN peacekeeping in intra-state conflicts. Their attempts at mitigation failed because there was no platform from which they can negotiate peace in such a chaotic conflict –and the use of force would contradict their intentions in every way. How can it be possible to get the conflicting parties to agree when you have an extremist group brutally attacking and killing innocent civilians? How can a compromise be reached when there are parties so driven by resentful values? Can sustainable peace be arrived at successfully amidst conflict and chaos? The UN is apparently only effective when there is a potential for "peace to keep" – Kofi Annan, the chief of the Department of Peacekeeping Operations (DPKO) at the time, stated that "peacekeeping works when you have a clear mandate, a will on part of the people to make peace. The inspiration for acceptable and viable peace can only spring from the leaders and people in the country".[23] And many of the problems that were initially caused by peacekeeping can be attributed to its increasing popularity as a tool of choice of the international community to contain conflict during this epoch.[24] The UN's successes with peacekeeping prior to the mid-1990s in addition to the growing confidence in the use of peacekeeping led to low expectations and weak mandates in Rwanda and other intrastate operations.

Another question of ethical concern that UN peacekeeping raises is this: is there such a thing as 'armed peace'? Traditionally, peacekeepers are soldiers –and armed peacekeeping forces and their relationship with civilians is a questionably interesting notion. Peacekeeping often operates in this grey area between conflict and peace where traditional 'Just War' ethics cannot be explicitly applied. Their responsibilities include: keeping conflicting groups apart, guarding designated safe zones, or protecting aid convoys. During the entire operation, it is imperative that they do not abandon impartiality or neutrality, or engage in the use aggressive force. Peacekeepers must win the trust of and cooperate with civilians as well as with local authorities and sometimes hostile forces. With peacekeeping soldiers coming from countries around the world, they are often required to work in environments in which the culture and civilian practices are unfamiliar. There are many ethical obligations when it comes to military peacekeeping, which tends to undermine what it is to be an actual soldier as they are expected to act in such a way that does not embody what they were trained to do in the first place. It also affects the rapport peacekeeping soldiers have with civilians. It is possible that they are often seen as incapable which can embed a paternalistic sentiment in peacekeepers and establish a hierarchy in which they operate with civilians – "how is it possible for soldiers to become successful peacekeepers in gendered and race hierarchical contexts?"[25] With this hierarchical sentiment, peacekeepers may also assume dominant roles that might end up causing more harm and undercut any trust civilians might confide in them. In this sense, true political neutrality is largely unattainable with the use of *armed* peacekeeping forces.[26]

Making decisions that are both ethical and justifiable under peacekeeping is challenging with internecine conflicts. On what grounds can the United Nations, as an outsider, intervene on local conflicts? Outsiders should be able to intervene in cases of internecine conflict if it is morally justifiable, as the 'Just War' theory states.[27] If there are gross human rights violations occurring upon civilians, then outsiders should undeniably intervene to mitigate and put an end to such conflict while establishing a potential for a more peaceful future. However, one may argue that outsiders may not have the right to interfere unless the conflict involves matters that are of direct concern to, or directly impact, the outsider. The United Nations is grounded on the principle of and responsibility to international peace and security, and upholding human rights and international law. Therefore, this does give the UN morally justifiable grounds upon which to intervene. What was unethical about Rwanda was *how* they intervened. The lack of a fuller scope of understanding of the conflict set the stage for failure, further inflicting damage.

The mid-1990s was deemed the "period of reassessment"[28] by the United Nations as its founding principles proved to be incompatible or insufficient in dealing with these conflicts. The United Nations is institutionally historical in structure, in which its constitutional Charter reflected the power configuration, and ideas and values of the international community at this particular moment in time right after World War II.[29] Its central responsibility is maintaining international peace and security under a global governance from which to deliberate. Its second most central responsibility is the development of peace.

The UN did not evolve to focus on internal conflicts until much later so it is possible that some of these constitutional values have become outdated or far too ideal to mediate complex situations such as the Rwandan conflict. What is needed is clearer and less abstract language, mandates, and goals in addition to a fuller and more holistic understanding of the root causes of war in conflict in these countries and regions. The root causes include systematic forces such as abusive government, economic policy or democratic absence that violate human rights. In addition, increasing use of deliberation in the Security Council's decision making processes could produce better mandates that could lend itself to more sustainable solutions.[30] Though there is a long way to go, there is still room for optimism.

Endnotes

[1] United Nations. *Charter of the United Nations*. 1945. http://www.un.org/en/charter-united- nations. Chapter I.

[2] Malone, D. M., & Thakur, R.. (2001). UN Peacekeeping: Lessons Learned?. *Global Governance*, 7(1), 12.

[3] United Nations. "What is Peacekeeping?". United Nations Peacekeeping.http://www.un.org/en/peacekeeping/operations/peacekeeping.shtml

[4] Durch, William J. *The Evolution of UN Peacekeeping: Case Studies and Comparative Analyses*. New York, NY: St. Martin's, 1993. Print. Pages 1-2.

[5] UN. What is Peacekeeping?

[6] United Nations. "The Early Years". United Nations Peacekeeping. http://www.un.org/en/peacekeeping/operations/early.shtml

[7] United Nations. "History of Peacekeeping". United Nations Peacekeeping. http://www.un.org/en/peacekeeping/operations/history.shtml

[8] United Nations. "Helping to bring stability in the Middle East". UNTSO: United Nations Truce Supervision Organization. http://www.un.org/en/peacekeeping/missions/untso/

[9] United Nations. "The Early Years".

[10] United Nations. "Post Cold-War Surge". United Nations Peacekeeping. http://www.un.org/en/peacekeeping/operations/surge.shtml

[11] Keating, Thomas F., and W. Andy. Knight. *Building Sustainable Peace*. New York: United Nations University Press, 2004. Print. Page XXXII.

[12] United Nations. "Post Cold-War Surge".

[13] Aksu, Esref. United Nations, *Intra-State Peacekeeping and Normative Change*. Manchester, UK: Manchester University Press, 2003. Print. Pages 1-2.

[14] Aksu, 27.

[15] Aksu, 25.

[16] United Nations. "Post Cold-War Surge".

[17] United Human Rights Council. "Genocide in Rwanda". UHRC: Genocide. http://www.unitedhumanrights.org/genocide/genocide_in_rwanda.htm

[18] United Nations. "Rwanda: UNAMIR Background". United Nations Peacekeeping http://www.un.org/en/peacekeeping/missions/past/unamirS.htm

[19] Barnett, Michael. *Eyewitness to a Genocide : The United Nations and Rwanda*. Ithaca, NY, USA: Cornell University Press, 2002. Page 65.

[20] Barnett, 72.

[21] Barnett, 76

[22] United Nations. "Letter dated 15 December 1999 from the Secretary-General addressed to the President of the Security Council". United Nations Security Council. Page 3. http://www.un.org/en/ga/search/view_doc.asp?symbol=S/1999/1257

[23] Barnett. 65.

[24] Durch, 2.

[25] Hutchings, Kimberly. *Global Ethics: An Introduction.* Cambridge, UK: Polity, 2010. Print. Pages 172-173.

[26] Malone, D. M., & Thakur, R. (2001). UN Peacekeeping: Lessons Learned. *Global Governance,* 7(1), Page 14.

[27] Hutchings, 172.

[28] United Nations. "Post Cold-War Surge".

[29] Aksu, 20.

[30] Malone, 12-14.

Works Cited

Aksu, Esref. United Nations, *Intra-State Peacekeeping and Normative Change.* Machester, UK: Manchester University Press, 2003. Print.

Barnett, Michael. *Eyewitness to a Genocide: The United Nations and Rwanda.* Ithaca, NY, USA: Cornell University Press, 2002. Print.

Durch, William J. *The Evolution of UN Peacekeeping: Case Studies and Comparative Analyses.* New York, NY: St. Martin's, 1993. Print.

Hutchings, Kimberly. *Global Ethics: An Introduction.* Cambridge, UK: Polity, 2010. Print.

Keating, Thomas F., and W. Andy. Knight. *Building Sustainable Peace.* New York: United Nations University Press, 2004. Print.

Malone, D. M., & Thakur, R.. (2001). UN Peacekeeping: Lessons Learned?. *Global Governance,* 7(1), 11–17.

United Human Rights Council. "Genocide in Rwanda". UHRC: Genocide. http://www.unitedhumanrights.org/genocide/genocide_in_rwanda.htm

United Nations. *Charter of the United Nations.* 1945. http://www.un.org/en/charter-united- nations

United Nations. "Helping to bring stability in the Middle East". UNTSO: United Nations Truce Supervision Organization. http://www.un.org/en/peacekeeping/missions/untso

United Nations. "History of Peacekeeping". United Nations Peacekeeping. http://www.un.org/en/peacekeeping/operations/history.shtml

United Nations. "Letter dated 15 December 1999 from the Secretary-General addressed to the President of the Security Council". United Nations Security Council. http://www.un.org/en/ga/search/view_doc.asp?symbol=S/1999/1257

United Nations. "Post Cold-War Surge". United Nations Peacekeeping. http://www.un.org/en/peacekeeping/operations/surge.shtml

United Nations. "Rwanda: UNAMIR Background". United Nations Peacekeeping. http://www.un.org/en/peacekeeping/missions/past/unamirS.htm

United Nations. "The Early Years". United Nations Peacekeeping. http://www.un.org/en/peacekeeping/operations/early.shtml

United Nations. "What is Peacekeeping?". United Nations Peacekeeping. http://www.un.org/en/peacekeeping/operations/peacekeeping.shtml

Caitlin McLaughlin

Female Sexuality in a Patriarchal Society: An Analysis of Victorian Era Feminist Texts

Women have been historically marginalized in Western society by the patriarchy; in Victorian England, men held all social and political power. Women were expected to maintain the household, take care of the children, and submit sexually to their husbands: their lives were defined by men. Women who did not take a husband, or lost a husband, had to either remarry or face financial insecurity. Some women turned to prostitution to support themselves, but these women were seen as morally deficient, because women were expected to uphold their virginity until marriage. Virginal women were seen as valuable for men to marry, although men were not held to the same standard. "Goblin Market" by Christina Rossetti and "The Great Social Evil" highlight the ways in which women's sexuality influenced their role in society.

In both narratives, women's morality is defined by whether or not she is sexually active out of wedlock. A woman who is a virgin is morally righteous, yet the author of "The Great Social Evil" asserts that virginity is "that which is commonly but untruly called virtue" ("Great Social Evil" 1621). The narrator is a prostitute, and therefore lacks so-called "virtue," yet she believes that the conflation of virginity to virtue is false. Therefore, a woman who is not virginal could still be virtuous. In "Goblin Market" Rossetti uses biblical imagery to illustrate the way that virginity is tied to morality:

> "...How fair the vine must grow
> Whose grapes are so luscious;
> How warm the wind must blow
> Thro' those fruit bushes" "No,"
> said Lizzie: "No, no no; Their offers
> should not charm us,
> Their evil gifts would harm us." ("Goblin Market" 60-66).

Just as the serpent in the Garden of Eden deceived Eve with the lure of the apple, the Goblin men lure Lizzie and Laura to eat their fruit. Fruit is representative of sex, and although both girls want to eat the fruit, to do so would "harm" them. Sex is framed as something "evil" that morally sound women can abstain. In both "The Great Social Evil" and "Goblin Market" virginity is framed as virtuous. To give in to one's sexual desires is to lose one's virtue. Although the author of "The Great Social Evil" dismisses the idea that virginity is tied to virtue, Lizzie in "Goblin Market" believes that for her sister to submit to the goblin men sexually would harm her morally.

In both works, sexuality is given value in economic terms. Power in the form of money comes from sex. The narrator in "The Great Social Evil" supports herself financially through prostitution, and although she is judged for her lifestyle, merchants "find my money as good and my pay better than that of Madam, my Lady" and goes on to say that, "if all circumstances and conditions of our lives had been reversed, would Madam, my Lady, have done better or been better than I?" ("Great Social Evil" 1622). The narrator's elevated lifestyle is paid for by her prostitution. She believes that she is better off financially in her life because of the work she does. If she were a "madam" living under her husband's salary, she might not be able to afford the lifestyle she has. She is in control because she uses her sexuality to make money. The merchants do not question her lifestyle because she can afford their goods. The narrator points out that the women in factories are exploited by capitalism. Anyone, including herself, who can afford the, "taste and elegance of that tradesman's show" do so because "of the poor creatures who wrought it" despite "what they were paid for it" ("Great Social Evil" 1623). Women who were just as exploited as prostitutes make the goods that are bought and enjoyed by those who condemn prostitution. The women in the factories are paid little, and lack agency. They feel that they too have "lost their virtue," yet these women are not thought to be immoral because they profit off of their labor, while the prostitute profits off of her "labor."

Men control women's class in society. In "Goblin Market" Lizzie has to pay the goblins for their fruit, but she does not have any money. She says, "I have no copper in my purse," to which the Goblin men reply, "You have much gold upon your head...Buy from us with a golden curl" ("Goblin Market" 118-125). Lizzie gives up a part of herself, her hair, to the goblins in exchange for their fruit. The goblins profit off Laura's hair, while Laura is left missing a part of her body. Hair, especially in Victorian England, was seen as a part of the self. Hair was important to women; it signified status. In Victorian England, men controlled the social status of women; women were expected to marry men of their class or higher. By taking Lizzie's hair, the Goblins have diminished her class status. However, the narrator in "The Great Social Evil" controls her own class status. She "pay[s] business visits to...the most fashionable of the West-end" ("Great Social Evil" 1622). If the narrator were to work in a factory like other unmarried women, she would not be able to afford the luxurious lifestyle she has. The factory women are poor because they have not taken a husband, or their husband is also poor. Men place them in their class. The narrator's lifestyle in "The Great Social Evil" controls her own status.

A woman who has sex is undesirable for marriage, and an unmarried woman in the Victorian era is financially insecure. In both circumstances, men wield the power. When women take control in a sexual situation, as the narrator does in "The Great Social Evil," the power structure is inverted. Men give money to women, and women profit off of male sexuality. When Laura decides to approach the goblin men, she says, "Give me much and many," then "Held out her apron" and "tossed them her penny," but does not stay to eat with the goblins ("Goblin Market" 365-366). Laura, taking ownership of her sexuality, tells the goblins what she wants, instead of allowing the goblins to guide her. She, like the narrator in "The Great Social Evil" controls what she spends her money on. Prostitution allows women to take ownership of their goods in a way that women of the time were not capable of.

In both pieces women who take charge of their sexuality are outcast by society, particularly by men. Laura is able to pay the goblin men for her fruit, taking charge of the situation in a way that Lizzie did not. She holds herself in a position of power over the men because she wants to take her fruit and return to her sister. She is the one telling the goblins what to do. The goblins do not take well to her dominance, they:

> Tore her gown and soiled her stocking,
> Twitched her hair out by the roots,
> Stamped upon her tender feet,
> Held her hands and squeezed their fruits
> Against her mouth to make her eat ("Goblin Market" 402-407).

The goblins force Laura to submit to their wills. Men rape women to show power, and the goblin men show their power over Laura by forcing her to eat their fruit in front of them when she asks to take it home with her instead. The goblins do not like that a woman would attempt to subvert the current power structure. In "The Great Social Evil" the narrator notes that while the wealthy who look down upon her, "stand on [their] eminence shouting that [the prostitutes] should be ashamed of [themselves]" they "deprive [them] of proper and harmless amusements to subject [them] in mass to the pressure of force ... to add the cruelty of active persecution to the cruelty of the passive indifference which made [them] what [they] are" ("Great Social Evil" 1624). Because men wield most of the power in society, women who are unmarried must decide to either find a husband, or work in horrendous conditions in factories. The same men who created the systems that forced them to turn to prostitution shame women who turn to prostitution for their livelihood. Prostitution threatens the power structure in the same way that Laura taking charge of the goblin men did. When women find a way to support themselves in the system created by men, they are shamed.

Women, in both pieces, stand in solidarity with other women. In "The Great Social Evil", the author draws attention to the plight of women in factories that work hard and are exploited by the patriarchal society they live in. She writes that, "These poor women toil on starvation wages, while penury, misery and famine clutch them by the throat and say, 'Rend up your body or die'" ("Great Social Evil" 1623). She stands up for factory workers in order to alter the social structure that causes women to be forced into prostitution. In "Goblin Market," Laura offers herself to the goblins in order to save Lizzie. In the last stanza, Lizzie says:

> "For there is no friend like a sister
> In calm or stormy weather;
> To cheer one on the tedious way,
> To fetch one if one goes astray
> To lift one if one totters down,
> To strengthen whilst one stands" ("Goblin Market" 563-568).

Women can help the situations of other women by offering their support. Women act as "sisters" to one another; they share in a mutual subjugation of the patriarchy. This solidarity among women allows for liberation. Women are liberated by the support of other women even while they are feeling powerful, and when they aren't, other women are around to help them. The narrator in "The Great Social Evil" creates this support network by granting a voice to the women in the factory who are often deprived of their voice by the patriarchy. Both works highlight the importance of female friendship and empowerment.

Women in the Victorian era were robbed of their agency through the patriarchy. They have been suppressed sexually for so long, that women who profit from their sexuality challenge the social order. As women began to express themselves through literature, they demanded the respect that they were denied historically. Not only were these women fighting for equality, but they fought to dismantle the systems that allowed men to stay in power. The narrator of "The Great Social Evil" implies that if women were not forced into low paying factory jobs, they would not be forced to sell their bodies. Furthermore, men fuel the sex industry, without the demand for prostitution; the narrator would have no job. In "Goblin Market," Rossetti explores the shame that is experienced internally and externally for women when they are sexually active. The goblins provoke women into eating their fruit, and yet shun the women once they submit. Both works point out a fundamental flaw in society: men use women for their own gain. When women gain bodily autonomy they become liberated. Both works call for the abolition of systems that prevent women from living an independent life.

Works Cited

Anonymous. "The Great Social Evil." *The Norton Anthology of English Literature: The Victorian Age*. Ed. Stephen Greenblatt. New York: W.W. Norton & Company, Inc, 2012. Print

Rossetti, Christina. "Goblin Market." *The Norton Anthology of English Literature: The Victorian Age*. Ed. Stephen Greenblatt. New York: W.W. Norton & Company, Inc, 2012. Print.

Shawn Mengel

Frankenstein and the Power of Privacy

In her work *Privacy and Private States*, Janna Smith defines solitude as "the most complete state of privacy." It is the one state where one can be completely alone with no one to intervene or affect their thoughts. It is a place where one can truly be themselves and act on their thoughts without giving in to the pressures of society. In many ways, this state can have either strongly positive or negative effects on an individual. Seeking solitude through isolation can be beneficial by allowing one to escape the sometimes overwhelming emotions of others. When alone, one can focus inward to reflect upon and discover more about who they really are. Conversely, when alone, there is no one to mediate between an individual's good and bad thoughts. Often the worse thoughts, ones that have never been revealed in the presence of others, can bounce around one's mind echoing louder and louder, drowning out the others. This negative side of solitude and privacy are most prominently displayed in Mary Shelley's renowned story *Frankenstein*, through the characters Victor Frankenstein and his creature. Both of these characters experience extended periods of isolation from society. In both cases, these periods of solitude change the characters for the worst thereby driving the story's tragic plot. In her novel *Frankenstein*, Mary Shelley demonstrates how isolation and solitude from others, whether forced or chosen, can cause one to lose their humanity and their mind.

In the beginning, the effects of solitude are shown solely on the protagonist, Dr. Victor Frankenstein. In order to pursue his research in galvanism and the creation of life, Frankenstein chooses to seclude himself from all of his family and friends. He hides in his apartment all day and night to conduct his experiments. He is very secretive with his work as a way of both preventing others from stealing his research and to prevent people from questioning the ethics of his work. Frankenstein has great plans to create a new, beautiful race of life and cannot let anyone stop him. As he works, Dr. Frankenstein becomes fully immersed and obsessed with his final goal of discovering the secret to life.

Shortly before Frankenstein left home to study at the University of Ingolstadt, his mother had died of scarlet fever. This becomes one of the primary motivations behind Frankenstein's studies. According to Steven Sanders, the death of his mother becomes "central to the psyche of Shelley's 'mad scientist'" (Sanders 79). Dr. Frankenstein leaves his family while still grieving. Because of this, his solitude does not allow him to properly deal with his emotions and they are quickly transformed into Frankenstein's apparent need to discover the secret to life and the cure to death. Had he been surrounded by people that cared for him, Frankenstein could have learned to better deal with the death of his mother rather than allowing it to become the inspiration and one of the driving forces in his research.

Through the results of Frankenstein's studies and research, Mary Shelley further reveals the harms of self-induced isolation and solitude. Humans cannot live in a constant state of privacy; they must interact and be social in order to emphasize and reinforce the more positive aspects of the human psyche over the negative ones. With no one around to talk to, Frankenstein loses a sense of ethics and morals. Isolation from society causes him to forget the responsibilities and consequences involved in pursuing knowledge, ultimately causing his downfall. Frankenstein forgets that in creating life, especially one of human form and understanding, he is creating something that will require care upon its conception. His monster, once made and alive cannot be simply abandoned. Frankenstein's solitude causes him to lose this sense of responsibility for his creation, a mistake that will torment him for the remainder of his life. Had he done his work surrounded by family, friends, and peers, they would have showed him the implications of his work and possibly convinced him to stop his work. Because of this, Frankenstein's privacy converts his love for science and the pursuit of knowledge into his tragic flaw as the product of his work later kills everyone he loves.

Although Frankenstein's time of solitude ends when he returns home, his privacy and its effects continue to haunt him. Upon returning home, Frankenstein discovers that his creation murdered his younger brother William and framed one of his most trusted maids, Justine, for the death. Justine is later executed for the crime she was thought to have committed. Following these two deaths, Frankenstein again becomes filled with grief, but this time his grief is accompanied by guilt as he feels responsible for what happened. After Justine is put to death, Frankenstein feels "a weight of despair and remorse pressed on [his] heart" (Shelley 101). In his mind, his actions that caused the creation of the monster were "deeds of mischief beyond description horrible" and he would never forgive himself. Although he is surrounded by family and friends, Frankenstein's mind retreats inward to form a sort of mental solitude. The melancholy caused by Frankenstein's guilt makes him distant from his family for the remainder of the story. Following each subsequent death, Frankenstein's guilt becomes more and more powerful within him. By the end of the story and his life, Frankenstein is a sad, broken man. His carefree and joyful nature from the beginning of his life has completely vanishes as everyone he loved dies as a direct result of the decisions he made while in his months of complete privacy.

When Victor Frankenstein first brought his creation into existence, he was appalled at the hideous being that had been the culmination of his work. He became startled and scared, causing him to flee his apartment. By the time Frankenstein returned, his creature was gone. As mentioned earlier, Frankenstein's impaired state of mind from his isolation then caused him to forget his responsibilities to the creature upon realizing it was gone. Because of this, Frankenstein never tried to pursue his creation and do whatever was necessary to either fully abort his experiment or take care of and raise the creature. Instead of being born in the presence of a family to nurture and provide for it, the creature was born alone and confused. Throughout the beginning of his life, Frankenstein's creature made repeated attempts to join society, to find a family, and to just be loved. However, every time he tried, his appearance horrified the people he encountered and they rejected him. When he entered a village, he was met with a barrage of stones. Upon saving a woman from drowning, he was rewarded with a gunshot wound. In regards to privacy, Frankenstein's creature represents the complete opposite of his creator. Frankenstein's creature hates the loneliness associated with his isolation while Frankenstein pursued it willingly. While Frankenstein chose to be in solitude, his creature was forced into it. Despite this difference between the characters' motivations, their extreme forms of privacy still affected both in similarly negative ways.

With each subsequent interaction with humans and their refusal to accept Frankenstein's creature based on its appearance, the creature becomes increasingly frustrated and angry toward the human race. At first, he remains hopeful that eventually someone would see him for who he really was rather than the "hideously deformed and loathsome" figure he appeared to be (Shelley 141). But over time, the creature's solitude and loneliness erodes his sense of hope. He begins to wonder if he truly is "a monster... from which all men fled and whom all men disowned" that everyone made him out to be (Shelly 141). After the De Lacey family rejects and beats him, Frankenstein's creature gives up trying to fit in and decides to declare "everlasting war against the species," especially against Frankenstein for bringing him into and abandoning him in this cruel world (Shelley 163). The creature's isolation and forced privacy therefore turn him into the monster that everyone already believed him to be. With no one to accompany him, the constant state of privacy drove him to madness, revenge, and murder.

In doing so, Mary Shelley shows that too much privacy will corrupt even the best, most pure-hearted individuals. Shelley's portrayal of Frankenstein's creature soon after its "birth" shows strong connections and inspirations from the works of the French philosopher Jean-Jacques Rousseau. In his book *Emile*, Rousseau states, "Coming from the hands of the Author of all things, everything is good; in the hands of man, everything degenerates" (Rousseau

11). Rousseau believed in the purity of nature and the innate goodness of newborn children. Mary Shelley reflects this idea through the early behavior of the creature. Shelley does her best to give Frankenstein's creature childish traits. After his birth, he is confused and frightened as expected of a neglected child. He does not know where he is or how to communicate with others. Then, during the creature's early encounters with humans, she depicts him as kind and gentle as possible. For instance, once Frankenstein's creature understands the poverty of Felix and his family, he decides to refrain from taking their food and begins to help the family by secretly cutting firewood for them. Upon learning how to understand words and tones, Frankenstein's creature learns to sympathize with the family. He feels joy when they are happy and gloom when they are sad. When the creature first learns of the idea of war and murder, he is appalled. All of this demonstrates that initially, Frankenstein's creature was pure-hearted and innately good.

By the end of the story though, Frankenstein's creature has lost that innate goodness and has become a murderous, monstrous fiend. However, Frankenstein's creature had no real relationships with anyone during most of the story. This raises the question of what had corrupted Frankenstein's creature into its homicidal rage. Following the beliefs of Rousseau, living in nature should have maintained the creature's purity, but this obviously did not happen. The only possibility is that the creature's forced state of solitude and privacy corrupted its mind thereby inciting its wrath against humanity. The unending isolation imposed by society changed Frankenstein's creature for the worst.

In Mary Shelley's novel *Frankenstein*, both the protagonist and antagonist are subjected to long periods of extreme privacy. Despite the differences in causes and motivations for the privacy, both characters experience harmful transformations in their behaviors as a direct result of their solitude. In the case of Dr. Victor Frankenstein, his self-chosen isolation drives him to insanity and the creation of his tormentor. As for Frankenstein's creature, the neglect and forced isolation from society drives him to murder and war against humanity. In the stories of both characters, had they not been excluded from society, a majority — if not all — of the conflicts would have never occurred creating a significantly less tragic plot.

Works Cited

Rousseau, Jean-Jacques. Emile. London: J.M. Dent, 1993. Print.

Sanders, Steven. *The Philosophy of Science Fiction Film*. Lexington: U of Kentucky, 2008. Print.

Shelley, Mary Wollstonecraft, and Patrick Nobes. *Frankenstein*. Oxford: Oxford UP, 2000. Print. Smith, Janna. "Privacy and Private States." *The Private I: Privacy in a Public World*. Ed. Molly Peacock. Saint Paul: Graywolf Press, 2001. 3-22. Print.

Ria Mulherkar

The Manmade Perils of Ambiguous Sexuality

Most societies place such a high value on the notion of sex, that any ambiguity in this department is perceived negatively. In fact, most parents take such offense to a child born with ambiguous sex, that they seek to immediately rectify all uncertainty and assign their child a definitive identity. However, there are a great number of difficulties associated with determining which sex to assign a child. Intersexuality is no light matter, and the determination of sex can have severe future ramifications. In a series of essays, the problems with current policies on intersexuality and sex determination are revealed.

Many individuals take issue with the prevailing need to categorize a sexually ambiguous child as male or female. Alice Dreger—in her essay "'Ambiguous Sex'—or Ambivalent Medicine?"—points out that "the 'true sex' of most individuals... [is]... settled nicely into one of the two great and preferred camps, no matter how confusing the rest of their sexual anatomies" (139). Dreger cites "contemporary theory," which states that "all children must have their gender identity fixed very early life for a consistent... gender identity to form, [and] that... the child's anatomy must match the 'standard' anatomy for her or his gender" (140). Individuals such as Anne Fausto-Sterling contest this norm: She suggests in her essay, "The Five Sexes, Revisited," that "the two-sex system embedded in our society is not adequate to encompass the full spectrum of human sexuality" (Henderson et al., 203). As an alternative, she suggests a "five-sex system," which accounts for not only males and females, but also true hermaphrodites (who she calls "herms"), individuals born with testes and female genitalia (termed "merms"), as well as individuals born with ovaries and male genitalia (termed "ferms") (Henderson et al., 203). Although Fausto-Sterling's proposed nomenclature may not have taken root, the subsequent emergence of "intersexuals" certainly insinuates a spectrum of sorts between the male and female sexual identity (Henderson et al., 203-204). This line of argument suggests that there may not even be a need to categorize an infant as definitively male or definitively female. In fact, to do so implies that there is something inherently wrong with ambiguous sexuality, and this conclusion has ethical ramifications of its own.

Regardless, the reality is that parents prefer to assign a definitive sex to a sexually ambiguous child. However, not only is this decision extremely difficult to make, the mechanics of intersex surgery often create a bias towards a female sex assignment. In "'Ambiguous Sex'— or Ambivalent Medicine?" Alice Dreger elaborates on these concerns. For one, when determining the sex, it is important to consider the future hormonal and physiological processes that may take place to influence the child's psychological perception of gender. Dreger mentions "a plethora of technologies" that are "used to create and maintain [a] sex in as believable a form as possible" (141). These include genital surgery, surgery on other parts such as breasts, hormonal treatments, and a fostering of the chosen gender via psychosocial means (141). However, maintenance is not the only concern when choosing which sex to assign. As Dreger states, "surgeons seem to demand far more for a penis to count as 'successful' than for a vagina to count as such" (142). This dominant protocol, which Dreger calls "arguably sexist" (143) biases the decision of sex determination, and thus doctors are more likely to encourage a female sex assignment. Considering the often unpredictable challenges associated with sex determination, as well as the inherent partiality involved, the current policy for dealing with intersexuality is further undermined.

An additional issue with the present guidelines regarding intersexuality is that they seem to hold sexuality to a different standard than other medical conditions. Dreger draws an interesting analogy to highlight the absurdity of decisions taken by parents: You wouldn't cut off a baby's arm if it was underdeveloped or mutated, so why would you do so with a penis? (144). She also points out that genitalia and reproductive organs, unlike other body parts, can be concealed with relative ease during childhood (145). Thus, she argues that there may not be a need for parents and physicians to make an executive decision regarding a child's gender so early on. Generally, infants are only operated on if absolutely necessary to sustain their lives. The fact that decisions regarding sexuality are not subject to the same ethical considerations as other medical conditions, again, casts doubt on the righteousness of existing policy.

The most compelling evidence against current policies on sex determination, however, lies in the psychological repercussions of these decisions on affected individuals. Both Dreger and Fausto-Sterling refer to the John/Joan case of a baby boy who was reassigned to the female sex as a result of an accidental penile ablation. Though raised as a girl, Joan was always uncomfortable in her body, and at the age of fourteen, came to resume life as a boy. The authors also offer several other examples of individuals subjected to sexual reassignment as infants coming to terms with their true identities as adults. In several cases, the children were raised in oblivion, either believing certain procedures had been done to save their lies, or simply not knowing that they had been born with a questionable sex. Such individuals are often psychologically disturbed, uncomfortable in their bodies and confused in terms of their identities. More often than not, learning the truth about their sexual identity causes them to become distanced from and mistrustful of their parents and physicians. Although sex reassignment surgeries are often conducted to provide a child with a definitive gender identity and protect him or her from sexual confusion, it is extremely difficult to predict how an individual will react psychologically to his or her assignment. Despite outward genitalia, hormonal treatments, and the societal imposition of gender, there are several cases where individuals assigned to a particular sex have been uncomfortable with this assignment. As such, there seems to be a need to reevaluate the existing practices in regards to intersexuality.

An interesting ethical dilemma pertaining to this topic is presented in the passage, "Case Study: Culture Clash Involving Intersex." The study describes a 13-year-old Middle Eastern boy who begins to develop breasts, menstruate, and is then discovered to have both a uterus and ovaries. His parents wish for the doctors to remove his female reproductive organs and to treat him so that he can retain his gender identity. They do not wish to inform their son of his female anatomy. The family insists that this is best for him, as they would have trouble accepting the boy if he were to become a girl; additionally, he risks being murdered by individuals of his community if he turns out to be a homosexual. After detailing the case, the passage then features responses from a series of informed individuals. David Diamond writes, "Given the significant cultural divide, the parents' own value system must be the guide" (Henderson et al., 213). Alice Dreger and Bruce Wilson have a polarized view. They refute the significance of cultural values in this context, citing the example of female genital mutation, and assert, "the physician should refuse to cooperate in the deception" (Henderson *et al.*, 217). They go so far as to suggest the parents' behavior may qualify as abuse or neglect (Henderson et al., 217). Sharon Sytsma takes a more moderate approach, advising that "the physicians should deliberate with the parents and explain the advantages of allowing the child to participate in decisions about his medical treatment" (Henderson *et al.*, 215). Aside from Diamond, all other authors seem to agree that, ideally, the child whose identity is in question should be informed. Perhaps Sytsma's methodology is most principled, as she asks the physicians to appeal not only to the parents, but also the populace to spread awareness about informed consent.

The aforementioned works all indicate a need for the establishment of discrete policies on intersexuality and sex determination. The ethical issues that they raise mandate a reform in the current policies on the matter. Sex assignment is a serious and challenging action that can have very dangerous psychological consequences. As such, physicians must reconsider the necessity of even performing a sex reassignment, and if deemed essential, proceed with incredible caution.

Works Cited

Diamond, David, Sharon Sytsma, Alice Dreger, And Bruce Wilson. "Case-Study: Culture Clash Involving Intersex." Henderson *et al.*, 211-217.

Dreger, Alice Domurat. "'Ambiguous Sex'—or Ambivalent Medicine?" *Health Disease and Illness: Concepts in Medicine*. Washington D.C.: Georgetown University Press, 2004. 137-152. Print.

Fausto-Sterling, Anne. "The Five Sexes, Revisited." Henderson *et al.*, 202-210.

Henderson, Gail E., Sue E. Estroff, Larry R. Churchill, Nancy M. P. King, Jonathan Oberlander, and Ronald P. Strauss, eds. *The Social Medicine Reader: Volume II*. Durham: Duke University Press, 2005. Print.

Raul Cooke Brossy

They Make You Stronger

It was 8th grade. I was attending a school for students with Learning Differences. Sitting in the back of the media lab I listened to my teacher as he explained our final project. We had to make a documentary about our Learning Differences and how we deal with them. I was listening while looking around the room. It was a long white room with two rows of white Macintosh computers mounted on tables. In front of the computers was a smart board. In the far corner, next to the smart board, sat my teacher, Roland Moe.

Roland was a medium height with a slightly muscular build. He had pale white skin, short brown hair, and a small goatee. He always wore a flannel shirt and jeans that made him look like he came out of Nirvana's "Smells Like Teen Spirit" music video. He was one of the friendliest teachers and always displayed an enthusiastic smile. At the moment he was sitting at his desk, leaning back with his feet up. "What is a learning disability?" he asked.

His question was met by the quiet humming of the computer fans. Finally, one of my classmates, Trent, raised his hand and said, "It is a problem in our brains that prevents us from doing something."

Roland smiled. "Good try, but no. A learning disability is a difference in our brains that make us learn differently. It is, in fact, not a disability, but an obstacle. For instance, having dyslexia does not prevent you from reading, it just makes it harder. Because it is harder to read, people with dyslexia often prefer listening or pictures as a learning alternative. Another example is ADD. I know many of you have difficulty keeping organized because of your ADD. However, you are not disorganized, just not neat. Let me show you. Trent! Ask me to find anything on my desk."

He pointed to the pile of random junk that covered his desk and the additional pile on the table behind him.

"How about the audio book I gave you last year?" Trent asked.

"Well," said Roland reaching into the pile and pulling out a disk, "do you want me to find the first disk? Or do you want the second disk?" Without looking, he reached into the pile behind him and pulled out another disk.

"See?" Roland smiled, "I have ADD, my stuff looks messy, but I can still find it." He stood up and started walking to the center of the room.

"Because Learning Disabilities are an obstacle, they make you stronger. For instance, take a normal brain versus a dyslexic brain. When reading, one part of the normal brain lights up with activity. On the other hand, multiple smaller parts of the dyslexic brain light up. The fact that the information has to travel further in the dyslexic brain makes it difficult to read, but it also makes the brain stronger. Also, people with learning disabilities think differently. People with dyslexia can be great artists and scientists. Thomas Edison, for example, had dyslexia, yet he is one of history's greatest scientists."

He paused and looked at me. "Raul!" he exclaimed. I jumped. "What are your learning disabilities?" "I have dysgraphia, ADD, and slow visual processing," I answered. "

And what do your disabilities do?"

I hated this. I hated being put on the spot in class. Why me? Why did he have to call on me? My heart was pounding; I felt all eyes on me. I had to answer.

"M-my dysgraphia makes it difficult for me to write, it makes my hand hurt and my handwriting is sloppy. My slow visual processing makes me read slower, and my ADD makes it difficult for me to pay attention in class."

"Those are the downsides," Roland said, "but what are the good sides?"

"I don't know," I mumbled.

"Think Raul," he said, "what are you good at?"

I shrugged.

"Let me tell you what I have noticed," Roland said. "You have difficulty writing but that makes you better at thinking what you want to do. For example, because you cannot write well, you are better at mental math and visualizing images in your head. Because you have difficulty reading, you learn better kinesthetically. Finally, because you have trouble focusing, you exercise your imagination, which helps you be creative. Tell me, how does this help you in life?"

I thought for a moment.

"Well my mental math obviously helps me in math and science. Kinesthetic learning helps me in sports. And my creativity helps me in writing stories and art. But I don't understand; if I'm supposed to be smarter, more creative, and better at math, how come my twin brother is smarter than me?"

It was a question I had asked myself many times. Why was my twin brother, Cosmo, more athletic, smarter, and more creative than me? Why was he the normal one?

Roland sighed, "You are not your brother and you do not have to be like him. You are both unique individuals. Just because he does better in school, it does not mean he is better than you in every way."

"But he is," I replied. "He is more popular than me, he is better at videogames, playing instruments, and stronger than me."

"It doesn't matter," Roland replied. "I'm sure he does not have your imagination, or tenacity, or outlook on life. You are who you are."

He turned to the whole class.

"You are all different. More so than average people. But that makes you special. Because your struggle, you have a tenacity that will allow you to succeed."

I don't remember the rest of class but his words will always stay with me. Because of what he said, I have accepted myself for me. I have made the most of what I have. I am able to advocate for myself, and I am determined to succeed.

Bhavya Sharma
Women in Baseball: The Legacy of AAGPBL

The All-American Girls Professional Baseball League was founded by Philip K. Wrigley, an executive in Major League Baseball, who founded the women's league to "sustain an interest in men's baseball, which he and other owners would restore when [World War II] was won" (Pierman, 71). The League was founded as a non-profit organization to sustain America's interest in baseball while the men of the country were at war with Germany. At the administrative level, Wrigley "basically used the Cubs' organizational structure to run the league" (Kenow, 5). To recruit the female players, he "launched an aggressive scouting campaign to recruit the best fastpitch players in the Unites States and Canada for a league founded on skill as well as femininity" (Pierman, 71). This paper will shed light on two major aspects of the AAGPBL – race and gender – and how they are portrayed in the film *A League of Their Own*. The paper will also cite reasons for the league's popularity until its demise in 1954.

1. Gender Issues in AAGPBL

According to Laura Kenow in "The All-American Professional Baseball League: A Review of Literature and Its Reflection of Gender Issues," AAGPBL was the first, and to date, the only women's professional baseball league in United States history (1). At the time of its conception, the administrative structure of the league was entirely male-dominated. Kenow states that women were marginalized from holding power positions within the league's administration (6). As a way to "court media coverage," the league had to depend on what came to be known as the "female apologetic" – a phrase suggesting "that female athletic participation is acceptable as long as traditional notions of femininity are present" (Kenow, 6). The public image of the women was essential to promote the AAGPBL. In her article "Baseball, Conduct and True Womanhood," Carol J. Pierman points out to a Time magazine report from 1943 which states that "part of [the athletes'] training was a compulsory course at Helena Rubinstein's Gold Coast salon – to learn about make-up, posture and other whatnots usually neglected by lady athletes. Athletes who would not compromise to enact the lessons of finishing school were cut before the end of spring training" (Pierman, 72). The players had to be talented and attractive to play in the league. In the movie *A League of Their Own,* the scene in which Ernie Capadino refuses to consider Marla Hooch because she is not attractive enough shows how the societal notions of beauty and femininity were tied to the AAGPBL games.

The movie has several scenes that show the challenges that were unique to women in baseball. There is a scene when the Rockford Peaches come out to play for their first game and are laughed at by the spectators in the bleachers. One man among the spectators derides the women for being too weak to swing a bat. There is also a radio announcer who discourages what she calls the "masculinization of women" through education and sports. Of course, by the end of the movie, the women prove the naysayers wrong by playing well and by drawing a huge fan following. There are other scenes that show the social pressures that existed for women during the 1940s – the "charm school lessons" that the women undergo in the movie were very much a real part of the players' training. According to Pierman, "for a population emerging from the Depression, with sponsors barely eking out an existence, any woman's team with uniquely designed uniforms, salaries, and travel and food allowances would be considered "classy" by comparison" (72). Pierman gathered interviews from various AAGPBL players according to whom the lessons "did them good" as they helped them at "achieving social fluency," even if it was at the cost of indoctrinating "an ideology of gender that undermined their athleticism" (75). This is to say that while the lessons did reinforce gender stereotype, they were seen as an opportunity for working-class women to become "classy" and move among the wealthy.

2. Race in AAGPBL

There is a scene in *A League of Their Own* in which an African-American woman pitches a ball to Dottie, which impresses the latter. While the scene only lasts a few seconds, it comments on the exclusion of non-white females from playing. During the time of the league's existence, white "feminine" women were considered as the ideals of beauty. It was not just non-white players who were excluded from the game, but "mannish-looking athletes were often cut or overlooked" as well (Kenow, 8). According to Kenow, "players who did not fit the white, middle-class definition of femininity were marginalized from participation" (7). Furthermore, while there were a few African-American women who did play baseball, not a single one of them could sign a contract with AAGPBL (8). Kenow writes that if African-American women were "allowed" to play baseball on a contractual basis like the white athletes, it "would have been a dual challenge to societal norms of femininity and may have affected the viability of the league" (8). This notion is represented in the film, in which the teams are comprised of white females who are groomed to fit the society's definition of female beauty.

3. The Rise in Popularity of AAGPBL

In her article, Kenow references surveys conducted by Wieller and Higgs in 1997 according to which, "fans most often attributed the league's success to the high quality of play (57%) followed by the unique entertainment it provided (28%)" (4). AAGPBL started as a unique movement that sustained the fans' interest in baseball through successful marketing strategies (such as the "female apologetic" and charm schools). That is not to discredit the women's athletic ability and qualitative play, but the aggressive marketing did play a huge part in attracting the crowds. Additionally, AAGPBL was composed of working-class women who were catapulted to sudden popularity and had a chance to interact with high-class people. Pierman states that baseball "represented one of the few paths of upward mobility open to the children of the dominated classes" (76). This chance at upward mobility was another factor that contributed to the popularity of the game. A third factor that led to the rise in popularity of AAGPBL was that the league was an opportunity that empowered women. Kenow cites survey researches done of Hensley in 1995 in her article according to which, AAGPBL "expanded players' vision of life possibilities and revealed options they hadn't previously considered" (4). Players had the opportunity to become educated, earn money and enter the workforce during the off-season. They also became "public figure[s] after the release of *A League of Their Own* (Abbott et al., 1992" (Kenow, 4).

The league came to an end by 1954 because of low attendance at the games and the managers' inability to earn profits from gate receipts (Kenow, 1). Television became the main source of entertainment, and people stopped attending AAGPBL games. Additionally, with the end of the war, there was a "social shift to a more conservative view of women's gender roles" (Kenow, 4). Once the veterans returned from war, the focus on men's baseball resumed and women were expected to resume their duties as housewives. In *A League of Their Own*, Lowenstein comments on how the league would be disbanded when the men return, to which Harvey responds that it would be more ridiculous to send the men who would "come back from war to the kitchen." The return of men to the workforce also perpetuated the stereotype that regarded women in masculine activities as homosexual (Kenow, 11). "Women playing baseball became increasingly peculiar as the league was no longer seen as fulfilling a patriotic duty in post-war times," and these factors ultimately led to the disbandment of the AAGPBL in 1954. Although the league no longer exists, *A League of Their Own* shows the importance of AAGPBL and documents the lives of players in the league. The movie also immortalizes the Rockford Peaches, which was one of the most successful teams that won the league championship four times.

Works Cited

Kenow, Laura J. "The All-American Professional Baseball League (AAGPBL): A Review of Literature and Its Reflection of Gender Issues." *Women in Sport & Physical Activity Journal* Spring 2010: 58+. *Biography in Context*. Web. 14 Feb. 2016.

A League of Their Own. Dir. Penny Marshall. Columbia Pictures. 1992. DVD.

Pierman, Carol J. "Baseball, Conduct, and True Womanhood". *Women's Studies Quarterly* 33.1/2 (2005): 68–85. Web. 14 Feb. 2016.

Wikipedia contributors. "Rockford Peaches." *Wikipedia, The Free Encyclopedia*. Wikipedia, The Free Encyclopedia, 9 Oct. 2015. Web. 14 Feb. 2016.

Yih-Chia Lam

Tools Themselves Do Not Have Morality

The potential of Clustered Regularly Interspaced Short Palindromic Repeat (CRISPR) seems borderline science fiction. In nature, these palindromic sequences are found and function in bacteria immune systems, cutting out foreign pieces of genetic elements inserted by invading viruses and phages. Simple, quick, and extremely effective, CRISPR has already revolutionized the application of gene-editing on model organisms used in disease studies. What if we took this a step further? If the use of CRISPR is perfected, then couldn't it also be used to cure humanity's ailments such as heritable diseases and mental illnesses? That's one direction that can be taken, but certainly not the only possible application of CRISPR. When dealing with such a powerful tool, one must think of the possible uses and implications of the revolutionary biotechnology. If improperly regulated, gene-editing may be a slippery slope. If it is possible to eradicate disorders from the genomes of future children, one may reason that parents could also be able to also choose or omit other traits as well – namely those pertaining to appearances, such as height, hair, and eye color – creating what is commonly referred to as a designer baby. That is not the only improper use of CRISPR. What if we took it in the opposite direction of disease eradication? If CRISPR could be used to fix illnesses, then couldn't it also be used to amplify them? Tools themselves do not have morality. If this biotechnology could revolutionize the medical field, then surely it could have a similarly profound effect on biological warfare as well. CRISPR has the potential to save and improve lives, but it could just easily be used to make designer babies or for malicious bioterrorism.

The mechanisms by which CRISPR is used on organisms' genomes is quite straightforward as compared to other gene-editing methods such as zinc-finger nucleases, a costly and time-consuming method popular before CRISPR's commercialization. Before introducing the gene-editing CRISPR molecule into an organism's body, scientists first synthesize fragments of CRISPR-associated protein 9 RNA (Cas9 RNA) that match the DNA they want to target in an organism's genome. CRISPR is then guided to the indicated location by the RNA sequence. Once CRISPR has arrived at the target location, it can edit genes or even silence them completely. The accuracy and simplicity of this process has been compared to opening up an individual's genome on a word processor to delete mutations and edit genes.

When used on microorganisms, CRISPR can make a disease much deadlier. Virologist Dr. Ron Fouchier and his team at The Erasmus University Medical Center in the Netherlands successfully engineered more virulent versions of the H5N1 bird flu. One resulting strain from the experiment is airborne and highly contagious – in contrast to the original disease that can only be spread through direct contact with an infected body – and has the potential to wipe out half of the human population. A statement from Fouchier himself admits that the airborne strain he created is "probably one of the most dangerous viruses you can make."

Ferrets were used to model how the virus would spread among human populations. The avian superflu was documented to be as contagious as strains of the human flu that many of us are familiar with – strains that often surface and spread like wildfire between the cold and dry months of October and March. The only difference is that the bird flu is much deadlier. In its original form, out of the 846 cases reported to World Health Organization to date, 449 cases resulted in death. This is roughly a 53 percent mortality rate. Fouchier wanted to publish his methods and findings, but colleagues urged against it in fear of the scientific blueprints being used for malicious intent. What if the research ended up in the wrong hands? Standing by his research, Fouchier argued that publishing his work would help steel the scientific community if an H5N1 pandemic were to surface. The resulting dilemma was a chicken and egg conundrum: if publishing the research could give bioterrorists a template from which they could recreate results, not publishing the research would leave scientists in the dark if an H5N1 outbreak were to ever surface.

Despite the debate, Fouchier's research was published in the U.S.-based journal Science in June 2012, but not without roadblocks set by the Dutch government that could hinder prospective research. The paper was treated as a dangerous document, setting a precedent for the treatment of the virologist's future work. Fouchier's team had to apply for an export license from the Dutch government that normally applies to technology that has the potential to be weaponized. Once the paper was cleared by the Dutch government, it was reviewed by the U.S. National Institute of Allergy and Infectious Diseases, which funded the research. "All that oversight causes delay," Fouchier said in response to the heavy supervision and legal handling. "That does not mean that we have reached general consensus about the need to do this type of work, and how to do it safely, but general consensus will be impossible to reach on any topic. We will keep the dialogues going with everyone, but at the same time need to continue this important line of work."

On the opposite end of the spectrum of applications for CRISPR is in the medical field to improve the quality of countless lives. CRISPR is already used on a large scale in the research of various diseases, and if perfected, could be used in gene therapy on humans. Scientists often run experiments on model organisms, which are non-human species that share a common ancestor with humans, thus retaining certain similar genes. These organisms, such as mice and zebrafish, are invaluable in the study of how certain genes affect the expression of an individual's phenotype, or expressed trait. From the results, scientists can then extrapolate how the same treatment would affect the human version of the disease. For example, in a case study conducted in 2014, bioengineer Dr. Daniel Anderson and his associates at MIT in Cambridge, Massachusetts used CRISPR on mice to correct a mutation associated with the human metabolic disease tyrosinemia, which results in disturbances of kidney and liver function, as well as mental retardation. This was the first time CRISPR was utilized to fix a disease-causing mutation in an adult animal – an important step towards using this biotechnology for gene therapy in humans.

In another field of disease research, when asked about the primary gene-editing method used in the study of Alzheimer's disease, Dr. Aleister J. Saunders of Drexel University replied, "CRISPR is being used extensively in a variety of models of Alzheimer's disease. These include human and non-human cells, invertebrate and vertebrate models." Alzheimer's disease is not always a result of inheritance, however, in certain cases of Alzheimer's – such as Familial Alzheimer's disease (FAD) – if one parent has a mutated gene that causes FAD, each child has a 50 percent chance of inheriting it. If predispositioned for it, the afflicted individual will eventually develop the disease, usually in their 40s or 50s. There is currently no cure for Alzheimer's disease, however, CRISPR could be a viable candidate if it is incorporated into the medical field. By targeting specific loci – positions of genes on a chromosome – linked to the heritability of Alzheimer's, the dementia could be eliminated from the individual's genome. All changes and permanent and heritable, ensuring that future descendants do not have to worry about the disease.

Along the lines of neurological diseases, mental disorders are a field that could heavily benefit from the application of CRISPR research. Aside from genetic disorders that result in physical defects, an almost unthinkable amount of people are predisposed to mental illnesses such as bipolar disorder, depression, and schizophrenia. The chances of developing such mental illnesses are not solely based on genetic predisposition, but according to Genome Wide Association Studies (GWAS), such factors increase the chances of mental illnesses an estimated 17 to 28 percent. For certain disorders, such as schizophrenia, the influence of genetic predisposition is simply too significant to be overlooked. Twin studies published in the American Journal of Medical Genetics have shown that schizophrenia has a staggering 80 to 85 percent of genetic heritability. Aside from heritability, environment and other existing conditions are known to trigger the development of mental illnesses as well. It is not uncommon for those coping with a physical illness to also develop mental illnesses such as depression or anxiety. According to the World Health Organization (WHO), depression alone is estimated to affect 350 million adults globally. This is just a conservative figure.

Between the two extremes of beneficial medical applications and bioterrorism is the possibility of exploiting gene-editing to make designer-babies – children whose genetic makeup have been altered to omit or express selected genes, chosen usually by the parents of the child. What was portrayed in the 1997 science-fiction film *Gattaca* may not be such a far-fetched future after all. If this biotechnology were to reach fertility clinics, there is little doubt that parents would be eager to choose the features of their children – be it height, eye color, or gender. Fellow classmate Moed Gerveni facetiously said that if gene-editing in embryos was made legal, he would want his son to be "6'6, 250 pounds, be able to run a 4.2-second 40-yard dash, and play football." Jokes aside, the abuse of gene-editing is without a doubt a possibility that would arise from the commercialization of this technology.

This possible exploitation is in the process of being addressed. The current plan is to keep genetic engineering away from fertility clinics until the uses of CRISPR can be understood in full. "You would be insane and criminally reckless to make a baby this way without 15 to 20 years of testing and proof it was safe," said Henry Greely, Director of the Center for Law and the Biosciences at Stanford University. This sentiment was shared by the 17 other prominent scientists and law and ethics experts who collectively published a letter in Science in 2015 calling for a moratorium on certain uses of the CRISPR biotechnology. This falls in line with the general consensus at the annual National Academy of Sciences and the National Academy of Medicine's Human Gene-Editing Initiative international summit in Washington DC the year before. "Research should only continue in line with existing laws and regulations," Dr. Eric Lander of MIT urged those in attendance. However, at that time, no experimental regulations had been established by any national federations, aside from the overall ban on the use of CRISPR on human cells.

The following year, in December 2015, Britain's Royal Society and the Chinese Academy of Sciences joined the US National Academy of Sciences and the US National Academy of Medicine to host the international summit once more. Dr. Tetsuya Ishii, a bioethicist at Hokkaido University in Sapporo, Japan gave a presentation covering his findings on the analysis of various national legislation and guidelines of 39 countries regarding the regulation of gene-editing on human embryos, much of which was from his article "International regulatory landscape and integration of corrective genome editing into in vitro fertilization" — which was co-authored with Motoko Araki and published in 2014. Out of the 39 surveyed countries, 29 have rules restricting genome editing for clinical and reproductive use — including the United States, where

CRISPR is regulated by the Food and Drug Administration (FDA) and National Institutes of Health (NIH) guidelines. However, the restrictions issued in several of these countries — namely Japan, China, and India — are not legally binding. In Japan alone, there are around 600 fertility clinics nationwide, and one out of every 27 children in Japan are born in vitro. Based on this, Dr. Tetsuya Ishii predicts that the countries with no enforceable rules on gene-editing – which also have the highest rates of in vitro fertilization – will be the first to attempt clinical applications. Dr. Qi Zhou, deputy director of the Institute of Zoology at the Chinese Academy of Science in Beijing, said, "I believe that in the near future, the Chinese government will publish rules that will be based on international conferences and symposiums." At the moment, Chinese guidelines prohibit manipulation of the genes in human gametes, zygotes, and embryos for the purpose of reproduction. Although, Dr. Qi Zhou admits, "the truth is, we have guidelines but some people never follow them." On paper there will be rules and regulations regarding the future usage of CRISPR on viable human embryos, however, the likelihood of CRISPR being abused seems inevitable. Even if the method is restricted or banned from fertility clinics in certain countries, as Dr. Tetsuya Ishii very simply stated, "rich people can go abroad."

In terms of CRISPR regulation in academia, on February 1, 2016, Developmental biologist Kathy Niakan at the Francis Crick Institute in London received approval for the use of CRISPR on human embryos by the UK Human Fertilisation and Embryology Authority (HFEA). It is important to note the conditions under which the experiments are allowed to proceed. Firstly, the research involving the use of CRISPR on human embryos is confined to studying errors in early embryonic development. Secondly, the experiments halt after seven days of testing, after which the embryos used in the experiment are promptly destroyed. "It's an important first," states Dr. George Daley, a stem-cell biologist at Boston Children's Hospital in Massachusetts. "The HFEA has been a very thoughtful, deliberative body that has provided rational oversight of sensitive research areas, and this establishes a strong precedent for allowing this type of research to go forward." Dr. Sarah Chan, a bioethics researcher at the University of Edinburgh, UK, is also hopeful for this pioneer case involving the use of CRISPR on human embryos. "Because of its history of successful regulation, the UK could serve as a model for other countries," Dr. Chan reasons. It is likely that firmer rules will be established and shaped based on the success of the current case in the UK. So far there have been no negative reports pertaining to the research and prospects are high. If the first approved usage of CRISPR on human cells is a success, a clean and transparent precedent will be set for the rest of the world.

The potential of CRISPR is seemingly boundless. With further research, the applications of this biotechnology could help eradicate diseases from the human genome. Permanent changes made to one's genome are heritable, ensuring that children of the future could live as the best possible versions of themselves, untethered by genetic disorders or predispositions. People could be happier and lives could be saved. It will still be years before we see the effects of CRISPR in the general population as the applications of the biotechnology have not been approved for the usage on viable human embryos yet. Further testing is still needed and regulations must be established. So far, 29 countries — including the United States — have restrictions on the usage of CRISPR on human cells, preventing legal and ethical mishaps for now. In the closing statement of Dr. Tetsuya Ishii and Motoko Araki's "International regulatory landscape and integration of corrective genome editing into in vitro fertilization," an ethical basis for the future usage of CRISPR for reproduction was suggested, saying, "a global consensus will need to be formed, because thinking about germline gene modification involves ethical, social, and evolutionary considerations for all of humankind." Until then, CRISPR will continue to be used in disease-related research and to further our understandings of the human genome. The misuse of CRISPR is a possibility, but with proper regulation of this biotechnology, this worry is eclipsed by its unfathomable benefits.

Works Cited

"Alzheimers Australia Home Page." *Alzheimer's Australia*. N.p., n.d. Web. 08 Mar. 2016.

Araki, Motoko, and Tetsuya Ishii. "International Regulatory Landscape and Integration of Corrective Genome Editing into in Vitro Fertilization." BioMed Central. BioMed Central Ltd, 24 Nov. 2014. Web. 14 Mar. 2016.

Callaway, Ewen. "UK Scientists Gain Licence to Edit Genes in Human Embryos." *Nature.com*. Nature Publishing Group, 1 Feb. 2016. Web. 12 Feb. 2016.

Cavell, Nic. "The UK Just Green-Lit Crispr Gene Editing in Human Embryos." *Wired.com*. Conde Nast Digital, 2 Feb. 2016. Web. 09 Mar. 2016.

Chyba, Christopher F. "*Microbe Warfare Hides the Enemy.*" Microbe Warfare Hides the Enemy. The New York Times, 10 Aug. 2001. Web. 22 Feb. 2016.

Cressey, Daniel, Alison Abbotl, and Heidi Ledford. "UK Scientists Apply for Licence to Edit Genes in Human Embryos." *Nature.com*. Nature Publishing Group, 18 Sept. 2015. Web. 08 Mar. 2016.

Enserink, Martin. "Flu Researcher Ron Fouchier Loses Legal Fight Over H5N1 Studies." *Science*. American Association for the Advancement of Science, 25 Sept. 2013. Web. 22 Feb. 2016.

Entine, Jon. "Ethical and Regulatory Reflections on CRISPR Gene Editing Revolution | Genetic Literacy Project." *Genetic Literacy Project*. Genetic Literacy Project, 25 June 2015. Web. 02 Mar. 2016.

Fyffe, Steve. "U.S. Needs a New Approach for Governance of Risky Research, Stanford Scholars Say." *Stanford University*. Stanford Report, 17 Dec. 2015. Web. 08 Apr. 2016.

Hayes, Jason. "The Bird Flu That Man Built: Controversial H5N1 Research to Be Published in Part | HealthMap." *The Bird Flu That Man Built: Controversial H5N1 Research to Be Published in Part | HealthMap*. Health Map, 18 Apr. 2012. Web. 09 Mar. 2016.

Herfst, Sander, Eefje J. A. Schrauwen, and Martin Linster. "Airborne Transmission of Influenza A/H5N1 Virus Between Ferrets." *Science*. American Association for the Advancement of Science, 22 June 2012. Web. 02 Mar. 2016.

Koebler, Jason. "Someone Will Eventually Use CRISPR to Try to Make a Dragon or Unicorn." *Motherboard*. Vice Media Inc., 8 Dec. 2015. Web. 08 Apr. 2016.

Ledford, Heidi. "Where in the World Could the First CRISPR Baby Be Born?" *Nature.com*. Nature Publishing Group, 13 Oct. 2015. Web. 02 Mar. 2016.

Lipsitch, Marc, and David A. Relman. "New Game, New Rules." *Foreign Affairs*. Council on Foreign Relations Inc, 31 Aug. 2015. Web. 08 Mar. 2016.

Niller, Eric. "Science Would Like Some Rules for Genome Editing, Please." *Wired.com*. Conde Nast Digital, 6 Oct. 2015. Web. 08 Mar. 2016.

Park, Alice. "UK Approves First Studies Using New Gene Editing Technique." *Time*. Time, 1 Feb.2016. Web. 20 Feb. 2016.

Philipkoski, Kristen. "Engineered Avian Flu Could Kill Half the World's Humans." *Gizmodo*. Gizmodo, 28 Nov. 2011. Web. 06 Mar. 2016.

Porterfield, Andrew. "Genetics May Open Door to New Treatments of Mental Disorders." *Genetic Literacy Project*. Genetic Literacy Project, 12 Aug. 2015. Web. 02 Mar. 2016.

Shanks, Pete. "CRISPR Opportunities ... For What? And for Whom?" *The Huffington Post*. TheHuffingtonPost.com, 10 Dec. 2014. Web. 19 Feb. 2016.

Faith Roser

There May Be No Answer

I've always been drawn to the sciences, especially medicine. As a deeply curious person, I'm always looking for answers. I take pleasure in gaining understanding through the problem solving and discovery processes that are so vital to scientific work. One of the most critical lessons I've learned in five years of undergraduate education is that the act of seeking understanding is as important as acquiring definitive knowledge. This concept is particularly relevant in the sciences, but the humanities introduced me to it.

Through my studies in the medical humanities, I was introduced to many writers with scientific backgrounds, particularly physicians. By reading what physicians have written about their work, I became acquainted with the art of medicine as a necessary compliment to the science. The unknown and the unanswerable were suddenly alluring; the difficulty of treating and attempting to heal unique individuals was suddenly intriguing. As I developed an appreciation for its gray areas, I knew that I could find a place for myself in the world of medicine. In this way, the humanities fueled my passion for a career in the sciences.

Medicine is an applied science. However, because medicine involves applying science to varied and complex living beings, it is not practiced in a vacuum, isolated from outside influence. We often think of the physician's role in an isolated scientific sense, however. From this perspective, physicians utilize a methodical approach, in which logic and detachment from emotions are prized. A patient's body is seen as a wealth of data waiting to be collected and analyzed. By viewing the body in this way, observing with precise attention to detail, the physician—as popularly perceived—is able to formulate a diagnosis (Flower 72).

Today, it seems obvious to say that science is the basis of the medical profession. Much of a physician's job does rely upon application of the scientific method and statistical analysis in order to arrive at a diagnosis and decide upon treatment options. Traditionally, however, the physician has practiced and perfected the art of healing, rather than the strict application of science. Physicians have historically relied upon their own interpretations of information gathered from patient testimony, physical examinations and diagnostic tests (Flower 72). Provided that their actions are "not provably, criminally fraudulent or negligent, physicians are free to operate as their training, experience, and personal bent move them" (Flower 74).

The foundation of the medical profession, then, is a focus on the art of diagnosing specific ailments and healing individuals, rather than scientifically treating or curing generalized conditions. Even in our current medical system—with an abundance of cutting-edge scientific and technological advancements—there is still a focus on the unique qualities that make patients individuals. A primary and ever-present hurdle in the physician's quest to apply medical training to human beings is learning to cope with the complexities and idiosyncrasies of the body. The physician must learn to master the decision-making process while avoiding mistakes in order to become a better medical practitioner. This involves learning to recognize signs in individual patients, and patterns across groups of patients, in order to prepare for treatment of future patients.

The surgeon Atul Gawande candidly struggles to determine the role a physician's intuition should play when making decisions steeped in uncertainty. Of successful decisions made under such circumstances, he notes that "[i]t is because intuition sometimes succeeds that we don't know what to do with it. Such successes are not quite the result of logical thinking. But they are not the result of mere luck, either" (247). He has no idea how physicians are able to make decisions that lead to desirable outcomes under uncertain circumstances, but he does recognize that "[h]uman beings have an ability to simply recognize the right thing to do sometimes" (Gawande 248).

The fact is, living beings can be generalized to a certain degree, and medicine can only be practiced by making assumptions about physiology. There will, however, always be enough variation between patients to create uncertainty. Recognizing and embracing this uncertainty is necessary in order to practice better medicine. Science may be objective, but it cannot be applied without some subjective judgment on the part of the practitioner. Part of learning how to apply scientific knowledge while practicing medicine, then, involves recognizing the judgments that physicians must make, and learning how to make better decisions.

The unpredictable nature of the medical profession extends beyond the realm of human medicine, as the writings of James Herriot illustrate. Herriot is the pen name of veterinarian James Alfred Wight, whose writing is based on his work as a rural veterinarian in North Yorkshire, England ("James Herriot Country"). Among the many juxtapositions and conflicting interests that populate All Creatures Great and Small, Herriot manages to convey continual wonder at the uncertainty that comes with his profession. Many anecdotes highlight Herriot's feelings of vulnerability, because he is unprepared or incapable of dealing with a difficult case. He writes, "They didn't say anything about this in the books…" (Herriot 1), but he clearly embraces unpredictability, never regretting his chosen vocation. After a happy ending to a tough calf delivery, Herriot sums up his passion for his work: "This was the bit I liked. The little miracle. I felt it was something that would never grow stale no matter how often I saw it" (Herriot 8).

Herriot displays a crucial virtue for a medical practitioner—the love of applying rigorous science to unpredictable living beings. He recounts a conversation in which he was warned that the veterinary profession is "a long tale of little triumphs and disasters and you've got to really like it to stick it" (Herriot 42). There is no sense of Herriot being dismayed at this idea in the retelling, however. He seems to take it all in stride, even when he is worn out and smelling after a hard day of testing cattle for tuberculosis. When "[his] ribs ached and [he] could feel the bruises of a dozen kicks on [his] legs," all he could do was lay down in a grassy field, and revel in his joy. He recognizes that this is "a strange way, in fact, to earn a living" (Herriot 57), but he relishes every minute of it.

Graduation looms, and I'm only months away from beginning veterinary school myself. I've been thinking a lot about the unscientific aspects of medicine that must be mastered in order to practice it successfully. For this reason, I'm revisiting the poems of cardiologist and writer John Stone, particularly "Gaudeamus Igitur: A Valediction"—an address to graduating medical students. I savor every line of this poem, which encourages fledgling physicians to rejoice in their achievements, while simultaneously preparing for a career filled with uncertainty:

> For this is the day you know too little
> against the day when you will know too much
> For you will be invincible
> and vulnerable in the same breath
> which is the breath of your patients
> For their breath is our breathing and our reason (Stone 8-13)

It doesn't matter that Stone worked in human medicine while I intend to work in veterinary medicine. This doesn't make his poetry any less relatable. The fundamental elements of both fields are, I believe, the same. My patients will be furrier, but their breathing will be just as essential to me. I will be equally "invincible and vulnerable" as I face my patients and their families. And I will, similarly, fail to come up with answers: "For there may be no answer / and [I] will know too little again / or there *will* be an answer and [I] will know too much forever" (Stone 18-20).

References

Flower, Joe. "What Is a "Doctor"." *The Physician Executive* (2008): 72-75. Print.

Gawande, Atul. Complications: A Surgeon's Notes on an Imperfect Science. New York: Picador, 2002. Print.

Herriot, James. *All Creatures Great and Small*. New York: St. Martin's Press, 1975. Print.

"James Herriot Country." *World of James Herriot*. 2015. Web. 9 Mar. 2015. Stone, John. "Gaudeamus Igitur: A Valediction." *Music from Apartment 8*. Baton Rouge: Lousiana State University Press, 2004. 102-05. Print.

Week of
Writing

The Week of Writing (WoW) is a week-long celebration of writing sponsored by the Department of English and Philosophy and the College of Arts and Sciences. Each Fall and Winter quarter, the Drexel Publishing Group runs the WoW Writing Contest, which is open to all students. Those winners are invited to read during the Week of Writing in May, and are published in the next section.

Introduction

Creative writing is among the most challenging fields; how do you tell a "truth?" Even experienced authors who have been writing for years often struggle to quell their inner voices that say "it can't be done." Creative writers are compelled to take experiences and observations and fine hone them into a larger vision. The writers whose work appears in this section have worked, and written, and rewritten, and sweated and maybe doubted. They have struggled to find the right words to drawn in their readers and bring their vision to life through fiction and nonfiction.

Julia Casciato

Open Waters

I never once glanced out a window while I raced against the clock to ready myself for work. As I stepped past the threshold of my front door, I looked up just in time to catch myself before falling into a sea of water. Not the puddle that usually casually sits on top of the sunken concrete walkway after a rainstorm like the one the night before, but an actual sea. I could see nothing else but crystalline blue water meeting the blue sky overhead. My house was floating in the ocean.

The yellow flowers detailing the walk down to the street were missing. The red Ford sedan absent from its usual parking spot. The street, the neighbors, the basketball hoop local kids played with after school: all gone.

I slowly backed up and closed the door. Was it a trick? My mind confusing me from all the tension and stress I've been under? I walked through the house to the back door, but instead of finding the brick patio and lawn chairs, I saw the same blue water meeting the blue sky.

I took a seat on the brown leather couch trying to remember if I felt anything unusual as I slept; I hadn't. I walked to the kitchen to brew a pot of coffee, staring out at the sea through the window above the sink. A few quiet minutes passed, the brewer beeped signaling the coffee ready, but the noise wasn't strong enough to break my curious gaze from the window.

My wife called from our bedroom above, "John can you grab the paper for me before you leave?" She asked the same question every morning. Sometimes I was here to answer and sometimes I wasn't. Could she tell the difference on those days?

I lifted the pot, the dark roasted coffee flowed into my mug, "Not today honey." I could hear her moving about as I leaned against the granite counter cautiously sipping my coffee not to burn my tongue. Dresser drawers banged close above, then the opening and closing of our bedroom door, the clacking of heels on the hardwood as she hurriedly climbed down the narrow staircase.

She went into our shared office and was placing stacks of files into her workbag when she asked me, "Why haven't you left for work yet? Won't you be late?"

"I decided to take the day off," I couldn't keep the grin from showing on my face as I tried to contain the fit of laughter bubbling inside of me. To hide my smirk I raised the mug to my lips. She stared at me with a look of confusion and annoyance as if she was waiting for the punch line.

As she moved to fill her own coffee mug she let out a scream and sent the mug crashing to the floor. "John! What is this?!" Her eyes and mouth open wide in shock expecting me to give her an explanation.

I lost it. I erupted into a fit of laughter. Tears streamed down my face as I doubled over clutching my stomach. "Why are you laughing? This isn't funny! What's going on?"

I couldn't stop laughing. She kept yelling, "We have to go to work!" After a few moments I was able to regain my composure to say, "Margaret our house is surrounded by water and you're worried about going to work?" She hadn't always been like this, so focused and obsessive about her job. There was a time she used to play hooky for no reason, take weekend vacations across the country. She used to be passionate about more than just the bottom line.

"I'm just being practical John. I have meetings all week, the firm needs me!" She looked at me with sad puppy dog eyes, as if I should pity the fact that she was going to be using up more than a couple sick days. Of course she wouldn't take into consideration the work I would be missing.

My work didn't matter—not to her. But we've had this argument countless times before, and I didn't think now was the appropriate time to have it again, not with bigger issues to deal with.

I took my coffee mug, carefully maneuvered around her broken one, and returned to my worn-in seat on the couch. I flipped on the television but there was only static. "What are you doing?" her unpleasing tone resonating throughout the house.

"I was hoping to watch the early morning talk shows that I never get a chance to see." My wife was sliding her finger across her iPhone but it was pointless. There was no way to connect with anyone outside of our single-family house that somehow moved from the middle of the continental U.S. to here. It's fascinating to see the electricity still worked. Hell, the whole damn thing was fascinating.

I sat looking around the living room: a stack of action movies and romantic comedies on the television stand, a bookshelf full of spines with titles from the 19th to 21st centuries that I've accumulated throughout the years (most that

I've never read), some outdated magazines and newspapers on the coffee table, a photo album from our wedding three years ago.

My wife opened the back door and getting down laid flat on her stomach. She looked silly laying there in her beige blazer and matching pencil skirt, both freshly ironed. She cautiously reached a fingertip out the glass door and touched the water, but retracted quickly as if she was afraid of it. It was impossible to tell if the house was moving or stationary. At least it wasn't sinking, for now.

"John...what do we do? We can't do nothing. We can't live like this." I could tell she

was scared. She still lay on the floor, but she had turned her head to face me. I wanted to reach

out and save her, but I couldn't.

I didn't have an answer for her, at least not the one she wanted to hear. I knew we couldn't live like this. We would run out of food. We would run out of things to watch, read, and do. We would even run out of things to say—if we hadn't already.

Sharan Walia

Entre les Lilas (Between the Lilacs)

The fields of lilac stretched on as far as her eyes could see; only stopping to rendezvous with their hue matching counterpart. The streaks of lilac that gripped the sky for a few quiet moments each morning appeared to be enveloping the vast fields of the barely budding flowers, the way old friends would embrace each other following a prolonged separation. Although, it'd only been a mere dozen hours since she'd last seen them greet one another.

She sighed at the simple, yet consumingly beautiful sight that displayed itself in front of her, like an Henri Zuber at the Louvre. Only this time the panes and the windowsill, in their rented bedroom at the antique bed and breakfast somewhere outside of Bordeaux, lent themselves as the frame to Nature's painting.

Somewhere, in the old abandoned-chateaux-turned-bed and breakfast, one of the seemingly hundreds of Ogar-sized, French Revolution era wooden doors thudded shut. The reverberation of the slamming door sent a creak and a shudder throughout the old building. The sound of which dragged her back from that infinitesimal space at the horizon that lay between the lilac fields and the now pink infused lilac sky.

She bent slightly over ledge of the screen-less window and plucked a single flower from the vine that quite nearly climbed into their room. Twisting the short stem of the delicate purple flower between her thumb and her index finger she turned her back on the rising sun to face the four-poster.

Her eyes scanned over the rest of the room, slowly, lazily almost. She'd always known she'd come here, she had always pictured herself in this place, even before she had known what it looked like. It was, of course, everything she had imagined it to be, yet nothing she'd dreamt it to be.

It felt as though the set director and the costume designer had taken the images right out of the never ending film reel that played in her head and meticulously prepared all the props for the frames of a scene. The people all looked the same but script they followed was foreign to her ears.

He remained exactly as she'd left him, still sleeping soundly on his stomach letting out a soft snore here and there. The longer she looked at him the more she remembered who he was.

When he slept he looked like the boy she knew from his visits to her dreams. The boy who entertained her thoughts during those long law school lectures in which an unmemorable professor's voice had seemed to drone on endlessly. The boy who danced through her mind during those preciously rare idle moments in the small desk of her corner cubicle at work.

When he slept she saw the boy who had once upon a time carried her books as they'd walked to class. She saw the boy with whom she'd feasted on a midnight picnic, which had been made up of the foreign towns' finest gas station cuisine and eaten at its local abandoned beach, before they'd slow danced only to the sound of crashing waves into the wee hours of the morning. She saw The Boy.

An early summer morning breeze passed through the room, leaving kisses of goosebumps all over her petite frame. She debated getting back into bed, but the risk of waking him combined with the overwhelming desire to linger in these moments, quickly triumphed over her temptation to seek warmth in him. It was as though she were trying to greedily elongate the final seconds of a wonderful, intangible dream that would inevitably be forgotten.

She opted to retrieve the warm woollen blanket that sat folded at the edge of the bed and retired to the bergère in corner of the room. It was placed across the bed but still perfectly angled to the view offered by the window she'd just departed.

She curled up, compressing herself to be as small as possible while still comfortable, the flower still in her hand, though its petals crinkled. Her gaze resettles on him again, just the same as it does in the most crowded of rooms. This thought pleases her, she smiles. It's a small thing, but it's a small thing that aligns.

She forced her fluttering eyes to remain open, as though doing so would pause this exact point in time. But she knew it would not be so, she drank in as much as she could before sleep overcame her. She savored the childlike mischief and innocence that melded together and danced across his face, unbeknownst to him, as he slept peacefully.

She relished in it, just a little while longer, she told herself. She knew when he awoke even the faintest glimmer of such expressions would be gone. His flawlessly sculpted face would be interrupted by the consistent furrowing of his thick brow only to be replaced by the thoughtful tightening and pursing of his perfectly shaped lips.

She drowned herself in his still startling features, his slightly lopsided nostrils, the result of a never fully healed broken nose, the permanent trophy from a subway fight ages ago etched front and center on his handsome face. He needed to shave; she studied the patterns of his stubble as though she'd be quizzed on them. The squinting it took to see the tiny hairs just brought her a step closer to allow sleep to dominate them shut.

The next time she would be conscious the boy in front of her would again disappear and be lost somewhere deep in the crevices of her mind. When she next looked at him she would see someone she no longer understood but loved nonetheless. She would see The Man. The man he is.

~~

She woke to the sound of him rustling through the cabinets of the French provincial armoire, undoubtedly selecting a polo for the day ahead of them.

She looks up at him, "Morning," she listens to herself say, hearing a tinge of sadness and nostalgia in her own voice, though she knew he would attest her tone to her grogginess.

She was among the fields of lilacs now. The same colored sky unreachable. And though they looked the same, in color and blended together even more so in the distance, they were unalike in all the ways that mattered.

Shalom Ikhena

Ash Wednesday

It is Ash Wednesday
The air smells of cold dust and morning birds
We wake up by 6 am, Fola, Kemi and I.
Fola is my best friend, well it is complicated now
But yes, Fola is my "best friend" who is sleeping over because his parents are
    out of town.
Kemi is my sister.

Mom and Dad woke us up at 6am. Although I was up already.
I heard the door of the bathroom in mum's room open.
That was when I ran back to my room.

It is Ash Wednesday.
My clothes have been picked out already.
The kind of white that brings the transfiguration to mind
It made me look pure. Like a virgin
Which I was, technically.

Mom and Dad went to bed at 10:18 pm.
I know, because I checked more than once.
Fola must have been checking too
Because he came into my room at 10:20,
To ask that I came over to his room to talk
One of our talks that rolled into dawn and left our days drowsy
A good kind of drowsy.

It is Ash Wednesday. Fola is an altar server,
I have never been one to serve in church.
Fola's white makes him look like an angel, a virgin
Which he was, technically.

Fola and I are in his room
Our intoxicating conversation is heating
He uses this as an opportunity to come close.
To make our conversation melt into a kiss
I do not know how.

But soon after the melting, our words were only being spoken in the language
of body parts.

Fola's hands are cold as they wrap
Caress
Speak
In tongues,
Vulgar tongues.
Our conversation was full of insides.
My hands in his pants.
His in my bra, Then my pants

And when it is over.
I am staring at this stranger
This part of him I had never met before
Fola's fingers are no longer virgins.
Neither is my mouth
Nor his mouth
Nor my fingers
and eyes.

But technically, we are virgins.

Because no one tells you that sometimes, your body parts lose their virginity
first.
That sometimes, on Ash Wednesday, you would wake up in a pool of regret.
Confused by your own curiosity
That you would brush your teeth until your tongue is bleeding but still unclean.

But we are in today
And it is Ash Wednesday
And my dress feels whiter than my soul
And Fola wraps the same fingers that have been in ungodly places around the
bowl containing ash
As the priest presses against my forehead.
"From dust you came and unto dust you shall return"

Tori Rae Davis

May

My mother used to grow red roses
the same color as her hair,
in the garden out back.

She would wake up every morning, rub the sleep from her eyes
and trim back the leaves in such precision
making sure that she handled the delicate flowers with care.
My mother was like this with everything she did.

Her small hands twisting the petals through her fingertips
with a face that longed for something more than a garden
and a three bedroom home
that wasn't even hers to keep.

Her hair just to her shoulders,
it never seems to grow any longer
no matter how hard she tries.

My mother is a woman that wants everything
and gets half of what she deserves.

She scrubs the floorboards of our home
till the splinters wear down,
unable to bury themselves in the soles of our feet
for at least 2 weeks.
Never longer though,
our home so old that it's spitting up the wood

My mother,
can't stand this.
Her frail fingers unwilling to wrap themselves
around sharp edges in fear of coming up with a fistful
of thorns.

cont.

My mother used to grow red roses
the same color as her hair,
in the garden out back.

Her fingers twisting through the petals,
she stands in the neighbor's yard,
longing.

Carly Smith

The White Whale

This work was also entered into the First-Year Writing Contest and won an honorable mention.
— Editor's Note.

The white whale. Somehow my passion for reading and literature arose, at least in part, from the story of Moby, the story of the white whale. It is critical to understand that upon reading *Moby Dick*, my thoughts were not of deep and abiding devotion to Melville, nor were they reflective to the point of adoration of the beauty and meticulous construct of his words and sentences that flowed and roiled like the sea itself. No, my immediate thought upon finishing one of the so-called greatest works ever written was "well that was dreadful." Mind, I was twelve years old at the time, and the circumstances under which I came to read the story were less than ideal.

Every evening, my Dad would read me a story (or a chapter from a book if the story was simply too cumbersome for a single evening). In such a way, I progressed through gorgeous works of literature such as *The Sneeches* by Dr. Seuss, the entire *Ramona* series by Beverly Cleary (twice...at least), many a random Christmas book in the middle of summer, the best of which featured a field mouse named Gus who got to sleep in Papa Noel's pocket because he hibernated through the receiving of gifts, and all seven *Harry Potter* books as they were released every two agonizingly slow years. I certainly enjoyed reading by myself at this time as well, but there was nothing quite like being read to. So as I got older, I would read books myself and my Dad would read books to me, and in this way I felt as though I could get through twice as many books twice as fast. Eventually, we began a sort of literary competition where we would read books and get the other to try them, just to see who was reading the best books. I was, and still am, perpetually losing this competition due to the fact that my father has at least a 40 year head start. However, at the age of twelve, I went for the big guns – a classic. I decided to read *Moby Dick* because I wanted to be as educated as my parents were. They would quote the story all the time: "watch the birds," my Dad would say. "Call me Ishmael." I longed to be able to engage with those who were smarter than me and to be seen not as a meek child, but someone who should be respected. I decided that becoming exceptionally well read was critical to achieving such elusive respect. I made a life changing decision by reaching for the archaic, leather-bound, barcode void, old paper scented copy at the very top of the old bookcase. I began.

Discovering how some things are just clichees, like

While it started decently enough, the book soon became to me like the faint taste of cough medicine clinging to the back of my throat – it was unpleasant bordering on unbearable the longer I was conscious of it, but I knew deep down that it was something that was good for me. I powered through. Halfway through the book, however, the unspeakable happened. Upon complaining to my mother of the book's tedium, she asked me why, then, was I reading it?

The answer was because she had read it, or course, and my father as well. "I've never read that book," she told me "at least not all the way though. Just bits and pieces for various English classes." That was a harsh blow, but the deception got deeper! Not only did I find out that my mother had never read the whole book, but my father, who had been quoting the thing at me for *years* had never read even a single sentence of it. He was quoting Gregory Peck's interpretation of Ahab in the movie! I was stuck.

I was up to my neck in the mire of a verbose and unappealing story, but if I finished it, I had bragging rights forever. Had I stopped then no one would have thought any less of me. I would have been a young child that tried her best with a difficult book. Nothing more. But I so desperately wanted the respect of an adult. Desire for glory won out, and after four weeks of absolute tedium and drudgery, the book finally ended. By that time, however, my mind was made up. I was firmly (and in hindsight rather rigidly) convinced that *Moby Dick* had no place among the "classics," and so I set out in pursuit of other such esteemed classic novels that did meet my impossibly high twelve-year-old expectations. There had to be one classic that was good and interesting, and I had already resigned myself to earning respect by becoming well read, so I decided to expand my literary quest beyond the seas.

Aldous Huxley, author of one of my favorite classics, *Brave New World*, uses the books that he reads to inspire him "about people in an actual environment," and how they interact with each other and their surroundings: knowledge of which he then uses to improve his own fictional writing (Huxley, "The Art of Fiction No. 24"). Realistic human interactions, such as those most meticulously included by Huxley in his work, are one of the most important aspects of a novel for me. My development into someone so intrigued by realistic fictional human interactions began when I was 15 with another manifestation of the white whale. I found myself in an argument with my English teacher, Mrs. Sams, over the symbolism in *Moby Dick*, a story which, I was not terribly unsurprised to learn, she had never read. Sams claimed, based solely on her knowledge of the single chapter she taught in class, that the whale was the symbol of evil in the story.

The *white* whale. The villain. I simply could not abide by that analysis. By her simplistic dichotomous analysis the white whale was the villain and Ahab was the hero. While I am far from a perfect literary analyst, by no stretch of my imagination could I imagine the mad sea captain, driven to complete obsession by the mere idea of exacting revenge on a whale, as the protagonist and the hunted creature, pursued across the globe, as the antagonist, regardless of the story's ending. Like Huxley, Melville includes human interactions in his story that are realistic, complex, and deep. *Moby Dick* is not a story of heroes and villains.

So, partially to spite her, and partially for my own gain, I began reading stories that she had never read, such as *The Great Gatsby*. I loved *Gatsby* but not for its symbols as most English teachers seem to, but for the importance of relationships between people in the story, of the bond between Tom and Daisy Buchanan and Gatsby himself. There was no clear line between protagonist and antagonist as I learned so often in school that there was. The characters in *Gatsby* interacted in ways that imitated the strange occurrences of real life. I soon realized that I enjoyed such blurred distinctions between good and evil. The grey area, at least in my experience, is a characteristic that distinguishes the classics from the rest. In classics the characters come to life. Words cannot give life to fictional characters unless there is realistic human interaction between them, and in the real world, there is no bold, straight line between good and evil.

My argument with Sams actually increased my interest in the interactions between characters, the line between protagonist and antagonist was not nearly as important to me as it had been before. I found myself reading more and more classics with strong personal interactions such as *Jane Eyre* and *Pride and Prejudice,* both of which have indistinct definitions of "protagonist" and "antagonist" or "good" and "evil." Somehow, *Moby Dick* managed to redefine my passion for literature for a second time, and yet still I considered it a loathsome story.

I thought I had finally left the white whale behind, but it came back one more time to change my way of thinking. At the age of 17, I was stuck in a tangible mentality where I had convinced myself that books had their plot and characters and nothing else. In English classes I could produce symbolism if I needed to, but ultimately as Joan Didion claims of herself, "my attention veered inexorably back to the specific, to the tangible" aspects of stories (Didion). I was of the firm mindset, as were most of my peers, that authors did not mean to include all of the symbols and connections in their stories, but rather such nonsense was the product of the over- analysis of the work by teachers who needed to meet a question quota for the next exam. I was wrong and it took a trip across the world to reveal it. I was offered the opportunity to travel with a friend to Greece around that time. Retrospectively, the trip was outstanding and expanded my worldview significantly, but at the time I was a miserable mess. My extraordinary dislike of air travel and the fact that it was my first prolonged period away from home "on my own" made me anxious. Loneliness and homesickness consumed me in the beginning, and I only began to calm down by the end of the trip, aided, in part, by a trip to a bookstore.

The store was the most quaint thing I have ever seen. It was built into the side of a house, which was built into the side of a cliff, partially underground, on the island of Santorini. It had whitewashed stone walls, narrow staircases, low plaster ceilings with exposed beams, and the beams that made the structure of the building had planks of wood nailed between them so they doubled as bookshelves for the store. Hand-painted quotes in all languages scrawled across the white plaster walls and ceilings in artistic patterns, and outside on the cobblestone street which was wide enough only for foot traffic hung a sign that read "rent a cat, $5." The first thing to catch my eye in this store full of foreign novels and bustling with quaint activity was an English copy of *Moby Dick*. It was facing out. Full cover facing the room, not just the spine. I picked it up and felt such an abiding sense of comfort that I was taken aback. I was halfway across the world and thousands of miles from home, and yet I was holding in my hands something that I had steadfastly loathed for the past 5 years and feeling comfort. Suddenly I had a thought that there must be more to *Moby Dick* than I understood. If it was actually as bad as I thought it was, then there would be no reason for it to be printed in English, in a bookstore on a Greek island, where English is not the primary language, and all supplies need to be brought in by boat from the mainland on a trip that takes at least 6 hours round trip. There must be more to it. From that moment I decided to look for deeper meaning in the classics that I read.

It is difficult. Like Didion, my attention is persistently drawn toward the tangible plot and away from those aspects of the story that require thought. I am, however, improving. I first noticed when reading *Maus* that I was getting better at finding images and determining what the author means when they say something in particular. Arguably *Maus* is the training wheels of imagery-seeking. The images of cat and mouse are literal and blatant, and the story is highly symbolic of a bigger problem. I will acknowledge though, that I would not have cared for the symbolism before finding *Moby Dick* tucked away on a shelf in a bookstore at the edge of the world. I have recently been concerned with what I have missed in other stories. What did I purposefully overlook in exchange for the simplicity of the tangible plot? I fear now that I will need to re-read *Moby Dick* because since my experience with it I have yet to discover a single classic that did not belong within its class.

Perhaps it was not the rest of the world with the misguided perception of the story, but instead I with the inability to appreciate it to the fullest. However, I have a theory about *Moby Dick*. I believe its fame comes from word of mouth. People believe it is a classic because they are told that it is. No one has actually read the entire book. Evidence of this comes from the fact that the most famous quote from the book, and arguably one of the most famous quotes of all time, "call me Ishmael" is the *first line*. It does not improve from the first line. No one revels in, or even mentions the 300 or so pages of technical instructions on proper whale butchering technique. The story is presented falsely as a thrilling tale on the high seas of the mad Captain Ahab who pursues the whale that wronged him across the globe in order to exact his revenge. The misperception is presented as fact and passed from person to person, none of whom ever read the book to see if what they were told is actually true. I want to form my own opinions about books. I do not want to accept what others tell me about them as fact because they may not even know if what they are saying is true.

I cannot entirely explain why reading a terrible book inspired me to read more classics. I know I still have a desire to be respected based on the books I have read. I use literature to engage with others on a deeper, more complex level, and I enjoy it. I have a deeper understanding of the world because of books. I no longer see events as "good" vs "evil" or "us" vs "them." Books have helped me grow as a person, and as much as I disliked *Moby Dick*, I felt such growth when I finished. While the story itself was dreadful, finishing it was an accomplishment. Something to talk about. Something to brag about. As shallow and pretentious as it sounds, I think I kept reading for bragging rights. To stand out. To be better. Reading classics has changed me for the better. I enjoy them now, and each book brings a different perspective on people and how they change over time. I read them now to form my own opinions rather than blindly following word of mouth. My world has expanded and I love it. However, there still is, and likely will always be, a small part of me that relishes in the surprised and impressed reactions I get when I say, "I read all of *Moby Dick* when I was twelve years old."

Works Cited

Didion, Joan. "Why I Write." *New York Times Book Review* [New York] 5 Dec. 1976: n. pag.Digital file.

Huxley, Aldous. "The Art of Fiction No. 24." Interview by Raymond Frasier and George Wickes. *The Paris Review*. 23rd ed. Paris Review, n.d. Web. 1 Nov. 2015

Lucas McLean

Shotgun with Franco

My best friend Scott lives in a condo complex about fifteen minutes from my house. Across the street from the condos is a wide field bordered by thick, gnarled trees: paradise for 11 year-olds with a *Lord of the Rings* obsession and too much time on their hands. Every time I visited Scott, the green would become a battlefield crawling with invisible elves and orcs, and if you took a wrong step, one of the woods' trees might stand from the ground and creak open its knotted eyes. Scott particularly thrust himself into the fantasy, gathering props and delivering speeches he'd clearly rehearsed before my arrival. His favorite part by far was the skirmish itself. Whether wielding a stick wand, sword, or anachronistic machine gun, he had an instinctive way with gratuitous fake violence.

That's why his father always puzzled me. Franco was in his early seventies when Scott and I met. His wispy gray hair sat atop a long face—wrinkled, sometimes tired, and with a pointed nose. A slight hunch accompanied his slow, methodical walk as he made his way around the house, although he was usually in the kitchen; he would make fresh Italian bread for Scott and me every time I came over, and would always have some small factoid to enthusiastically share in his flowery accent. He was a professor of literature; his desk in the basement where Scott and I played computer games was covered in scholarly biblical analyses and books of ancient poetry. I'd always admired him, but I don't think I ever thought about him with any actual depth. He was my friend's father, your typical wise old man. Kids think of old people as a different species; they're there to complain about computers and come up with games to play in a traffic jam. The real question was how Franco, this human bottle of fine wine, helped produce a child as rambunctious as Scott.

At around 10 in the morning on a pleasant Saturday during the summer after eighth grade, Franco was at the wheel of the Masciandaros' 2007 white Toyota Camry, curving it around rural back roads at the pace of a moderately excited turtle. He'd made Scott and me bread that morning after a sleepover and offered to bring me home.

The first few minutes of the ride were scored by a silent radio, as I fiddled with a water bottle wrapper I'd found shoved into the passenger side door and looked out the window at the slowly passing oaks. I was never really one for small talk, let alone with the unusually generation-gapped father of my best friend.

"Do you know what you want to do after high school?" he spoke up, adopting a friendly inquisitive smile. "Scotty doesn't know yet. I try to ask him all the time." He chuckled. I forced one in response, then hardly thought for a beat before churning out my neatly-scripted default response, which, at the time, was:

"I want to be an English teacher."

I looked down to tear off a small corner of the water bottle wrapper, but my peripheral vision revealed him beaming from ear to ear.

"Aah!" he said, a trademark of his that made him sound like a Hogwarts professor. "That's wonderful! Very interesting stuff, you know? And important too."

I nodded. Given his area of expertise, I'd assumed my aspiration would impress him. I then braced myself for the inevitable long-winded oration about how to choose a college; I doubted he would urge the Ivy Leagues just yet, but he'd have some perfect equation for finding my best fit. Next would come the necessity of succeeding in high school to prove my standardized academic worth, and how I should never skip classes or drop out, and whatnot—

"You know, my town was bombed during World War II."

Oh!

That was new!

I cautiously looked at him. His spry eyes were aimed right ahead, his hands were at
2 o'clock/10 o'clock position on the wheel, and a youthful smile was shining through his wrinkles. I shifted in my seat and looked down.

"Oh yeah?" I said stupidly.

"My friends and I were riding our bikes. And then- aah! You know?" He chuckled and threw his arms up in mock terror. He looked at me, so I attempted to return his smile. As we turned onto Jared Sparks and the local church came into view, I realized there were still ten minutes left until home.

"Oh...yeah." I repeated. Stupidly. "Aah."

He nodded, his gray eyes looking off nostalgically. I cleared my throat and returned to my wrapper pickings.

"You know, I didn't move to America until I was seventeen," he said. "And I didn't even know English."

English! There was his connection. I wanted to be an *English* teacher! I breathed an internal sigh of relief. Now he would ask me if I'd started looking at colleges yet and—

"I don't want you to think I was in the mafia or anything. Although I could be." He laughed. I didn't. "Back in Italy, when Mussolini's soldiers came into our town, my friends and I hid behind buildings and threw rocks at them. We were very young. But it was a lot of fun!"

"Yeah," I said.

Stupidly.

He nodded. "But I think you'd make a very good English teacher."

I paused for a beat. "Thank you." I pushed my glasses up the bridge of my nose and watched the forest pass.

He nodded and smiled. "Mine was shot."

We arrived at my house about five minutes later, I thanked him for the ride, and he drove off up the rough gravel driveway. As I turned to face my woods-nestled home, his story was still running through my head. The funny thing about that is that when you're told something of that nature, you don't imagine a little kid; you imagine a 72 year-old Italian man chucking rocks at Nazis.

Franco was the same after that—save for a new spice on his bread every now and then.

He would still greet me with a smile and invite me back to stay again. He would let Scott and me binge-play *Age of Empires* in his study and then venture out into Middle-earth across the street for as long as we wanted. But I don't think I ever really looked at him the same way.

Oh, but who am I kidding? He's just an old man.

Gina Vitale

The Greatest American Coward

The *Rocky* theme song goes off like a goddamn foghorn in the middle of an otherwise silent lecture hall. This, I am certain, is God's way of punishing me for daydreaming in the middle of class. Nineteen years of an overactive imagination (as my parents so lovingly refer to it) and I haven't done poorly in a class since seventh grade Phys Ed.

You'd think the big bastard in the sky would have cut me some slack by now.

My physics teacher glares at me with distinctly Russian disdain as I scramble to hit the red 'reject' button as quickly as I can without knocking over all the shit on my tiny fold-out desk.

When you're in elementary school, you get a desk so big you can't reach your chubby arms all the way across it. But when you pay fifty-eight grand a year – "the tassel is worth the hassle" and all that bullshit – you barely get enough space to rest one goddamn elbow. There are people on the other side of the world, a little voice in the back of my head reminds me as my half-full thermos of cheap coffee goes crashing to the ground, who have it far worse than I do. I'm sure I would do well to acknowledge this voice, but I listen to music at a volume that's probably high enough to cause small earthquakes and my hearing just isn't what it once was.

I rush to pick up the thermos before the brown puddle on the floor grows big enough that it can actually be seen from space. I nearly drop it right into my lap when I lift my head to find my professor's sneer less than two feet away from my own face. For a few excruciating seconds it's nothing more than a staring contest. Although I like to believe my eyes bore into him like lasers and my jaw set like solid steel, in all probability my facial expression would have made a deer in headlights look unfazed by comparison.

"Do you know what right hand rule is?" His harsh, thick accent breaks into the silence like scissors would cut through honey. It's everything I have not to wince.

"Uhh...yes," I recover quickly and elegantly, all poise intact. Said no one ever. "It's this," I separate my pointer finger and thumb and imitate a turning motion, fumbling to validate my claim using only vague gestures. It's a particularly worthless talent of mine. "The thumb points in the direction of the axis of rotation."

His permanent grimace widens slightly as he considers this explanation, and my shoulders sag in relief when he finally turns his suffocating glare in another direction. "Correct," he states in a tone that still somehow makes it sound wrong. "I would refer to it as screwdriver rule, as motion is similar to turning screwdriver, but women might not understand. Women don't use screwdriver."

Of course he doesn't make eye contact with me now, the Siberian chicken, or so I call him in my head. In truth, it wouldn't matter even if he did. I'm one of those people who plays out a hundred different scenarios in my head of ways that I would rip someone a new asshole if they ever said something to me that was even tangentially offensive. But if that same person were to come up to me in real life and spit directly at my face – hock a loogie right into my left cornea, let's say – in all likelihood I would just stammer an apology and stumble off in the opposite direction. The Greatest American Coward, that's what they'd call me in the newspapers. Italian-American, if we're really going to split hairs.

I wait until after the lecture is over to look at my cell phone. I don't want to risk my comic book villain professor challenging me to another game of eye contact roulette that I will inevitably lose. *Mom* is the name displayed next to the missed call symbol, and I lift the phone to my ear to return the call as I file out of the classroom.

"Hello?"

"Hi, Mom. It's me."

"Hi sweetie. How are you doing?" she asks with her characteristic level of excessive cheer.

"I'm great. What's up?"

"I just wanted to see if you got the package I sent you."

I remember with a shallow twinge of guilt the box I had received in the mail a few days prior. I had every intention of calling to say thanks – then again, I had every intention of getting six hours of sleep last night. Intentions are not my strong suit.

"Yes, I did. Thank you," I answer stiffly, hoping that'll be the end of it. It never is.

"Did you like it?" she presses, and I can hear the excited smile in her voice. I make the mistake of sighing as I push open the door to exit the building and enter out onto the street. "Did you just sigh? Why, what was wrong with it? Do you not like scarves anymore?"

"No, Mom, I love scarves. And it's a great scarf. Thank you for knitting it for me." I assure her with as genuine a tone as I can muster as I stand at the corner and wait for the walking sign.

"But you don't like it." She presumes, disappointment in her voice.

"It's not that I don't like it," I bite my lip in hesitation as I deliberate whether it's worth having this discussion again. "It's just…"

"What?"

"It's *rainbow*."

"What's wrong with rainbows?" her tone is just a touch too defensive, and I roll my eyes at her attempt to feign innocence. "Don't even pretend you didn't do it on purpose. You know exactly what rainbows mean in this day and age."

Checkmate. The momentary silence on the other end of the line is confirmation enough. "I'm just trying to support you, honey," she offers gently. I push my glasses up against my forehead as I pinch the bridge of my nose between my thumb and forefinger in exasperation.

"I appreciate that, Mom. I really do," I assuage her as I replace my glasses. "But we've been over this. I'm not a lesbian."

"Whatever you say, sweetie."

Another sigh of futility escapes my lips as the light turns green and the crowd at the corner begins to shuffle forward. "Is there anything else you wanted to talk about? Because my girlfriend and I have a pride parade to get to. I'm actually the keynote speaker."

"Fine, I get it. No more rainbows. I'll let you – wait, sorry, your father's saying something– I think he wants to talk to you. Do you have a minute?"

"Sure."

"Okay. I love you sweetie."

"Love you too."

"No matter who you love."

"Still not gay, Mom.

"Hello?" A slightly more masculine voice calls through the receiver.

"Hey, Dad."

"What's wrong?" he asks suddenly, suspicion clear in his tone.

"How do you know something's wrong?"

"You sound dejected. I can hear it in your voice." He says matter-of-factly, and I raise my hands to gesture a rebuttal before I remember he can't see it.

"I'm not dejected!"

"I sent you five cat pictures this morning and you didn't answer any of them." "You know I've been in class all morning."

"They were good ones though. One of them was playing guitar – and it had a hat on!"

"That one was pretty cool," I grant him with a small smile, shaking my head at the fact that this is a typical exchange for a fifty-year-old man and his twenty-year-old daughter.

"I know it was. And you didn't answer. So what's going on?"

"I don't know. My physics professor was being a jerk."

"It's probably because he has to study physics for a living."

"Yeah, maybe," I concede, pulling open the door to my apartment building. "Hey, you've seen me use a screwdriver, right? Like I can definitely do it?"

"Sure you can, why?"

I run my hand through my hair and try to clear my mind of misogynistic physics teachers. There's no point in crying over spilled coffee. "No reason."

"Listen, don't let this physics guy bother you. Some people just get their kicks out of
making other people feel bad. They're called bullies."

"You're supposed to stand up to bullies, Dad. I never say anything," I confess, internally kicking myself for how much I sound like a second-grader from some cheesy '80's sitcom.

"You know, sometimes the bravest thing you can do is just grit your teeth." He says in an extra dad-like voice, and I grin at the fact that he's just as much of a sitcom character as I am.

"Thanks, Dad. Hey, my elevator's here – can I call you back later?"

"Sure thing. Bye honey."

"Bye Dad." I hang up and replace the phone in my pocket as the slowest elevator in all of creation struggles its way up four floors. The hallway to my apartment, lined with cheap, 1993- style carpet and off-white concrete walls, seems even longer than usual. It's not even 3:00 pm and I can already feel my soul groaning in relief as I finally reach the door and step inside.

"Hey, how was physics?" My roommate calls from the kitchen as she tosses some leftovers into our microwave.

I offer a small grimace as I pull my arms out of my fleece jacket. "As expected."

"That bad, huh?"

I shrug in either resignation or defeat. I'm not sure which one. "It is what it is."

"That's the attitude. Hey, did you know your mom sent me a knitted hat?" she mentions casually, her lips turning up at the corners in mild amusement.

"Jesus Christ." I let my face fall into my hands, thinking I really shouldn't have referred to god as a bastard earlier because this is clearly his retaliation.

"So, does she just really like rainbows, or does she still think we're secretly dating?"

I exhale deeply through my fingers. Sighing is my action of the day, apparently. "Please don't ask."

"I see. By the way, not to make your day worse, but the vent in our room is like, falling off the wall," she comments idly as she turns her attention back to the microwave.

This brings me to lift my head back up, and I consider it for a moment before coming to a decision. "I'll fix it," I declare resolutely.

"Really?" she raises her eyebrows in surprise. My dad used to be a mechanic but we're both aware that I never inherited any of his skill with repairs. "Look at you, being the hero."

"That's what they call me," I shoot her a wink as I head off in the direction of our utility closet to grab the necessary tools.

"Do your thing, superwoman. Just to warn you, I think some of the screws in the metal frame are coming out."

I fold out a stepstool just below the vent and climb it with gritted teeth, doing my best to ignore the way the old metal joints complain under my weight.

"Oh, I think I can handle a few loose screws."

Christian N. Schill

KFC Filibuster Schisms Washington Along Partisan Lines

WASHINGTON- Saturday evening Senate party lines were clearly drawn down the aisle. The decision as to whether the group should order Original Recipe or Grilled Chicken from a local K.F.C.© lead to one of the most heated debates in Congress history. Eventually giving way to Senator Marco Rubio (R- Florida) filibustering the decision before a vote was taken.

Arizona senator John McCain (R.) first proposed the group order from the fast food joint after coming down with what he claims was a severe case of the "munchies." Quickly each senator voted in favor in this decision, before Massachusetts senator Elizabeth Warren (D.) offered to the legislative chamber: "Okay, but let's get Grilled Chicken. I don't need to swell up and look like Chris Christie after a fascist potluck." This retort was quickly combated by Texas senator and presidential hopeful, Ted Cruz (R.) who said: "I ain't eatin' any hipster K.F.C."

Soon the congressional meeting turned into a heated, and at moments, tearful debate. While both parties agreed on the restaurant's mashed potatoes and cornbread as sides, none of the congressional members would budge on chicken recipes. Florida senator Marco Rubio (R.) came to the rescue of the Republican Party after standing on the congressional floor and speaking for over 4 hours about the culinary prowess of the original recipe chicken and the dull flavors of the Grilled Recipe chicken. This move was later admitted to be a filibuster, to quote: "starve the Democrats out."

President Obama and other White House officials were said to be watching the debate restlessly. When contacted for comments on the debate, the president said the following: "I think Michelle and I both agree that the Grilled Chicken is the way to go on this one."

When contacted for her opinion over the phone, Secretary Hillary Clinton stated the following: "Trevor what the hell do you want I was measuring the Oval Office drapes... Oh, this is being recorded? .... Oh yeah that filibuster thing. Why the hell don't they just get both?"

Local K.F.C.© manager Rob Kent was asked to comment on the hearing but offered only: "I really don't give a shit. It is chicken. It's literally chicken. Why is this a big deal?"

The Filibuster came to an end when Senate Majority leader Mitch McConnel (R.) suggested the group order the new "Nashville Hot Chicken". To which Presidential hopeful and Vermont senator Bernie Sanders (I.) replied: "It is time for some real change in this country! Wall Street is not too big to fail! The Nashville Hot Chicken it is!"

When asked about how the meal was Senator Rand Paul (R.) said only: "Eh, I'd like it to be spicier."

Presidential hopeful Donald Trump stated the following on Twitter during the filibuster: "The real issue that no one is talking about is that they let just any chicken into the congressional floor. Why are the chickens not going through a screening process to weed out high risk chickens? It's called terrorism, people. "

Safa Aman

404 [Females] Not Found: A Look at Women in Computing

I clenched my hands into fists. Then I unclenched them. I reached my fingers over my keyboard and tap-tapped a few more words into the console on my computer screen. I dragged the cursor up to the antiquated floppy disk symbol, waited less than a moment, and then refreshed the webpage that occupied the left side of the screen. My brows furrowed, and I glared at the screen as if it would cower in fear and do just as I willed. But instead, I clenched my hands into fists. Then I unclenched them. Tap-tap. Save. Refresh. Glare. Clench, unclench. Tap-tap. Save. Refresh. Glare. At some iteration of this brutal cycle, a thought creeped into my head, "Maybe you should ask someone for help." My pride, however, took great offense to this idea. I pressed on. Tap-Tap. Save. Refresh. This time, doubt's voice floated in. "This could be because you're a girl and you're trying to program." Though I knew that this was unlikely to be true, I did not have any concrete evidence to deny it. Maybe I *was* struggling because I just wasn't calibrated to do such tasks. But at that point, all I could do was press on, tap-tapping more incorrect code, hoping at some point it would become correct.

The voice I hear during my biggest struggles as a computer science student is one heard by so many of the women who pursue computing as a career. In 2012, the number of women pursuing undergraduate computing degrees was 19%, down nearly 10% since 1998 (Dubow 90). A smaller proportion of women is electing to pursue studies in computing fields, yet the total number of women in all science, technology, engineering, and mathematics (known collectively as STEM) actually increased between 2000 and 2009. The number of female engineers, biologists, chemists, and even STEM managers increased, yet the number of female computer scientists and mathematicians saw an overall decrease (Beede et al.). While all other STEM fields seem to find themselves on a trajectory to open themselves up to women, computing is moving in the opposite direction. Such a thought is worrying when one considers that computer scientists have their hands in essentially every new technology that emerges. Women offer a set of perspectives that their male counterparts may not necessarily be equipped to provide, and the lack of women in computing means that, in many instances, this perspective is inadequately represented or even missing completely. In order to understand why this matters, we first have to understand the cause of what is often dubbed the "gender gap." If we can see why women seldom find themselves in computing, then we will also see why they are so essential for the advancement of computing as a field.

The most obvious way that males and females differentiate themselves in computing is by the way they approach the subject. In 2000, Carnegie Mellon University published the results of a four year study on its computer science students, both male and female. The researchers found that the female students focused more on how the computer could "do something useful for society." The study juxtaposed this approach to computing with a "male fascination with the machine" (Fisher et al. 14-15). In other words, a female in computing may ask herself the human-oriented question, "How can I use this technology to help someone?" while a corresponding male student will ask the machine-oriented version, "How can I improve this technology to run faster?" I have found that male and female computing still distinguish themselves in very similar ways today, and that generally, we tend to look at computing from a machine-oriented perspective. Andrea Forte is an information sciences professor here at Drexel who specializes in a subset of human-computer interaction called social computing. Her work often concerns the way humans interact on popular social media websites like Facebook and Instagram. When I spoke with her, she mentioned that growing up, she never knew that computing offered disciplines that were simply about people. She speculated that more females would be interested in computing if they knew readily that such human-oriented applications existed. In fact, Professor Forte's undergraduate degree is not in computing, but in philosophy; she directly entered human-centered computing at a graduate level. I was drawn to her work because I found it so pertinent to my own life and the life of individuals like me. This draw implies that I, too, adopt that human-centered approach the Carnegie Mellon researchers found relevant over a decade ago.

The machine-oriented predisposition that males in computing display has directly created a "hacker subculture" within computing. The quintessential image of an individual who "does computers" is of one who holes himself up in his room to play video games and write various computer programs in his free time. These individuals do not have auxiliary interests outside of computing and computers, and are content to have their lives revolve solely around them. A key component of this image is that it always features a male; however, more than just this stereotype is what keeps women in computing to conform to the hacker image. Women in computing often have difficulty consuming themselves with computers like their male counterparts are able to do. The Carnegie Mellon researchers noted that they saw how "women's confidence erode when they compare their attachment to computing to that of their male peers" (Fisher et al. 19). One student they interviewed remarked that "when I have free time, I don't spend it reading machine learning books...I'm just not like that at all." When I surveyed computing students at Drexel, I found that their responses reflected this as well; one student wrote that she doesn't like coding and learning theoretical computer science concepts "all day, every day," and she felt that she "wouldn't make it if [she] didn't love it all the time" as her male peers did. Women in computing focus on the human-oriented side of computing, which means that they concern themselves more with context, and they therefore see computing as an interdisciplinary field. The hacker subculture directly opposes this, causing a contradiction between how women need to approach computing and how society says that they should.

Although most women in computing are fundamentally unable to adhere to what we consider a hacker and often by extension, a computer scientist, this fact alone cannot perpetuate the lack of women in computing. Ultimately, the discrepancies between what society expects individuals in computing to be and what these individuals actually are causes women in computing to exit the field because they lose hope that they could ever be sufficient or accepted in their careers. One student in my survey noted that being a female in computing "makes [her] even more afraid to fail, because [she] feel[s] like [she] will be judged for it." Another student remarked that when she sees male students around her succeed, she feels that her struggles "make women in computing look bad." While these thoughts may not hold any truth, the uncertainty and lack of confidence in these women make them the catalysts that drive these women to study different disciplines. Thus, if a women never grew up to know the archetype of a hacker, she would have trouble experiencing the same doubts and fears. This topic arose when I talked with Professor Forte. While she acknowledges the gender gap, she told me that she'd never been compelled to support Women in Computing groups because growing up, "[her] mom was the one who sat at the computer and programmed." She grew up without the idea that men were the individuals who excelled with computers, and as a result, never felt inadequate as a woman in computing. Professor Forte's thoughts reveal just how much the gender gap is caused not by the malevolent male students who don't believe women belong in computing, but by the women who lack the confidence to assert that they do.

Each time I clench and unclench my fists, tap code into a console, and glare at a disobedient computer screen, some voice in my head gets louder. My pride tells me that I am capable of anything, while doubt reminds me that I'm not meant to succeed. My biggest opponent will always be myself. I have to overcome this, and realize that I bring a perspective to computing that, if it grows, could possibly usurp that hacker stereotype, and make it easier for individuals like me to have the confidence to stay in this exciting field. I cannot hope to help people with my software creations unless my male counterpart also strives to make these innovations faster and more powerful.

Unfortunately, we still see a polarization between male and female computer scientists, and there isn't a visible end to this trend. If these discrepancies can somehow fade, we will see a symbiosis of male and female programmers working together. Even if they don't, I know that only persistence will garner me the self-respect and audacity to challenge what it is to be an individual who studies computing. And perhaps someday, the cycle I push through with every programming assignment will evolve into something more. Clench, unclench. Tap-tap. Save. Refresh. Repeat. Create. Change the world.

Works Cited

Aman, Safa. "Demographics and Motivations for Entering Computing Fields." Survey. 04-10 Nov 2015.

Beede, David N., et al. "Women in STEM: A Gender Gap to Innovation" *Economics and Statistics Administration Issue Brief No. 04-11.* (2011). Print.

Forte, Andrea. Personal Interview.13 October 2015.

DuBow, W. "Attracting and Retaining Women in Computing." *Computer* 47:10 (2014): 90-93. Print.

Fisher, Allan, Jane Margolis, Faye Miller. "Caring about connections: gender and computing." *Technology and Society Magazine*, IEEE 18.4 (1999-2000): 13-20. Print.

Faculty
Writing

Faculty writing reflects current, published work by professors in the College of Arts and Sciences. These texts have previously appeared in academic and scholarly journals, books, conference papers, magazines, and websites. They are often thought provoking, sometimes poignant, and at other times funny; but they serve always as a living demonstration of the many forms writing can inhabit.

andré m. carrington

Afrofuturism, and *Fear of a Black Planet* at 25

Twenty-five years after *Do the Right Thing* was nominated but overlooked for Best Picture, Spike Lee is about to receive an Academy Award.[i] At the beginning of that modern classic, Rosie Perez danced into our collective imaginations to the sounds of Public Enemy. Branford Marsalis's saxophone squealing, bass guitar revving up, she sprung into action in front of a row of Bed-Stuy brownstones. Voices stutter to life: "Get—get—get—get down," says one singer, before another entreats, "Come on and get down," punctuated by James Brown's grunt, letting us know we're in for some hard work as ever-more-insistent sounds join the overture. In unison, Chuck D and Flavor Flav place us in time: "Nineteen eighty-nine! The number, another summer..." The track's structure, barely held in place by the guitar riff and a snare, accommodates Marsalis's saxophone playing continuously during the chorus, but intermittent scratches and split-second samples make up the plurality of the sounds. The two rappers' words take back the foreground in each verse, and their cooperative and repetitive style reinforces the song's message during the chorus, when they trade calls and responses of "Fight the power!"

Throughout the credits, lyrics and musical elements are shot through with noise: machine guns, helicopters, jet engines—even the sax, the only conventional instrument at work, seems to cede ground to these disruptions. The dancing form of Perez, unlike the other figures taking part in the performance, is silent but visible, and she's the only one who seems fully in control of the relationship between her body and the sounds. The solo female dancer is a countermeasure to the pattern Afrofuturist critic Nabeel Zuberi observes, "In a great deal of popular commentary, the people who move on the dancefloor are described as an amorphous singular body manipulated by the DJ's control of the record decks."[ii] In a critique of discourse on Black music that resists the "differential agency [of] women's experience and pleasure on the dancefloor" as technological strategies worthy of examination, Zuberi locates fantasies of masculine technological mastery, Ecstasy-driven trance states, and anti-technological notions of rootedness that naturalize athletic male bodies and the heteronormative relations they dominate.[iii] Perez's performance of "Fight the Power" is an antidote: her movements, while sometimes syncopated, are discrete to the point of appearing martial—the steps are improvised but the skills are practiced. She executes the motions demanded by the song literally, as well: in boxing gloves, with footwork and aerobic thrusts timed to her own interpretation of the beat, she seems ready to step into the ring and fight the powers that be.

One line foreshadows the confrontation that will play out between Black and White popular imaginaries attempting to occupy the same space in the film: "Elvis was a hero to most, but he never meant shit to me as he's straight out racist/The sucka was simple and plain," says Chuck. But the judgment isn't complete until Flav makes it rhyme: "Mother fuck him and John Wayne!" This line and its response are the counterpart to the incredulous rage that drives Buggin' Out to ask the rhetorical question, "How come you ain't got no brothers on the wall?" at Sal's Famous Pizzeria: the celebratory iconography of whiteness obscures the indispensable presence of Blackness in America—indispensable in imagery, movement, sound, and in silence—and PE is here to cut through the noise with a new sound.[iv]

"Fight the Power," which fulfilled Spike Lee's request to Public Enemy to provide a theme for the movie, made it onto the group's iconic album *Fear of a Black Planet* the following year. Shana Redmond names the song "perhaps the last Black anthem of the twentieth century," noting that it bridges divides like the space between East and West Coast.[v] It does so as part of the film's opening sequence through juxtapositions: the sound of helicopters, a signature of LAPD surveillance, crosses the New York City streetscape in stereo. On the album, however, a radically different opening sets the tone for the track. A speech by Thomas Todd taunts, "Yet our best trained, best equipped, best prepared, troops refuse to fight. Matter of fact, it's safe to say that they would rather *switch* than fight." The speaker draws out the breathy, sibilant ending of the word "switch" to create a double entendre; voiced this way, "they would rather *switch*" connotes both disloyalty in the "fight" and a swishy movement of the hips attributed to effeminate men. In later years, the crystal-clear sample would resurface across genres; it was the only lyrical component of DJ Frankie Bones's "Refuse to Fight" in 1997, a track purely intended for dancing in the blissful atmosphere of the rave scene, which evacuated militancy to make room for "Peace, Love, Unity, and Respect."[vi] On PE's album, the version of the song introduced by this sample strikes a stark contrast with its rendition in the film as the vehicle for an inexhaustible and defiant female dancer in a neighborhood wracked by disempowerment.

Identifying *Fear of a Black Planet* as "the first true rap concept album," Tom Moon of *The Philadelphia Inquirer* recognizes the role of the DJ and production team in achieving a unique synthesis between melodic and meaning elements. At first he calls the sample-heavy stage for the rap performance "a bed of raw noise not unlike radio static," but he later parses out how this "noise" actually consists of a rich informational emulsion:

> an environment that can include snippets of speeches, talk shows, arguments, chanting, background harmonies, cowbells and other percussion, drum machine, treble-heavy solo guitar, jazz trumpet, and any number of recorded samples.[vii]

This soundscape includes Lee's 1989 Bed-Stuy, where "Fight the Power" blasts over Radio Raheem's boombox, but in 1990, the album as a whole encompasses what Josh Kun has called an "audiotopia." Whereas Kun identifies autotopias as "almost-places of cultural encounter that may not be physical spaces but nevertheless exist in their own auditory somewhere,"[viii] echoing Thomas More's original conflation of the homophones "*eutopia*" (a better place) and "*outopia*" (no place) with the phonetically identical title *Utopia*, it's fair to say that PE's Black Planet is decisively dystopian in nature. The underlying concept driving the album is the ominous encounter between Blackness and whiteness, which has become an object of fear and fascination throughout centuries of American culture. As the role of their anthem in the film about a neighborhood undergoing violent transformation indicates, the meeting of Black and white is not a fearsome future to come, but a present giving way to both reactionary and revolutionary possibilities. And it goes a little something like this.

As the first song, "Contract on the World Love Jam," insists, in one of the "'forty-five to fifty voices'" Chuck D recalls sampling for this track alone,[ix] "If you don't know your past, then you don't know your future." *Fear of a Black Planet* contributes to Afrofuturism through the prophetic speech it invokes and through its place on the cultural landscape as a touchstone for the beginning of the 1990s, a moment that has become a "future past" full of resources to draw on, in the words of Nabeel Zuberi.[x] Unbeknownst to us at the time, this moment continues to resonate in the present as a repository of ideas and modes of expression we still need. Along with the hypnotic efficacy of rhetoric like "Laser, anesthesia, 'maze ya/ Ways to blaze your brain and train ya," and Flavor Flav's subversive humor, I would argue that *Fear of A Black Planet* participates in Afrofuturism by using sound to instigate the kind of "disjuncture" that Arjun Apparurai called characteristic of culture under late modern global capitalism. Coining the term "technoscapes," Appadurai cited "the fact that technology, both high and low, both mechanical and informational, now moves at high speeds across various kinds of previously impervious boundaries."[xi] This kind of practice thematizes *Fear of a Black Planet:* it uses sound to confront the boundaries of information, desire, and power on decisively African Americanist terms.

Sampling is an indispensable strategy on *Fear of a Black Planet*. Yet as Tricia Rose contends, the sound of hip-hop arises out of a systematic way of moving through the world rather than as a "by-product" of factors of production. Mark Katz identifies Public Enemy's sampling with "the pre-digital, pre-phonographic practice of signifying that arose in the African American community"[xii]. Scholarly treatments of works from the era that gave rise to the album employ the periodizing notion of a "golden age" of digital sampling, a moment when new technology made it possible for musical composition to rely on audio appropriated from a panoply of sources but before the financial and methodological obstacles of copyright clearance emerged in force. The challenges imposed by the cost of licensing fees now associated with sampling make contemporary critics doubtful that the same album could be produced today without incurring significant commercial losses.[xiii] In retrospect, the album shows us how the "financescape" of popular music has evolved out of sync with the technoscape: by placing property rights in the way of the further development of the tradition inaugurated by the Bomb Squad (PE DJs Terminator X, Hank and Keith Shocklee, and Eric "Vietnam" Sadler), we have forestalled the democratizing potential of their innovations.

In 2011, when asked about sampling as an art form, Hank Shocklee pointed out that, "as we start to move more toward into the future and technology starts to increase, these things have to metamorphosize, have to change," further insisting that this means, "everything should be fair use, except for taking the entire record and mass producing it and selling it yourself."[xiv] Realizing how sampling entails not just the use of sound but its transformation, he stakes out a radical position on intellectual property, extending his critique to countenance broad takings, "a chorus, if you take the entire intro from a record, eight bars of whatever it takes," and rebutting the dubious framing of the interview, which is titled "Digital Sampling: Creativity or Criminality?" Shocklee arrives at the same analysis as Siva Vaidyanathan regarding the interests behind intellectual property enforcement, that "the creator is a straw man in copyright debates," by noting that the law tends to protect record companies rather than performers.[xv]

> Stubblefield, [the drummer], is not a copyright owner. James Brown is not a copyright owner. George Clinton is not a copyright owner. The copyright owners are corporations... when we talk about artists, you know, that term is being used, but that's not really the case here. We're really talking about corporations.

Driven by such a skeptical orientation to the notion of sound as property, *Fear of a Black Planet* is both unapologetic and unforgiving in its sonic promiscuity. It weds a dizzying repertoire of references from the past to a sharp political critique of the present, embodying the role of hip-hop in transforming the relationship between sound and knowledge through whatever means the moment makes available.

A different Spike Lee joint (*Jungle Fever*, 1991, with a soundtrack by Stevie Wonder) enacts the spectacle behind the title track on *Fear of a Black Planet*. Interracial sexuality, as one of many dimensions of living together across the color line, is the most explicit "fear" a Black Planet has in store, but the track undercuts the flawed notions of white purity at the heart of the issue. Chuck D dismisses the concerns of an imaginary white man at the start of each verse: "your daughter? No she's not my type... I don't need your sister... man, I don't want your wife!" He subsequently shifts focus to the questions of "what is pure? who is pure?" what would be "wrong with some color in your family tree?" and finally, whether it might be desirable for future generations to become more Black, owing to the adaptive value of "skins protected against the ozone layers/ breakdown." Chuck's line of questioning assuages the anxiety that the imagined white interlocutor might feel in order to address more fundamental planetary concerns, like environmental degradation. In addition to staging a conversation in which a Black man enjoins a white man to listen to reason, the structure of the track involves Flavor Flav in a parallel dialogue. Flav replies to each of Chuck's initial reassurances regarding the prospect of white women as intimate partners with the same playful counterpoint: "but suppose she says she loves me?" He keeps posing the hypothetical in one verse after another, despite Chuck D's repeated insistences that he isn't interested in white women, suggesting that "love," an irrational but undeniably powerful motivation for interracial encounter, is just as compelling as a putatively rational browning of the planet's people.

The hypotheticals spoken by the two MCs on *Fear of a Black Planet* rehearse the argument of the other vocal elements paired on the track. After the first verse, a speaker's voice in a recorded sample catalogs the progeny of different unions: "white man, white woman, white baby/white man, Black woman, Black baby/Black man, white woman, Black baby," and after the second verse, a highly distorted voice synthesizes the conclusion to be drawn from the previous interlude: "Excuse us for the news/You might not be amused/But did you know white comes from Black/No need to be confused." The interludes recur following the next two verses by Chuck and Flav. Together, they expound the theory of hypodescent, in which having one Black direct ancestor, no matter how distant, identifies any individual and all their descendants as Black. By confronting this logic directly, through the phrasing "white comes from Black," the critique of purity, and playful exhortations to peace and love, the track skips the oppressive corollaries that accompany the "one drop" rule. "Pollywannacracka" riffs on the same subject with hauntingly distorted vocals and a chorus that includes a mocking crowd calling the Black woman or man who desires a "cracka" out their name (the drawn out refrain is the word "Polly...") and a teasing whistle. These derisions reduce the taboo topic of interracial liaisons to the stuff of schoolyard taunts while playing out tense confrontations among Black men and Black women in between the verses.

The group greets controversy as an old friend on *Fear of a Black Planet,* having earned notoriety for comments that a former manager, Professor Griff, made in an interview in 1988. Griff's anti-Semitic "Jews control the media" remarks struck an importune chord that was all too familiar among Black nationalists in the era and disrupted the group's promotional schedule right before the release of *It Takes a Nation of Millions*.[xvi] *Black Planet* presented the first opportunity for PE to reconstruct their reputation through new music. They take the public's temperature on "Incident at 66.6 FM," which reiterates snippets from listeners calling in to radio broadcasts; most of the callers represented excoriate the group but a few defend them, including erstwhile DJ Terminator X, who shouts himself out in a call to a station. This inward-facing archive acquires more material on the album's most self-referential track, "Welcome to the Terrordome." Veteran critic Robert Christgau illuminates "Terrordome" as a frustrating but understandable accounting of the group's sins. The song elliptically places the scrutiny the group has faced in perspective through allusions that are rendered even more involuted through repetition and internal rhyme: "Every brother ain't a brother... Crucifixion ain't no fiction... the shooting of Huey Newton/from the hand of a nig that pulled the trig." The brother who allegedly ain't one was David Mills, the music journalist who publicized Griff's comments. Noting Chuck's rather transparent analogy between this betrayal and the myth that the Jewish community was responsible for killing Jesus, Christgau concludes that "the hard question isn't whether 'Terrordome' is anti-Semitic—it's whether that's the end of the story."[xvii] It isn't.

"War at 33 1/3" redraws these same lines by advising that "any other rapper who's a brother/Tries to speak to one another/Gets smothered by the other kind," hearkening back to the earlier song's assertion not all skinfolk are kinfolk. The song samples speech from Nation of Islam leader Louis Farrakhan that frames the titular "war" as a rhetorical contest. Farrakhan names various disciplines, including theology, political thinking, education, and science, in which Black practitioners demonstrate superior knowledge, and PE testifies to this belief at 33 1/3 RPM.

The most collaborative jam on the album, since remixed by Rage Against the Machine's Zack De La Rocha, "Burn Hollywood Burn" enacts an acerbic critique of media representations of Blackness against the most party-perfect hooks on the album, including a sampled crowd repeating the three words of the refrain like a protest chant, a timeline provided by a pea whistle, and a horn sample looped for the gods. Sustaining a militant ideal of Black masculinity in defiance of Hollywood's Stepin' Fetchit and *Driving Miss Daisy* scripts (both referenced by name on the track), featured MCs Ice Cube and Big Daddy Kane occupy the foreground throughout most of the track. Their forward-leaning posture demands that they be taken seriously, like Chuck D, rather than coming off as whimsical and indulgent like Flavor Flav. Yet PE's sound is unrecognizable without Flav's flavor to carry out the call-and-response structure of their performances. Flav voices a skit on the final verse of "Burn

Hollywood Burn" in which he is invited to portray a "controversial Negro" as an actor; he asks if the role calls on him to identify with Huey P. Newton or H. Rap Brown, but to his chagrin, the invitation calls for "a servant character that chuckles a little bit and sings." Contemporary audiences might associate Flavor Flav with the latter, based on his reality TV persona, but the comic wit he brings to PE knowingly undermines their strident posture and demands that the audience listen more closely.

Despite the comparatively trivial content of his lyrical presence on most tracks, Flav actually enhances the repertoire of knowledge at work across *Fear of a Black Planet,* deepening its cultural frame of reference and accentuating different elements of its sonic structure. On "Who Stole the Soul," for example, after Chuck says, "Banned from many arenas/ Word from the Motherland/ Has anybody seen her," Flav repeats after him, "Have you seen her," to emphasize the allusion to "Have You Seen Her?" by the Chi-Lites. Then, before Chuck has finished his next line, Flav repeats *himself,* stylizing the question "Have You Seen Her" with the same melody used in the chorus of the Chi-Lites song: "Have you seen her?/Tell me have you seen her?" Ingeniously, Flav modifies the allusion that Chuck makes in verbal form by using the timing and melodic structure of his repetition to produce a new timeframe within the existing track, doubling the ways in which this line alludes to a prior work. A seemingly effortless mastery of flow proves as essential to the group's participation in sound practices that subvert time, space, and property as the skills of the Bomb Squad.

On his own, Flav's performances on *Black Planet* laugh through the pain of urban dystopia. Concentrated poverty, premature death, and alienation from the amenities of citizenship are the subject matter of "911 is a Joke" and "Can't Do Nuttin' For Ya Man," on which Flav takes center stage. "911" is especially notable for coupling Flav's cynical appraisal of life and death in the hood to repetitive verse structures, a tight rhyme scheme consisting mostly of couplets, a chart-ready beat (the song reached #1 on the Billboard Hot Rap Singles list), and an unforgettable quatrain as the hook: "Get up, get, get, get down/911 is a joke in your town/ Get up, get, get, get get down/Late 911 wears the late crown." The notion of getting down to misery is disturbing, but that's all you can do. Despite the emergencies underway, Flav's persona on "911" purports to rap in medias res, with the matter-of-fact opening, "I dialed 911 a long time ago" and gestures throughout the three minutes to suffering contemporaries: "You can ask my man right here with the broken neck." The absurd music video for the track depicts Flav rapping from inside his own coffin while a church choir sings; although he's wearing his trademark clock medallion, he glances at a wristwatch to mark the time since he called for help. The track also features a particularly macabre sample: the laughter of Vincent Price, the same heard at the harrowing conclusion of Michael Jackson's "Thriller."

While "911" ironizes the withdrawal of public resources from "your town" amid concentrated poverty, "Can't Do Nuttin' For Ya Man" is a send-up of misfortunes the urban denizen has brought upon himself. The main instrumental elements cited on the track are a highly truncated pipe organ sample, a snare, cowbell, and a bass guitar loop, which shake together and apart during the breaks and give way to a highly danceable bridge before Flav dismisses the listener. The music fades out after his final blows, "You on welfare... You got a rip in your couch" and concludes with his raspy laughter. The funky tune profanes the serious concerns of a man who's fallen into a life of crime, offering none of the self-help Chuck D might endorse but only "Bass for your face."

Mark Anthony Neal has called the generation that came of age in the 1990s the "Post-Soul" generation, and the many funk and soul references on *Fear of a Black Planet*, from the preceding sounds to the rallying cry of "Who Stole the Soul," connect the first hip-hop of the decade to the prior generation of Black music. Repetition with difference allows the group to maintain a dialogue between their precedents in socially conscious popular music and the new intervention they intend to make. If "Fight the Power" signals the dawn of new era, so does the largely-forgotten "Reggie Jax," the downtempo freestyle on which Chuck D coins the term "P-E-FUNK." Whereas digital sampling made the former possible then and impossible now, the latter perpetuates a signifying tradition constantly reiterated throughout Black modernity. Chuck's neologism, which he introduces by spelling it out, "P-E-F-U-N and the K," is a performative citation linking PE's brand of hip-hop to the P-Funk of the 1970s: perhaps the defining expression of Afrofuturism in popular music. The morphology of "P-E FUNK" is highly novel, infixing a new element within an existing word and also facilitating the flow between the terms by enunciating their assonant sounds. Like Eshun's Afrofuturist criticism, Chuck's account of PE's sound "mobilizes a new jargon to replace academic vocabulary," in this case, displacing prevailing concepts of genre with a hybrid category of his own invention.[xviii] This tactic for naming the fusion of hip-hop and P-Funk allows PE to continue a pattern initiated by their predecessor Afrika Bambaataa, whom they sample on "Fight the Power," by inserting themselves into a particular artistic genealogy animated by George Clinton, Bootsy Collins, and the mind-expanding antics of Parliament/Funkadelic.[xix]

The intense polyrhythmic edifice of *Fear of a Black Planet* supports many more interpolations that link past to future, engaging in a radically heteroglossic practice of treating sound as information. Deploying the sound of knowledge and the knowledge of sound in the service of envisioning the world as it is, the album charts a dystopian itinerary for the 1990s that we need in order to comprehend how we arrived at the present. Rather than worrying that a collision with a Black Planet is something to fear, we might consider the lessons that emerged from past efforts to cope with developments already underway. If we listen to Flavor Flav and find that coping strategies are futile, at least we can party. And if we were right to call Chuck a prophet, then the dawn of the Black Planet he warned us about—characterized by neoliberal governance, gentrification, and boundaries that demand to be crossed—is a moment when the avant-garde tactics critics have identified with Afrofuturism are becoming important to everyone. Citizens of Earth: Welcome to the Terrordome.

[i]   Ben Child, "Spike Lee to Get Honorary Oscar 25 Years After Do the Right Thing," *The Guardian*, August 28, 2015.

[ii]   Nabeel Zuberi, "Is this the Future? Black Music and Technology Discourse" *Science Fiction Studies* 34, no. 2 (July 2007), 291.

[iii]   Ibid, 292.

[iv]   Lasana Hotep, "'No Brothers on the Wall': Black Male Icons in Spike Lee's *Do The Right Thing*" Ph.D. dissertation (Arizona State University, 2012), 14.

[v]   Shana Redmond, *Anthem: Social Movements and the Sound of Solidarity in the African Diaspora* (New York: New York University Press, 2014), 261-262.

[vi]   Dan Wender, "How Frankie Bones' Storm Rave Birthed the 'PLUR' Movement," Vice, May 13, 2015.

[vii]   Tom Moon, "'Fear of a Black Planet'-Concept Rap from Public Enemy," *Philadelphia Inquirer*, April 10, 1990.

[viii] Josh Kun, *Audiotopia: Music, Race, and America* (Berkeley: University of California Press, 2005), 2-3.

[ix]   Kembrew McCleod and Peter DiCola, "Creative License: The Law and Culture of Digital Sampling," reprinted from Creative License: *The Law and Culture of Digital Sampling* (Durham: Duke University Press: 2012).

[x]   Zuberi, 286.

[xi]   Arjun Appadurai, "Disjuncture and Difference in the Global Cultural Economy," In Daya Kishan Thussu, ed. *International Communication: A Reader* (New York: Routledge, 2010), 384.

[xii]   Mark Katz, *Capturing Sound: How Technology Has Changed Music* (Berkeley: University of California Press, 2010), 164.

[xiii]   McCleod and DiCola, 14.

[xiv]   Ira Flatow, interview with Dean Garfield, Kembrew McLeod, and Hank Shocklee, "Digital Music Sampling: Creativity or Criminality" NPR's Talk of the Nation, January 28, 2011, http://www.npr.org/2011/01/28/133306353/Digital-Music-Sampling-Creativity-Or-Criminality.

[xv]   Katz, 201.

[xvi]   Robert Christgau, "The Shit Storm" Robert Christgau: Dean of American Rock Critics http://www.robertchristgau.com/xg/music/pe-law.php.

[xvii]   Robert Christgau, "Looking for the Perfect Public Enemy," in *Grown up all wrong: 75 Great Rock and Pop Artists from Vaudeville to Techno* (Cambridge: Harvard University Press), 270-271.

[xviii]   Zuberi, 289.

[xix]   Ytasha Womack, *Afrofuturism: The World of Black Sci-Fi and Fantasy Culture* (Chicago: Lawrence Hill Books, 2013), 63.

Valerie Fox

Insomnia

But lately, we are all afraid

to call upon one another

unless the meeting has been pre-arranged.

Must mean someone's personal

Dark Age is looming across

the countryside,

heading toward the cities,

dragging blood and bone.

What did Dali paint

when he couldn't sleep?

I must've been drunk or invisible

when I used to know facts,

like that.

Valerie Fox in collaboration with Arlene Ang

There Are Worms and There Are Butterflies

Some of you will always be worms.
You may end up eating rotten flesh off burn victims

and saving lives. Butterflies often get the net.
Someone, probably with a mustache, invented a killing jar

so butterflies don't damage their wings trying to escape.
No one will tack you on a board and hang you

on their wall after you're dead. This doesn't mean
you shouldn't stop wishing to be a butterfly.

For every thirty-three breaths, there's a wish bubble.
There's time enough later to stop breathing.

If you will always be a worm,
you should try to be your best worm.

On the inside we are all the same
and we all want what is best for everyone (and you too).

Henry Israeli

Blame the French

1.

Whatever you do
the French did first.
Whatever you say
the French said first.
Whatever you wear
the French wore first.
You see the pattern?
There is nothing in life
that the French did
not do first. Nothing.
Can you think of anything?
Wrong. The French
did it first. Say what?
The French already said that.
You saw something
original in a film once?
Then you never saw
Renoir or Cocteau.
You read something?
Zola, Baudelaire, Rimbaud,
de Beauvoir, take your pick.
Food? Don't even go
there, wise guy.
You had a dream
after which you awoke
amazed at the veracity
of your complicated mind?
Get over yourself.
The French dreamt it
long before you.
Everything you've done
in the bedroom—
I'll simply say, the French,
and waste no time
humiliating you further.
Everything you ever
encounter or experience

in this short-long life
you may thank or blame
the French for,
take your pick.

2.

But, for god's sake,
pity the French, will you?
For they have no one
to praise, no one to fault.
They are doomed to
the boredom of
self-containment.
When a Frenchman
looks in the mirror
he sees no reflection,
nothing whatsoever,
for there is nothing
to reflect upon.
As the originator of all
he can only,
as Descartes said
more eloquently, be.
A Frenchwoman can
never experience
the joy of being told
she looks French,
for that is a vile
(or as the French
say, vil) redundancy,
and holds no logic
for the French mind.
It is like kissing your
own ghost and falling
into an ethereal abyss
of self-referential absurdity,
which is, after all,
typically French.

Kirsten Kaschock

Theater in the Wake

Sometimes you do not control the circumstances surrounding your entrance into a theater.
Sometimes you are not in control of what wells up inside of you in response to art.
Sometimes, maybe that's what art is.

*

My sister Mary's mother died Friday.

Mary came to live with me two months after I turned 13 and one month before she turned 14. When she came to live with me I called her cousin.

None of this has anything to do with the show I'm about to see.

*

In Bronx Gothic, Okwui Okpokwasili tells the story of two girls coming of age in hate-love. She tells this story through her body, through reading their loose-leaf letters, through threading together snatches of song. The girls' bestfriendship demands and flaunts its honesty, the kind that can be cruel but never heartless. This intersection of oppositional energies is the excruciation of adolescence.

One of the girls recounts a grown man telling her her black is so ugly she's almost beautiful.

*

When I met Okwui, we were 18, and she was stunning. I was in my dorm room at Yale with my parents (who'd done this same song and dance at American University with my sister Mary a year earlier) and my roommate walked in—a six-foot-tall drink of water, dark-skinned, a smile that lit up the whole hallway. She was self-composed with a deep velvet voice meant for the stage or for a different era of radio, and my mom and dad immediately adored her and her family. With our parents at ease and chatting, Okwui and I decided on bunks. She took the top and me, the bottom.

*

My sister Mary and I shared a bedroom for three years. Sometimes, after the lights went out we'd talk. My memory of these late night sessions was that—as the slightly younger and less mature—I was always trying to glean something from her: the undisclosed details of her difficult past, some recipe of how to be with boys (it seemed to me she knew all the secrets), what guy she was crushing on... flirting with... dreaming of. In short, I wanted pieces of my new sister. I felt entitled to them.

Mary wrote in a diary with a lock, and I was not entitled.

She'd been dropped unwittingly into our large family, her younger brother and sister (whom she'd been parenting before her time) living a few miles away now in another relative's house. Her young mother Moira had given her children to her cousin and her sister to finish raising. These are some of the complexities of family love.

*

As the audience walks into New York Live Arts (where Okwui is performing this sold out encore performance after being named NYLA's Resident Commissioned Artist in July), they see her in a knee-length halter dress, trembling, dancing, muttering, and posturing into a corner draped in white fabric. She doesn't stop moving and by the time she turns and makes her way towards the microphone thirty minutes later, still vibrating like an engine, the ropy muscles of her back, legs, and arms are drenched with sweat. Her embodiment of this story will be won through hard physical labor. The girls' voices she engages (one tremulous and childish, the other not), the fragmentary songs, the gestures she uses to identify side characters (mother and mother's predatory boyfriend and Ricardo, one of the girl's firsts): every bit of fractured narrative is starkly defined in her body. The pieces don't come easily, but like shards of a broken mirror—glued back together—they reflect a sharp and bloody time. The time when a girl is becoming a woman... sometimes without full understanding, sometimes against her will.

*

When we left home for college, my sister Mary and I were not what anyone would call friends.

*

I emailed Okwui a few days before I came to New York. I haven't seen her in two decades. We were not close in college, though she always welcomed me into her circles. A force of nature, a dancer and actress and singer, she was cast contra-gender as Judas in the Yale Mainstage production of Jesus Christ Superstar senior year, defying easy description then as now, mildly androgynous and magnanimous and utterly magnetic. Three years after our first fall together I was still known to some as Okwui's roommate—a tighter bud, smaller in ways that had nothing to do with our relative heights. In our email exchange she mentioned that at that time she'd felt riddled with holes. I wrote back, "and who was not?"

*

Mary's mother Moira was 15 when she had Mary and 60 when she died. I was in Chelsea, heading to the show, when my mom called. She told me Moira had passed. After a long up-and-down illness, her last few hours were peaceful, and her three children were at her side.

Nearly a year ago, my sister Mary brought her dying mother into her home to ease the coming transition.

Mary's own children—my niece and nephew—they have a remarkable mother.

*

Okwui's show is about brown girls in the Bronx in the 1980s. The specifics— the taste of Newport loosies, the smell of Vaseline Intensive Care, ripped-out note pages passed in class, fire-drenched dreams of Orchard Beach—conjure a very particular time and place. But the girls themselves and the way they alternately bloom against one other and are blocked, the way they hate-love and share-shame and intertwine and thrash inside each other's narratives: this is a sister story. A story of sisters made not born. Girls so hungry they suck on each other's dreams as if they were the last of the grape Now & Laters at the close of a long school day.

Bronx Gothic ends with two girls so close they sometimes seem one, and so far apart we doubt they ever really knew one another.

Except—of course they did.

*

My sister Mary got pregnant with her first child six months before I did. She decided (she's the decider) that our sons would grow up to be close. Then she made sure it happened. During the same period, we too became friends. I am so grateful. My nephew lived for a month this summer (his sixteenth) at my house while he did lab research at Drexel. He and my son talked every night, played videos, did whatever teenage boys do when their parents aren't bearing down on them. Not too long from now, they will be leaving home for their respective colleges.

*

There are people against whom you measure yourself as a person. People who live side-by-side with you during the time when you are becoming yourself, for better or for ill. They serve as both your mirror and your negative image. You fill in the gaps they leave. Once they are out of the room you shadowbox their phantom or sucker slap their imagined face or you try on their bra. It doesn't fit. You are the shy one or the short one or the darker one or the ugly one. And they are the center.

Sometimes, later, you are lucky enough to learn that—during that same time—they were piecing themselves together through the same incomplete processes, using the same Elmer's glue, the same glitter, the same tiny broken mirrors.

We are all we have.

*

Okwui Okpokwasili tells two stories with one body. That's how storytelling works. It's also how anyone comes to know anyone else, by learning their story from the inside out. We rewrite the other's text on our own inner walls until we are—until we have no choice but to be—each other's.

Bronx Gothic finds its grace in the hardest moments of girldeath, in its reversals and betrayals and gaps, the dark places in each other we never do get to read.

Yet the work never lets go of this idea—the fact of our holes does not negate nor erase what we were capable of sharing... no matter how riddled.

*

Broken glass, glinting off asphalt, catching starlight.

Scott Knowles & Charles B. Strozier

How to Honor the Dead We Cannot Name
The problems with the Sept. 11 memorial museum.

On Saturday, May 10, a solemn procession marked the transfer of the unidentified human remains of the World Trade Center disaster from the New York City medical examiner's office to a "remains repository" in the National September 11 Memorial and Museum. Many Sept. 11 victims' family members had worked for years, through protest and legal proceedings, to halt the placement of the remains in the underground museum. Nevertheless, after many delays, the museum is set to open on May 21, and when it does tourists will pay $24 each to mill around just yards away from the fragments of those who died on that day.

While the New York City medical examiner will retain legal stewardship over the remains, the repository is situated in the museum complex, located between the footprints of the Twin Towers. The location is marked only by a quotation from the *Aeneid* ("No day shall erase you from the memory of time"), yet many visitors will know what's behind that wall.

Is the new repository a part of the museum, a cemetery, a forensics lab, or a tomb for the unknown who will never be identified? This lack of clarity is troubling. As of today, the Sept. 11 memorial museum is the only museum in the world in which unidentified human remains constitute a central, and yet tragically unacknowledged, feature. History shows that it need not have turned out this way.

Hiroshima shows a different possibility. The bomb obliterated more than 100,000 people in a fraction of a second. The bomb also dismembered, burned, and poisoned countless thousands of others. The Peace Memorial Park, built in the 1950s, is a moving and appropriate memorial to the disaster. At one end is the A-bomb dome, a municipal building below the hypocenter that was badly damaged but not destroyed. It was left to stand with bricks lying about and holes in its walls, a meaningful and understandable memorial to the effects of the first atomic bomb. At the other end of the park is a remarkable museum that honors the dead. Its exhibits also grapple in intelligent ways with the responsibility of Japan's military government for starting the war.

Do the dead have the right to be preserved (in whole or in part) until they can be identified?

Along the path of the park lies a special memorial that one can almost miss. A "memorial mound" about 10 feet high and 48 feet in diameter contains a vault with the remains of 70,000 unidentified victims of the atomic bombing. They were cremated at various sites around the city in the horrific days and weeks after the attack, before they could be identified by family. A small pagoda finial stands at the top of the mound that is otherwise simple and plain. The grass that has been allowed to grow on the mound is kept cut but is not manicured. One can come near to but not tread on the mound. There is no charge to pay one's respects. It is simple, powerful, and present—a constant reminder of the human costs of war.

At Auschwitz, the location of millions of deaths, one could say that the entire site is a final resting ground for human remains. One can dig even now just below the grass and find fragments of bones. The crematoria, badly damaged and decaying, attest to the mass production of murder. Exhibits of hair shaved from prisoners' heads have long served to help visitors understand the humanity of the victims. With almost a million and a half visitors annually, Auschwitz has folded the museum and memorial functions into one—it is hard to imagine it functioning in any other way. Visitors walk the grounds where countless prisoners were housed and where their incinerated remains lie embedded in the soil. Visitors are deeply immersed in exhibits of victims' shoes, children's toys, and a vast store of other personal items taken from the newly arrived. The connection between mourning and learning is explicit.

Hiroshima and Auschwitz are sites of disasters that predate modern DNA-identification techniques. The possibility of DNA analysis changed forever our relationship to the human remains of historical disasters. Many victims caught in the inferno of the World Trade Center were incinerated, turned to dust that floated into the air that New Yorkers breathed, literally taking the victims into their lungs and bodies. Death's work lent the disaster echoes of Auschwitz. For the rest, death left parts of bodies, sometimes as much as a limb but often as little as a fingernail. These fragments mostly came from those who fell or jumped from the fires in the upper floors, those who somehow ended up in cracks or crevices of the twisted steel, or those who were on the ground near the collapsing towers that crushed and dismembered them. These dead left 22,000 body parts scattered and buried in the pile. In time and through careful DNA analysis, more than half of those pieces of flesh and bone were identified, many for the same victim (for one person investigators found 300 parts). Some families had multiple funerals in the course of this process. Yet despite the advances in DNA identification, 8,000 body parts for what are now 1,115 victims could not be identified by current techniques.

The ability and responsibility to perform effective disaster victim identification, or DVI, is today a central feature of international humanitarian relief. Interpol and the International Committee of the Red Cross have in recent years established guidelines to aid disaster relief agencies and emergency managers when they are faced with identifying mass disaster victims. After horrors such as the Indian Ocean tsunami in 2004, local officials are expected to preserve and identify their own citizens and also the bodies of visitors—and to repatriate remains if and when possible. Advances in the speed and accuracy of DNA testing (pushed forward by the scale of the post-Sept. 11 identification work) and the use of digital photography and social media have encouraged the practitioners of DVI. But each new technological advance increases concerns over security and privacy. Do the dead have a right to privacy, do they have a right to be buried individually, do they have the right to be preserved (in whole or in part) until they can be identified? International protocols on DVI raise more questions than answers on these thorny ethical questions, and they offer no real guidance on what to do when the will to memorialize runs ahead of the time required to identify the dead, as it does today in lower Manhattan.

Chip Colwell-Chanthaphonh, curator of anthropology at the Denver Museum of Nature and Science, says that useful models are available in the long history of Native American attempts to regain and maintain control over sacred sites. "The key concept," he notes, "is consultation. Native Americans have insisted on their rights to help determine the ultimate fate of their ancestors' remains. Museum professionals do this through conversation, by seeking to include descendants and kin, so that [Native Americans] have a voice and choice in how human remains are cared for." Colwell-Chanthaphonh points out that Sept. 11 museum officials did not hold extensive discussions with victims' families before moving ahead with their plans to store the remains at the museum complex. "Family members have the right to decide the fate of their loved ones," Colwell-Chanthaphonh says. "No city official or museum administrator should be empowered to make exclusive decisions without the consent of the families. How would consent be determined? Through consultation and open dialogue. This is why the 9/11 museum has violated the rights of so many victims' families."

Another path was possible. In the days and weeks following the crash of Flight 93 into a field in Shanksville, Pennsylvania, the county coroner worked to identify the victims. As with the other Sept. 11 crash sites, the human remains were mostly destroyed and scattered. Only 8 percent of the remains recovered at Shanksville could be identified (though this was enough to account for each victim). When identification efforts ceased, the entire crash site was designated as a final resting place. The chasm left by the plane was filled in, and grass was planted. Today this "field of honor" is open only to families of the victims who died in the crash. The field is visible to visitors, but it is clearly demarcated from the line of marble slabs bearing the names of the dead, the groves of memorial trees, and the site of the future museum. The division of sacred from non-sacred space may seem arbitrary, and yet the division matters to families and to those who wish to pay their respects without treading on the dead.

No such clarity is available in lower Manhattan. Everything seems jarring and contradictory at ground zero. It will be, but also won't be, a cemetery. It will be a museum with lots of noisy visitors, children wanting to touch the bruised fire engine, crying babies, people snacking and taking photographs. And the museum is an integral part of the memorial itself, where water falls for no particular reason from 70 feet high into two ominous square holes. The memorial is a wildly abstract, massively expensive and grandiose tribute to the lost buildings more than to the dead. Will the museum be flooded again, as it was during Hurricane Sandy? And how exactly are visitors expected to behave knowing that the unknown dead from that day remain just behind the wall? Kai Erikson's chilling observation about the lasting effects of nuclear radiation seems applicable here: "The book of accounts is never closed." The capacity to identify the dead using DNA analysis is extraordinary, yet it has apparently given us no guidance on how to build a meaningful memorial to the dead we cannot name.

Miriam N. Kotzin

Aviary

My heart had become home
to Brooklyn's bright flocks of feral
parakeets flown from their perch
on freezing wires and winter-bare
branches. Left to themselves they
kept a noisy wordless communion.

       Old women wrap themselves
       in a rainbow of acrylic and fling open
       their windows. They cover their sills
       with crumbs and seeds, croon budgie
       budgie to the empty air. Gone,

gone all the small sojourners, improbably
to roost awhile in the four dark
chambers of my heart. No heart can
hold a feathered riot long.

They flicked their tails and went, a merry
metastasis, a mess of molt and shit—
a grip of beak and claw.

                        I hold out my arm
and watch the clear cocktail in its slow
drip through the tube. We sit in a row,
each of us tethered breath by breath
keeping time.

Miriam N. Kotzin

Goldenrod

Well, then, consider the proud goldenrod.
It lords the pasture and roadways while all

summer long it busies itself with hoarding
the heat and the sunlight. It holds them up

as an offering, all the gathered summer gold
as if to say, "This! Just this! Just this and no more!"

And the hot sky responds
"This! Just this and no more!"

But this happens, and then that comes to pass
as you guessed it would: Summer wanes. Then

the goldenrod holds up its summer's store of greed
like a measured sacrifice, "This! Just this and no more."

The regardless sky responds, "Just this and no more."
Now along the roadway and over all the wide pasture

goldenrod offers up these soft gray curls,
its question, a plea, "This? Just this?

Just this and no more?" And the cold sky answers
as you know it will.

Miriam N. Kotzin

The Letter "C"

Dizzy with courtship, carpenter
bees hover around the eves,
all day darning the sunlit air.

> *A shower of white petals*
> *falls from the pear tree.*

When I sit on the porch, a bee
bumps my shoulder in false
camaraderie, then buzzes away.

> *The fallen petals only feel like*
> *loss today. This is a masque of loss.*

Untreated, the nest-
tunnels in the rafters
will bring down my house.

> *A friend refuses my illness, even its name;*
> *she asks in whispers about the "C."*

I need a second lethal remedy:
a puff of poison per tunneled bee;
I've had five chemo cocktails mixed for me.

> *My hair fell out, a shower like white*
> *petals from a pear tree.*

> *This is no mask of sorrow.*

> *In last-night's dream, bees cluster*
> *in my belly, hang like an over-ripe pear.*

Lynn Levin

Buying Produce from the Marked-Down Cart

I rescue them at times from the back of the store—
cellophaned oranges and apples
packaged good-side-up.
I imagine them as little brains
thinking of the days when they were on the tree
and full of promise.

Mostly I leave the rusty beans, blotched pears
to the gleaners, calling to mind my days
as a gleaner at Dominicks and Star
when I approached with furtive hunch
the scratched and bruised, bought them

with my meager pay. What a bounty of salads and pies
they made me who saved them from the heap.
More than anything I hate waste
and yet how much
of my own life have I let go unused.

Lynn Levin

On Knowing One's Goblet at the Banquet Table

Glum the lady to your left
whose goblet you grab
at the company banquet.
When she summons the waiter
for another water glass,
you grin like an ass
and tell her how much you
hate the pettiness of etiquette.
Now she is as chilly to you
as the shrimp cocktail.
Mister, if eat left, drink right is
such a small thing, why not
learn the small thing?
It's not like this is about forks.
No one can solve the cipher of forks.

Lynn Levin
Spending Small Change

I praise the spenders of small change
for they give the humblest their due.
They hold themselves not above pennies
but love thrift and exactitude.
On their bureaus one finds no
Abes, Toms, Georges, or FDRs
sequestered in jars, calling out:
Are we not worthy? Do we not amount to much?
And when at the checkout those spenders
place coins in the palm of a clerk
hands might touch
the human gain purchase.

Harriet Levin Millan

Axis Mundi

Where in the church of the mind,
the mind's sawn down trees,

where hardwood's stacked up,
quartered and milled where under the nave

the painting is placed,
in the left-hand side aisle,

the viewpoint from which one approaches the altar
do the putti recover us and give us wings?

The figures are over life size,
their heart beats thump through the church

in the direction of the brushstroke,
drift at the edge of fields left to the shape it takes.

Sometimes it's rain the reach of rain.
Sometimes it's purer, less mixed. Jubilance.

I felt it running down the hill in the rain
running so as not to get wet but getting wet.

Pause to tie my shoelace,
as if, tying it, I might actually pull together—finding it undone.

Harriet Levin Millan

Just Before

This was before the cockle head's shadow
crept across my shelf. Soft, the sheets I lay on.
Naked I lay amid a mecca of bird choirs,
"chway" "clee-ip" "cleeer,"
before X-ACTO knife cuts dragged
across canvases and stinging hot liquid
spilled onto my thighs, chiggers bore into my skin,
the eggs they deposited, the larvae
And if life seeps through like dirt under a fingernail,
hammers me back into place—
telltale the nails— and succeeds in retrieving me,
every morning I brew coffee, the sound
of the pot percolating will roar like thunder
and the house shake to its foundation
while the coffee drips into the pot
Every morning the same teaspoons spread out
on linen like a faceless corpse.
All that Spanish moss clinging to the living
vine— shoeless and naked from the waist down.

Harriet Levin Millan

The Road Between the Rims

The badminton racket is a manifestation of myself, lying deep
down in the bottom of a creek. The kind that snaps back, taut.
Resilient, strong enough to strike back and smash a birdie.

I walk around to the back of the building and peer in through the windows.
Wood floors, metal desks, a chair on metal coasters, an orange extension
cord bundled into the corner. There I am again, wound up, back in the moment,

shock and after shock. The wind bores through me.
Swaying branches make a cleft in the road, forge a route.
I used to want a souvenir—maple syrup, maple candy,

maple sugar, everything's maple in Vermont, or one last cappuccino
in the café, but I don't now. Now I defer to the weather, to blankness
spuming and the gas station attendant's oily hands when I ask for change.

When I was keeping herself away from poetry, getting manicures and haircuts,
I'd open up bottles of nail polish in different shades and brush them on,
then remove them, until I couldn't decide which color I wanted.

After the manicurist massaged my skin with oil,
she fitted me with gloves—the final sword thrust in the bull's hide.
Money cusped the conversation, a clavicle supporting its neck and head.

A pick-up parked in the driveway. The house facing me with all its blinds.
I hope the driver won't haul away the junk that's been accumulating in the yard.
Wood scraps, blackened garden gloves, cracked terra cotta, ice skates, wagons.

That's the stuff I like to think about. Whose gloves were they
and do they still mold to skin? Someone's essence arrived at by focusing on the
    gloves, earth
ground in. The things someone might throw in a fire

to listen to the sizzle and restore oneself to reason. So the
gloves, pelted with flames, turn out to be inflammable.
Reason is not restored—there I am again.

Gwen Ottinger

Citizen Engineers at the Fenceline

Environmental regulators would do a better job protecting air quality and public health if they worked with local communities.

On August 22, 1994, the Unocal refinery in Rodeo, California, along the north end of the San Francisco Bay, began to leak a solution of Catacarb through a small hole in a processing unit. While the prevailing winds blew the toxic gas (used by the refinery to separate carbon dioxide from other gases) over the neighboring community of Crockett, Unocal workers were instructed to contain the release by hosing down the unit, but to keep operating. Unaware of the ever-expanding leak, Crockett residents began to experience sore throats, nausea, headaches, dizziness, and other problems, their symptoms worsening over the next two weeks. Unocal finally shut down the unit on September 6, when a neighboring industrial facility, the Wickland Oil Terminal, complained that the refinery's expanding leak was sickening its workers.

The 16-day release made the shortcomings of ambient air monitoring, which residents of Rodeo, Crockett, and other so-called "fenceline communities" had been complaining about for years, suddenly very visible. If there had been regular air monitoring in the area, or even if residents had had the capacity to test the air once they started to suspect that their symptoms stemmed from chemical exposures, the release likely would have been detected sooner, and the damage to workers' and community members' health—which in many cases seems to have been permanent—would have been mitigated.

Community-led innovation

The release galvanized residents of Crockett and Rodeo, who until that point had largely been complacent about the refinery's presence. As a result of their activism, two new community-centered monitoring techniques emerged. Residents' lawyers commissioned an engineering firm to develop an inexpensive, easy-to-use air sampler to give them a way to quantify chemical levels when air quality seemed particularly bad. The device, known as the "bucket," was subsequently adapted by engineers and organizers with the non-profit Communities for a Better Environment (CBE) for widespread dissemination, and it is currently used by fenceline communities around the world. Beyond helping neighborhoods closest to refineries know what they're breathing, the bucket has become a cornerstone of advocacy for more comprehensive air monitoring: users take each bucket sample as an occasion to point out the lack of information being generated in their communities during potentially dangerous releases and to criticize industry and government agencies for their apparent lack of interest in finding out what fenceline communities are breathing.

The second innovation in air monitoring that arose from the Catacarb release, although less well known, has been an important complement to the bucket. In the wake of the accident, Crockett and Rodeo residents successfully demanded that Unocal's land-use permit not be renewed unless a real-time, "state-of-the-art" air monitoring system was installed at the refinery's fenceline. Residents were instrumental in designing "the Fenceline," as the system has come to be known locally, and for nearly two decades it has been held up by bucket users around the country as the "gold standard" for air monitoring that should be required of all petrochemical facilities.

These two new monitoring technologies partially addressed and amplified fenceline communities' long-standing criticisms of the way environmental regulators measured air quality. Monitoring sites established by state and regional agencies to assess compliance with the Clean Air Act are set up away from large sources like refineries with the aim of getting data that would represent the airshed as a whole. And the little monitoring that was being done by agencies in fenceline communities was only conducted after residents complained about odors, flaring, or other releases from neighboring facilities—and always, residents charged, many hours after the worst pollution had dissipated. Fenceline communities thus were left without information about what they were breathing.

With the invention of the bucket, community members suddenly had the ability to respond to releases themselves, taking 5-minute samples that represented air quality during the worst periods of pollution. These data helped fill the information gap. When regulators and industry criticized bucket data—raising questions about their credibility or arguing that they painted a skewed picture of air quality—community groups took it as an opportunity to highlight the shortcomings of agency monitoring, pointing out that, in most cases, the supposed experts had no data at all. Simultaneously, the development of the Fenceline not only gave Crockett and Rodeo residents continuous information about their air quality in real time; it also offered a concrete example of what regulators could and, according to residents, should be doing to assess air quality and protect communities.

Yet it still took two decades of sustained community activism around air monitoring to push regulators to change their approach. In 2013, the Bay Area Air Quality Management District (BAAQMD) proposed a new refinery rule that would require monitoring at the fencelines of the five northern California oil refineries it regulates (including the Rodeo refinery, now owned by ConocoPhillips spin-off Phillips 66) and in nearby residential areas. Fenceline air monitoring requirements are also a feature of the U.S. Environmental Protection Agency's (EPA) new refinery rules, adopted in September 2015. (The BAAQMD's rule was still in the process of getting final approval at the time this article went to press.)

The specifics of the air monitoring required by the two rules are very different: the BAAQMD rule calls for real-time monitoring of a number of chemicals, whereas the EPA rule requires benzene sampling that triggers remedial action if measured concentrations exceed a specified level. Although the very inclusion of monitoring in these rules is a victory for fenceline communities, arguably neither is up to the task of protecting air quality and, ultimately, residents' health. Looking back to the story of how the Fenceline was set up and how it has evolved points to two important ways that the rules should be strengthened—if not now, then in subsequent iterations: by creating better mechanisms for presenting, interpreting, and using monitoring data, and by including neighboring communities in the design and operational oversight of fenceline monitors.

Issued by Contra Costa County just a few months after the Catacarb release, Unocal's 1994 renewal of its land-use permit stipulated that the company would design, install, and test "an improved air pollution monitoring system" that would "include infrared or other state-of-the-art remote sensing technology." But when Unocal brought its design to the county, residents found that "their [Unocal's] idea of what state-of-the-art was and our idea of what state-of-the-art was were considerably different," according to Jay Gunkelman, who lived in Crockett at the time of the release. Unocal wanted to use technology already common in the industry: hydrocarbon monitors at a few points around the refinery's perimeter. Residents—including Gunkelman, a self-described "geek" who at one time developed brainwave biofeedback instruments and now specializes in computer analyses of electroencephalograms (EEGs), and Howard Adams, a Ph.D. chemist who worked in the research department at Chevron for 20 years before moving to Crockett in the mid-1980s—wanted instead to adopt remote sensing devices used by the military to detect chemical weapons in the first Gulf War. The monitors used infrared or ultraviolet (UV) beams of light in conjunction with advanced sensor technology to measure chemical concentrations along a section of the refinery fenceline, not just at a single point, by analyzing the wavelengths absorbed by chemicals along the light beam's path. The residents' proposal also included Tunable Diode Lasers (TDLs) to measure hydrogen sulfide and ammonia and, because "open-path" monitors of this sort don't function well in inclement weather, hydrocarbon monitors similar to the ones in Unocal's proposed system.

In the disagreement over what counted as "state-of-the-art," county officials sided with the community, and Unocal was sent back to create a detailed plan that included elements of the community's proposal. Meanwhile, Crockett residents worked with CBE engineer Julia May to do their own testing of the instruments for which they had advocated. Andy Mechling, who in his job at a camera shop was always the one to set up new equipment when it came in, found that testing out the monitors was right up his alley. Although he had moved away from Crockett with his family when a 1995 tank fire exacerbated chemical sensitivities they had developed in the wake of the Catacarb release, he commuted back to town to operate a borrowed infrared open-path monitor, known as an FTIR, on a neighbor's roof.

The battle for data access

In the end, residents got the system they wanted. The final Memorandum of Understanding (MOU) that spelled out the monitoring required by Unocal's permit included FTIRs, comparable UV systems, the TDLs, and organic gas detectors for both the Crockett and Rodeo sides of the refinery. But the residents' fight for information about what was in the air wasn't over, because the agreement did not provide for open access to the data. Instead, a video of the monitors' computer interface was transmitted by modem to a terminal in one resident's home. That resident, according to the terms of the MOU, could monitor measured chemical levels but was restricted from sharing any of the data until three business days after they were recorded.

The arrangement was cooked up to quell refinery official's fears that data—especially data which had not undergone thorough quality assurance—might panic the public. To resident Ed Tannenbaum, it was technologically backwards: "I saw this screen and I said 'Well, why isn't this online?' This was 2000 by now." An electronic artist who already had experience building websites, Tannenbaum found a way to capture screenshots from the terminal in his neighbor's house and put them on the web where anyone could look at the air data. Technically, his website violated the terms of the MOU between the refinery and the community. So the county stepped in: the government was also entitled to the data but not bound by the same rules. They agreed that the data should be made public, and Tannenbaum developed his website—which posted a .gif file every few minutes—under the auspices of the county. As Tannenbaum remembers it, the refinery was finally forced to allow the site to pull actual data directly from the monitors to make the website compliant with disability access law: his screenshots couldn't be read by assistive technologies for the visually impaired, whereas the numbers could be. Still under pressure from the county, the refinery contracted with Argos Scientific to build a real-time website as part of satisfying requirements for a new land use permit in 2002. When Argos's design did not meet with community members' approval, the company helped Tannenbaum incorporate a real-time feed into a site he had designed.

As residents were trying to improve their access to data from the Fenceline, the limitations of the system were becoming clear. The TDLs could only detect large-scale releases of chemicals, making them good for emergency response but not for giving residents information about the odors they periodically experienced. The FTIRs went offline frequently because they had been set up with a path length that was too long, which resulted in too little light reaching the sensor for the system to quantify the chemicals in the air. And the UV systems couldn't tell the difference between benzene and ozone.

Community members pushed for upgrades to the system, but—as with the initial installation of the Fenceline—the refinery only agreed when it needed permits for new land uses. The UV monitors were replaced in 2002, in conjunction with a new Ultra Low Sulfur Diesel project at the refinery; and when ConocoPhillips applied for a land-use permit for its Clean Fuel Project in 2006, residents used the company's eagerness to get on with the project to negotiate an updated MOU: the FTIRs would be replaced, the UV systems upgraded, and all of the monitors would have to be online and operational an average of 95% of the time. Under the terms of the new agreement, Conoco also agreed to pay for a portable open-path monitor to be operated by residents and for laboratory analysis of a fixed number of ad hoc, short-term air samples collected at residents' discretion—creating the possibility of representing air quality in the community itself and not just at the refinery's fenceline.

The spread of fenceline monitoring

Crockett and Rodeo residents' struggle to get and maintain a working fenceline monitoring system had ripple effects in other refinery communities. Even early in the history of the Fenceline, Denny Larson, former CBE organizer and founder of Global Community Monitor, a nonprofit that spreads buckets to communities around the world, was portraying the system in Crockett to communities in Texas, Louisiana, and elsewhere as an example of what the refineries next door to them could—and should—be doing. Communities wanting to emulate Crockett's example gained an important resource and ally when the contract for operating the Crockett-Rodeo Fenceline was taken over by Cerex Environmental Services. Co-owner Don Gamiles, a physicist and entrepreneur with a passion for open-path monitors like the ones deployed in the Fenceline, saw in fenceline communities an important new market: although community groups could not afford to purchase and maintain the sophisticated instruments, organized communities could still create business for Gamiles by compelling companies to agree to monitoring.

With Cerex—and Gamiles's next company, Argos Scientific—willing to rent monitors to community groups for demonstration projects, provide technical support to communities, and work with refineries compelled to develop monitoring systems that would satisfy residents, other communities began to advocate for, and win, fenceline monitoring. In Chalmette, Louisiana, residents working with the Louisiana Bucket Brigade, an environmental justice non-profit that offers technical and organizing assistance to communities, independently operated an open-path UV monitor for several months, documenting a violation of the EPA's 24-hour sulfur dioxide standard in the process. Their efforts not only prompted an enforcement action against nearby Exxon-Mobil, they helped residents win a real-time fenceline monitoring system that the Louisiana Department of Environmental Quality (LDEQ) operated for the next several years. Activists in Port Arthur, Texas, and Benicia, California, also successfully fought for real-time monitoring.

All of these projects were, however, plagued to some extent by the same issues that Crockett residents faced. How the information would be provided was a frequent bone of contention. In Benicia, for example, monitors operated for two years without data ever becoming available to the public because residents and the Valero refinery could not agree on a data-presentation format. A significant issue, which had also arisen in Crockett, was whether monitoring readings should in some way be flagged as dangerous ("red") or potentially dangerous ("yellow") when they reached certain concentrations— and, if so, what concentrations would mark the change from safe to unsafe. The sustainability of the monitoring programs was also a problem: Crockett and Rodeo residents had to remain active on the monitoring issue, at times appealing to the county's authority to withhold the refinery's land-use permit, to ensure that the Fenceline was kept up-to-date and in good repair. In Benicia, residents were not able to convince Valero to extend the monitoring program beyond their initial two-year commitment, nor could they persuade the city government to take it over. And the LDEQ-run monitoring program in Chalmette was pared back dramatically after a "final report" concluded that air quality met all relevant standards.

Imperfect regulations

On August 6, 2012, the Bay area saw another major refinery accident. At the Chevron refinery in Richmond, a corroded pipe ruptured, releasing flammable gas which subsequently ignited and sent up a large smoky cloud over the East Bay. Hundreds of residents went to area emergency rooms to treat respiratory problems and vomiting presumably caused by exposure to the large amounts of sulfuric acid and nitrogen dioxide released by the fire. Yet in the immediate aftermath of the accident, residents did not have access to information about the chemicals they were breathing. Contra Costa County officials told reporters and the public that their monitors had detected no hazardous chemicals. No fenceline monitoring was in place at the time of the accident, either: Chevron had been talking for years to residents, City of Richmond officials, and Don Gamiles about establishing a system similar to the one at the Rodeo refinery but, in the absence of a deadline from the city, it had not been completed.

Where the Catacarb release catalyzed innovations in community monitoring technology, the Richmond fire spurred a new wave of efforts to make fenceline monitoring standard at refineries. Chevron moved quickly to establish real-time air monitoring at its perimeter and in the community with the help of Argos Scientific, whose design for the system was informed by the company's experience with the fenceline at Rodeo. By the spring of 2013, residents could look at real-time data on a website, modeled on the one developed for Benicia but never made public.

The fire also prompted the BAAQMD to make the development of new refinery rules a priority. In March 2013, they released a draft rule that, among other things, requires the five refineries in its jurisdiction to establish fenceline and community air monitoring systems. The accompanying guidelines for monitoring, informed by both public comments and an "expert panel" that included Gunkelman and Larson, clearly reflect lessons learned from residents' experience with the Fenceline in Crockett and Rodeo. Guidelines include requirements for data completeness—a minimum of 75%—and specify that refineries' monitoring plans must provide for making monitoring data available to the public in real time, via a website or some similar means.

During the same period, the EPA was revising its own refinery regulations. The rule it put out for comment in May 2014 and adopted in September 2015 also calls for ambient air monitoring at refinery fencelines, but its focus is on controlling "fugitive emissions" from leaky valves and seals. Real-time, open-path monitoring is among the approaches the rule considers, but it concludes that fenceline monitoring with open-path UV systems, although technically feasible, is cost prohibitive. The rule opts instead for passive sampling for just one chemical, benzene, with each sample representing a two-week period. Environmental justice activists, including those associated with Bay area refinery communities, have criticized the proposed requirements for their limited scope and their poor temporal resolution, both clear weaknesses of the strategy relative to the kind of fenceline systems the BAAQMD rule calls for.

But the EPA's monitoring scheme has an additional feature that highlights weaknesses in BAAQMD's rule. While the Bay area rule focuses exclusively on generating and providing air quality information, the EPA's rule lays out a plan for assessing and acting on the air data generated. Data from two-week samples are to be compiled into an annual average, which in turn is compared to a "concentration action level." If the average benzene concentration at a refinery's fenceline exceeds nine micrograms per meter cubed for any 26-sample (52-week) period, the refinery must take action to reduce its fugitive emissions.

Despite its other shortcomings, then, the EPA's rule addresses one problem that has plagued fenceline systems: how the data should be interpreted and presented to the public. Where communities like Crockett and Benicia have struggled with refineries over the levels at which readings should be coded "yellow" or "red," the EPA's rule specifies exactly what concentration is considered to be of concern. It remains unclear whether the presence of the Fenceline in Crockett and Rodeo has resulted in any change at the refinery. Although residents maintain that the refinery is more vigilant because it knows it is being watched, there is no evidence that the data are informing refinery practices, or even that refinery officials pay attention to the data. In contrast, the monitoring required by the EPA rule has the potential to trigger corrective action that would measurably reduce the refinery's fugitive emissions, which, because they occur at or near ground level, are thought to have an especially significant impact on community health.

If government agencies are going to succeed in protecting the health and safety of fenceline and other communities vulnerable to airborne toxic chemical releases, rules for air monitoring at refineries and other large point sources will need to incorporate the best features of both the EPA rule and the BAAQMD's regulation. As in the BAAQMD's guidelines, air quality measurements should be taken often enough and be available quickly enough to bring to light releases from accidents and inform emergency response. Residents should also have information about the highest levels of pollutants they are being exposed to and the durations over which they are exposed—information not available from long-term sampling strategies. And monitoring should measure as many as possible of the potentially deleterious chemicals released by refineries, not just a single proxy chemical, no matter how strategically chosen. However, for extensive, temporally fine-grained monitoring programs to be effective in reducing communities' exposure to toxic chemicals, they need to be implemented in the context of a well-specified framework for understanding the results, one that identifies not only what levels may be a cause for concern—as websites for data from Crockett-Rodeo and Richmond monitors now do—but also what levels require action to be taken by facilities responsible for the pollution.

The still-missing masses

Different as they are in their visions for fenceline monitoring, the BAAQMD and EPA regulations share one feature that misses a larger lesson of the Crockett-Rodeo Fenceline: monitoring design and implementation is left up to experts. The EPA rule prescribes in detail the monitoring approach to be used and lays out the site selection and data analysis tasks to be undertaken by technical people at the refinery. Community groups do not figure into the process of siting, sampling, or evaluation (although the rule-making itself, of course, included a public comment period). The BAAQMD's rule is less prescriptive, outlining basic components of an acceptable monitoring system and requiring each refinery to make a plan and submit it for the agency's approval. To the agency's credit, its expectations for monitoring plans have been informed by residents' experience designing and trouble-shooting the Fenceline in Crockett and Rodeo. In addition, refineries are expected to invite public comment on their monitoring plans—but BAAQMD's guidelines suggest that community involvement is to happen after refinery experts have come up with a plan.

BAAQMD and the EPA fail to learn from the crucial contributions that residents played in setting up the fenceline air monitoring system in Crockett and Rodeo, and, just as importantly, the contributions that members of the Fenceline's Community Working Group continue to make in overseeing the system's operations and understanding its results. Engaged citizens were integral to designing a fast, sensitive monitoring system, at a time when there were no models for fenceline monitoring at refineries. They also catalyzed further improvements to the system by identifying weaknesses in the original design and remedies for them. They created means for data from the monitors to reach the community at large, and they now work with Argos on improvements to the website—most recently by asking the company to show wind direction on a map alongside readings from the monitors. Residents' on-going engagement with air monitoring issues has even helped improve local emergency managers' understanding of the effects of chemical exposures on human health: in June 2012, the refinery released hydrogen sulfide from a sour water tank, which stores wastewater during its treatment process. Monitors at Philips 66's north fenceline and a monitor in a residential area of Crockett registered high levels of the gas, and many residents felt ill as a result of the incident. Yet the measured levels of about 10 parts per million (ppm) hydrogen sulfide did not trigger a shelter-in-place warning that would have indicated to residents that conditions were potentially dangerous to their health; such a warning would have been triggered at 15 ppm. Because fenceline monitoring enabled residents to make a clear link between the 10 ppm level and adverse health effects, they were subsequently able to convince Philips 66 to lower the threshold for a shelter-in-place specified in its MOU, thus improving the health benefits of the local Community Warning System.

Neither the BAAQMD nor EPA rules seem designed to encourage the kinds of opportunities to improve the Fenceline that Crockett and Rodeo residents have had as members of the Fenceline Community Working Group, and that they have made for themselves through their attention to local permitting processes. Community groups are not invited into the design of monitoring systems. Opportunities for public comment, where they exist at all, happen after a monitoring plan has already been sketched out. And public involvement ends once a plan is in place, suggesting that the plan can be implemented in its optimal form by experts with no need to learn from subsequent experience.

The history of community involvement in Crockett and Rodeo shows the limits of that approach. Community members' experimentation with the system and knowledge of its operations were critical in the design phase, not just to ensuring the acceptability of the system to the community, but also to creating a robust system. And once operational, community involvement helped to improve the system, and to highlight data that could feed back into local government policy to improve outcomes. Given the particular geography and chemical profile of every refinery, the lesson from Crockett and Rodeo is as much about the value of community involvement and local learning and innovation as it is about the technical specifications of a monitoring system.

More effective government regulations would set up the design of fenceline and community monitoring systems as a collaborative process from the start—one in which community members, industry, contractors, and regulators have the opportunity to learn from each other. In the Bay area case, for example, this could be accomplished through monitoring guidelines that require community members to sign onto a monitoring plan before it can be approved. Regulators could further facilitate these collaborations by offering to lend their expertise in both air monitoring and community collaborations; both BAAQMD and the EPA can now point to projects that have been quite successful in the latter regard.

Regulations should also make provisions for ongoing community involvement. Oversight, in particular, should be a collaborative process, since community members have different incentives than refineries to keep monitoring systems up-to-date and operating well; their outside-the-fenceline perspective could also offer insight into how adequately the monitoring system, once it is up and running, is representing local conditions. The most recent MOU between Phillips 66 and Crockett and Rodeo residents builds in opportunities for continued involvement by stipulating that the company will meet with the Community Working Group at least quarterly "to review fenceline monitoring system performance." Agency rules could specify that a similar agreement should be one component of a company's monitoring plan.

Finally, although making fenceline data available online was an important step in the development of monitoring systems, more work remains to be done to create interfaces that allow members of the public to explore the data, query it, look for trends, and connect it to what they see, hear, smell, and feel when chemical concentrations spike. As part of creating frameworks for interpreting and acting on data, regulatory agencies should attend to this need for better interfaces, whether that means expanding monitoring guidelines to include issues of accessibility and ease-of-use, or finding ways to integrate fenceline monitoring data into the interactive tools for accessing environmental information that the EPA and other agencies already host. In any case, of course, members of fenceline communities will be important contributors to design teams for the interfaces.

In the realm of fenceline air monitoring, the 1994 Catacarb release was a seminal event. It inspired the buckets, which have become a potent symbol of activists' calls for better air monitoring in fenceline communities. And, equally important, it led to the behind-the-scenes work that produced a "gold standard" fenceline monitoring system that bucket activists could advocate for—and that at least one California regulatory agency is now using as a model for the fenceline monitoring that it hopes to require of all oil refineries. But just as the fenceline monitoring requirements in the EPA's proposed refinery rules would benefit from the BAAQMD's more comprehensive monitoring approach, the BAAQMD rules would be strengthened considerably by the development of predetermined thresholds that trigger action to address toxic releases. And both should make provisions for community participation in all stages of monitoring design, implementation, oversight, improvement, and data interpretation. Not every resident of a fenceline community will have the interest, dedication, or time to delve into the intricacies of ambient air toxics monitoring. But as the history of the toxic releases in Rodeo and Crockett shows, local knowledge and motivation can be powerful sources of technological and policy innovation on behalf of public health and the public good at fencelines that separate everyday life from chemical hazards.

Recommended reading

Christine Overdevest and Brian Mayer, "Harnessing the Power of Information through Community Monitoring: Insights from Social Science," *Texas Law Review 86*, no. 7 (2008): 1493-1526.

Gwen Ottinger and Rachel Zurer, "New Voices, New Approaches: Drowning in Data," *Issues in Science and Technology* 27, no. 3 (2011).

Don Riggs

Alice in the 21st Century

When C. L. Dodgson metamorphosed himself into Lewis Carroll, he proceeded to transform much of his contemporary culture into what many have called "nonsense." But as Martin Gardner's *The Annotated Alice* reveals, Carroll took many sententious works of literature and other contemporary cultural artifacts and "turned them on their heads" through verbal paraphrases and distortions. Contemporaries, familiar with the originals being mocked, could laugh at the parodical changes.

Standing on Carroll's shoulders, John Langdon has recently done the same with his new version of Alice's adventures, *Alice and the Graceful White Rabbit*. Both Carroll and Langdon are translators, who imitate their original text, in John Dryden's words, "... not to translate his words, or to be confined to his sense, but only to set him as a pattern, and to write, as he supposes that author would have done, had he lived in our age, and in our country" (19).

Langdon's text at times sets the events in the late twentieth century, setting up parallels and oppositions with Carroll's original text, and at times uses the original text verbatim. Thus there are a series of shocks experienced by the reader very familiar with the original, who is alternately lulled by the familiarity of some passages and caught off-guard by variations. Carroll's first chapter is titled "Down the Rabbit-Hole," while Langdon's version is titled "Subterranean, Homesick, and a Little Blue," both characterizing Alice's adventure under ground emotionally and alluding to Bob Dylan's "Subterranean Homesick Blues." In both cases, Alice is with an older woman: in the original, she is with her older sister, on "the bank" of the river on that "golden afternoon" when Carroll first told the tale to Alice and her sisters; in the more recent version, she is with her mother "who had been in line at the Riverside Bank" (1), obviously a financial institution rather than a body of water flowing through the landscape. In the outdoor setting, Alice considers making a daisy-chain, but decides against it because it would not be worth the trouble of picking the daisies; in the indoor setting, Alice considers making a chain of paper clips, wondering whether it would be worth the trouble needed for collecting them in the bank (2). A bit later in the original version, Alice, having fallen down the rabbit-hole, beginning "to get rather sleepy," starts wondering "'Do cats eat bats? Do cats eat bats?' and sometimes 'Do bats eat cats?'" In this she anticipates Saussure by half a century, playing with the phonemes so as to give a variable value to the word meanings; as the narrator puts it, "as she couldn't answer either question, it didn't much matter which way she put it" (14).

Langdon places his version of Alice's "bats and cats" question a bit earlier in the plot, as Alice has not yet met the White Rabbit when, bored at having been left in the bank lobby with nothing to do and her mother standing in line, she begins to make up a nonsense song: "I hate to wait I hate to wait I hate towait I hate twowait I hate two ait I hate twoeight," until, "amused by discovering that she could change the words without changing the way they sounded," (1) that she appropriates the bank's complimentary paper and pen and writes "the very first poem she had ever written in her life" which explores the boundaries of meaning that shift when the spellings are changed. Langdon extends this to the realm of textspeak when he has Alice write "U might hate it 2." Not only does the capital U replace the second person pronoun "you," but the "too," meaning "also," is replaced by its homonym, the number 2. The "U" and "2" surrounding "might hate it" suggest the rock band U2, named after the spy plane shot down over Soviet Russia in 1960. This, of course, is a very dense set of puns and allusions for a ten-year-old girl, but she is simply generating text and the reader is the one who makes the associations. However, the narrator does comment that the poem "reminded her of some people's poetic license plates" (2), alluding both to what are generally known in the U.S. as "vanity plates" and the concept of poetic license.

While Carroll has Alice have "not the slightest idea what Latitude was, or Longitude either" (13), Langdon's Alice "could always remember which was longitude and which was latitude, because latitude went back and forth sideways, and it rhymed with flatitude. On the other hand, she thought that the opposite of longitude should be called shortitude." This seems like a practical mnemonic device for a child learning geography. Another geographical figure occurs when Alice, having first shrunk herself by drinking from a bottle, then eats a bit of cake and grows so tall that she thinks she will have to send things to her feet through the mail. Carroll has Alice conceive of the address as:

> *Alice's Right Foot, Esq.*
> *Hearthrug,*
> > *near the Fender,* (21)

while Langdon has her imagine the address as:

> Alice's feet
> 10 Little Piggies Way
> The Foothills, Patagonia (12)

While Carroll's "address" places Alice's feet in a Victorian parlor, Langdon's recalls the Mother Goose rhyme "This Little Pig Went to Market," which is recited when someone is tweaking each of a child's toes, and the final line of the address situates Alice's location in the Western hemisphere, as Patagonia is at the southern tip of South America, including parts of both Argentina and Chile. "The Foothills," of course, is yet another unconscionable pun. Langdon notes: "There is a 'questionable,' though oft repeated notion that the name Patagonia means "the land of the people with big feet" (personal email, 8/31/2015).

At times, Langdon changes the original wording slightly, so as to work in a pun or an allusion. For example, when Carroll's Alice inadvertently scares off the White Rabbit, she says, "'Dear, dear! How queer everything is today! And yesterday things went on just as usual" (22). Langdon's Alice says, "Yesterday things were just as they usually are." His original text quoted a line from Paul McCartney's song "Yesterday." Langdon notes: "Copyright issues with 'Now it looks as if I'm here to stay' forced me to drop that quote. It now reads 'Wow! How very strange everything is today! Yesterday things were just as they usually are. Now it seems I'm stuck here!'" (personal email, ibid.)

That Carroll has been deliberately metamorphosing elements of his contemporary culture in this alternate reality is made evident when Alice, in an external world that is so different from her usual one, starts to question who she herself is, tries to assert her Aliceness on the basis of what she knows. She attempts to recite Isaac Watts's poem "Against Idleness and Mischief" beginning with the line "How doth the little busy bee" but says, "How doth the little crocodile" and ends up reciting a sly satire of the original. While Martin Gardner comments that "Carroll has chosen the lazy, slow-moving crocodile as a creature far removed from the rapid-flying ever-busy bee" (24, n.5), there is also a rather nasty, possibly Darwinian element in the crocodile's welcoming "little fishes in, / With gently smiling jaws!" (23)

Langdon takes this opportunity to imitate Carroll's parodical practice by transforming "How Doth the Little Crocodile" into the following metatextual poem, which describes Langdon's — and, by extension, Carroll's — literary approach:

> How doth the little linguaphile
> Refresh a classic tale,
> And vex the purists all the while
> On a stupendous scale.
>
> How cheerfully he drops a pun
> in a dependent clause
> and does it merely 'cause it's fun
> regardless of its flaws.

How blithely he'll ignore the rules
Of grammar and of diction.
But no! He never ridicules
A classic work of fiction. (15-16)

Langdon here points out that there is a tension between the need to
"refresh a classic tale," in the case of *Alice in Wonderland* because the original
sources of Carroll's parody have been forgotten, so much of the humor in it has
been lost, but at the same time, this "refreshing" activity is not a denigration,
but an act of homage.

At times, Langdon carefully sets up a context for a pun. When the
menagerie of birds and other animals crowds around Alice in the pool created
from her tears, she leads them all to shore, where they congregate. Langdon's
text continues:

> Alice thought the dodo seemed familiar somehow, but she couldn't
> seem to figure out why. But after a minute, from somewhere deep
> in her deepest memory — perhaps it had been in a dream — Alice
> remembered seeing a painting of herself standing next to a dodo.
> Pausing a moment, and treading water, Alice turned and said, "Well,
> Dodo, it looks like we're not on canvas anymore!" (20)

To any American child raised in the era of the Baby Boomers, this
statement recalls the statement that Dorothy makes to her dog, Toto, in the
1939 film *The Wizard of Oz*: "Toto, I've a feeling we aren't in Kansas anymore."
In fact, according to Wikiquotes, "[t]his line is ranked #4 in the American Film
Institute's list of the top 100 movie quotations in American cinema." In tying
Alice's adventures under ground with Dorothy's adventures over the rainbow,
Langdon underscores that both are now canonical stories which utilize female
protagonists in the Monomythic quest narrative, a function usually reserved
for males.

The matter of the painting, which is necessary for the pun on canvas/
Kansas, may make the reader smile indulgently, as the famous image of Alice
with the Dodo is most likely to be John Tenniel's illustration of Alice speaking
to the Dodo, which is a black-and-white drawing rather than a painting on
canvas. However, Martin Gardner comments that "the Oxford University
Museum, which Carroll often visited with the Liddell children, contained...the
remains of a dodo, and a famous painting of the bird by John Savory" (27, n.10).
At the same time, Langdon admits that Alice's memory of the scene could have
"been in a dream — " which describes Alice's adventures as well as the film
version of *The Wizard of Oz*.

Throughout *Alice and the Graceful White Rabbit*, Langdon has woven allusions to rock and folk music, particularly of the 1960s and 1970s. The title itself alludes to Grace Slick, the lead singer for the Great Society, then for the Jefferson Airplane, subsequently Jefferson Starship, and the song "White Rabbit," which attributes countercultural psychedelic drug interpretations to elements of Carroll's *Alice* books. Whether such interpretations correspond to the author's original intentions, head shops in the 'sixties sold posters of the caterpillar sitting on a mushroom and smoking a hookah, and the Firesign Theater radio comedy group used the phrases "Eat me" and "Drink me" to imply the temptation to alter one's consciousness through ingesting psychotropic substances, as in Grace Slick's misquoting of the dormouse, "Feed your head!" in "White Rabbit."

As Carroll leads up to Alice's encounter with the caterpillar, he writes that she "looked all round her at the flowers and the blades of grass" (46), while Langdon has her look at "the enormous flowers and their little flower children and the grass" (47), an obvious reference to "flower children" as a synonym of "hippies" in the late 1960s San Francisco, and the "grass" as a reference to marijuana. After her encounter with the caterpillar, Alice eats of the mushroom and grows so rapidly that all sight of the ground is lost: "'Where have the flowers all gone?' Alice asked herself, gravely" (58). This is an allusion to Pete Seeger and Joe Hickerson's 1960 song "Where have all the flowers gone?" The circular song has the flowers go to young girls, the young girls to young men, the young men go for soldiers, the soldiers go to graveyards, and the graveyards go to flowers.

Langdon's Alice walks under the mushroom and sees "a doorbell on the stem," which she pushes, and thinks she might "have heard a bong" (48), which conflates the sound of a doorbell when heard from outside with a type of water pipe used to smoke marijuana since the 1960s. Alice looks over the edge of the mushroom cap and sees a caterpillar who, in the original, is blue, but in the adaptation, is "of a rather mellow yellow," an allusion to the song "Mellow Yellow" by Donovan. There was a popular myth that "mellow yellow" referred to banana peels, which when dried could be smoked to get someone high, but this was invented by Country Joe MacDonald and the Fish, who advertised a concert of theirs in San Francisco by appropriating a large model of a banana and driving around town with it. They said smoking banana peels could get you high, and shortly thereafter Donovan's song "Mellow Yellow" was released, establishing the erroneous connection in the popular imagination.

Langdon brings the series of rock allusions full circle through his transformation of "You are old, Father William," itself a parody of Robert Southey's "The Old Man's Comforts and How He Gained Them," into a portrait of an aging rocker, "You are old, Uncle Ernie:"

"You are old, Uncle Ernie, the young man said,
"And your hair has become very white.
And yet you continue to play rock and roll.
Do you think, at your age, it is right?"
"In my youth," Ernie calmly replied to the lad,
"It seemed that my morals might crumble.
But now that I'm perfectly sure I have none,
I'm as ready as ever to rumble." (52-54)

It goes on to comment on the rocker's appetite and weight, with Ernie finally snapping at the youth, "Get lost, or you can't have the car!" The Caterpillar pronounces that "It is wrong from the very bigending...But you can't have your cadence and edit, too, I suppose" (55).

It is not necessary to read John Langdon's *Alice and the Graceful White Rabbit* with a copy of Alice in Wonderland close by any more than it is to read Lewis Carroll's *Alice* in Martin Gardner's *The Annotated Alice*. Just as relatively few readers today know "How Doth the Little Busy Bee" but still enjoy Alice's unconscious transformation of it on its own merits, so will many readers who do not have "You are old, Uncle William" by heart enjoy "You are old, Uncle Ernie," as it supplies its own context. However, the intertextual nature of Langdon's more recent text, by the very process that Dryden would have called "imitation" (19) reminds us of the process that the Rev. C.L. Dodgson had used nearly a century and a half before, and such a reading cannot help but enrich both works for us.

Works Cited

Carroll, Lewis. *The Annotated Alice.* ed. Martin Gardner. New York: Norton, 2000.

Dryden, John. *Preface to Ovid's Epistles, Translated by Several Hands*, 1680.

Langdon, John. *Alice and the Graceful White Rabbit.* 2012. TS.

John Langdon (l.), the White Rabbit (c.), and Don Riggs (r.) at Cambridge University in Sept., 2015 at the international conference on the 150th anniversary of the publication of Alice in Wonderland.

Gail D. Rosen

Whedon's Women and the Law: Parallels from *Slayers* to *S.H.I.E.L.D.*

Does the law have gender? How does a female approach differ from the male, especially for Whedon? In Buffy the Vampire Slayer, Buffy is bound by the rules of the Watcher's Council, and Buffy and Willow are bound by the laws of man. Similarly, in Marvel's Agents of S.H.I.E.L.D, Skye and Melinda May must adhere to the rules of S.H.I.E.L.D. In both television shows, these characters often confront the tension between the obligation to blindly follow the rules and the need to disregard them when justice and fairness demands.

In Buffy the Vampire Slayer, both Buffy and Willow (at different times) achieve the status of single most powerful person in the world. Yet both characters make most of their important decisions by consulting with their circle of friends. This group functions more like a family, and their love for each other informs their choices, and allows them to sometimes create their own laws. This is also true of Skye and May in Marvel's Agents of S.H.I.E.L.D. The characters in this television show are family — much more than co-workers or even friends. Both Skye and May subvert the law and rules of S.H.I.E.L.D. in order to protect fellow members. In both Buffy the Vampire Slayer and Marvel's Agents of S.H.I.E.L.D., the "family" becomes both the law and a court of equity — in both cases, due to Buffy, Willow, May and Skye with their ethics of care, equity and love.

In his book *Law and Literature*, legal scholar Richard Posner discusses Carol Gilligan's book In a Different Voice, which distinguishes between "ethics of justice" (masculine) and "ethics of care" (feminine). Gilligan uses a study of boys and girls about enforcement of rules in games. She found that boys want to strictly enforce rules where girls want to look at contexts, relationships and feelings rather than formal rules/rule breaking. When adjudicating an infraction in the game, girls paid particular attention to preventing problems in the relationships (124). Posner also sees these same ideas in Susan Glaspell's "A Jury of Her Peers" (1917), (based on the 1900 murder trial of Margaret Hossack) in which two women hide evidence during a murder investigation in order to protect the accused wife. He concludes that women prefer to look at the circumstances of the case and do not feel the need to conform to neutral principles of law. Posner noted that women were virtually excluded from the legal system at time "A Jury of Her Peers" was written (122-124). For women, justice was not blind. But did ethics of care inform the way women view the law solely because women were excluded from legal processes? Is the ethics of care principle still relevant in world where women actively participate in all aspects of the legal system?

In "Myth, Morality; and the Women of the X-Men," Rebecca Housel sees Gilligan's "ethics of care" in Storm and Jean Grey (80-87). It appears that although times have changed since Glaspell wrote "Jury of Her Peers," the "ethics of care" has not. We can see this dramatically illustrated in the world of Buffy the Vampire Slayer. In the Buffy universe, Buffy Summers and Willow Rosenberg, the two most powerful women in the world, continue to use ethics of care when applying laws.

Destiny has chosen Buffy to be the slayer. The slayer's mission is to kill vampires, demons and the forces of evil, following the dictates of the Watchers Council and their representative, Giles. But early on, Buffy shows that she is a woman who does not follow rules blindly. Buffy defies the Council on several occasions to save the lives of her vampire boyfriend Angel and her friend Willow. In the latter case, Buffy's new watcher Wesley and the Watchers Council oppose a hostage negotiation in which Buffy must trade the deadly Box of Gavrok for Willow. The Council insist it is better to save many lives than one. But Buffy ignores their commands ("Choices," B3.19). She's shown in contrast with the other slayer, Kendra, who eagerly follows rules. When Kendra insists that they check in with the Watchers Council before helping Angel, she cites procedure. Buffy objects to this, telling Kendra, "I don't take orders, I do things my way" ("What's My Line," B2.10). Buffy further explains to Kendra that "my emotions give me power."

Near the end of season 3, in "Graduation Day Part 1" (B3.21), Buffy finally quits the Watchers Council when they refuse to find a cure for a poisoned Angel. Wesley justifies his actions, saying that, "It is not council policy to cure vampires." Giles, using the ethics of care principles adopted by Buffy and Willow, asks if Wesley explained to the Council that "these are special circumstances" ("Graduation Day Part 1," B3.21). Contexts, relationships and feelings are more important for Buffy than neutral principles of law; even if those laws have, as Wesley says, "existed longer than civilization." In the episode, Buffy quits the Council for good, declaring, "I don't think I am going to be taking any more orders from the Council. I am not working for them." When Wesley describes her actions as "mutiny" she replies, "I like to think of it as graduation" ("Graduation Day Part 1," B3.21). This strained relationship with the Council continues throughout the series.

As the series progresses, Buffy extends the ethics of care principles to others beyond her intimate circle. She makes exceptions to the "kill vampires, demons and the forces of evil" slayer mission for those certain beings (Spike, Anya, Clem and others) by examining the specific circumstances and considering the feelings of her friends. Even when Spike and Anya commit murder, she forgives them as they are part of her inner circle.

Unlike Buffy who begins the series as a slayer, Willow becomes more powerful magically each year. Willow's relationship to the law evolves as her power grows. Early in the first season, a shocked "good girl" Willow learns of the existence of vampires and suggests calling the police to help battle them. "They couldn't handle it. They'd only show up with guns," Buffy answers ("The Harvest," B1.2). Through the early seasons, she uses ethics of care, comforting Buffy through romantic troubles. When Angel (once murderous, now good) returns from death and Buffy conceals this fact, Buffy's friends stage an intervention. Willow explains that instead of making accusations, the group should express their feelings by making "I" statements. Willow, using ethics of care, begins by saying, "This isn't about attacking Buffy." The feelings of the group members (in this case Buffy) are more important than following the rules and punishing Buffy for breaking those rules.

Buffy and Willow move beyond looking at the feelings of those in their inner circle, and begin to apply the principles of equity to those they do not know. Equity dictates that strict rules of law should be applied with sensitivity, so that the intention is not sacrificed to the letter of the law, as with Portia's insistence in *The Merchant of Venice* that taking a pound of flesh will be murder and therefore unjust. Willow, more than Buffy, leads the charge for equity. In season two, a ghost, a former student who had an affair with and then killed his teacher and then himself, is haunting the school. Willow investigates the ghost and empathizes with him. Thus, Willow combines the principles of ethics of care and equity by looking at the circumstances of the ghost and advocating for equity in this case. Willow feels that the ghost is not an ordinary killer acting without remorse. She urges others to find out what the ghost wants, instead of trying to destroy him ("I Only Have Eyes For You," B2.19). Buffy is especially angry and only wants to kill this ghost. Buffy says the ghost should be serving a long jail sentence and "making friends with Roscoe the weightlifter." Her anger prompts Xander to reply, "The quality of mercy is not Buffy." The reference to Portia and her quality of mercy speech shows how far apart Buffy and Willow are when it comes to equity in this case. When Buffy realizes that the ghost needs forgiveness to move on, she balks, but only because she cannot forgive herself for her relationship with Angel who has reverted to being an evil vampire and killer. In the end, Buffy accepts Willow's teaching that the best way to get rid of the ghost is to forgive him and thus saves the school. Equity is not only the just solution, but the best solution to the problem of the murdering ghost.

An even stronger demonstration of equity can be seen in season four. During Thanksgiving, a Native American spirit from the Chumash tribe wants vengeance for his people ("Pangs," B4.8). Although the spirit has killed innocents, Willow spends time reading about the atrocities committed again this tribe. After this, Willow thinks they should be helping spirit redress these wrongs and should bring the atrocities to light, rather than stopping him. Even after the spirit gives Xander a disease, Willow continues to defend the spirit. For Willow, the principles of equity are clear here. The many wrongs committed against his tribe mitigate the Native American spirit's crimes. Buffy has conflicting feelings about the Native American spirit, as she does not "like her evil mixed up with guilt and destruction of indigenous people" ("Pangs," B4.8). Buffy is finally convinced by Willow and tries to apologize to the spirit. When the spirit tries to kill all of them, Buffy is forced to destroy him – but she first tried for a more equitable solution.

In "It's About Power: Law in the Fictional Setting of a Quaker Meeting and in the Everyday Reality of Buffy the Vampire Slayer," Anthony Bradney posits that "Law in the latter half of Buffy the Vampire Slayer is arrived at through discussion with one's intimate friends and requires their assent. "Law is connected with and supplemented by love" (15). We see that this idea of Buffy's family as a court of law solidifies by season four. In "Pangs" (B.4.8), a heated discussion takes place about the Native American spirit. When Xander asks the group when they will kill the spirit, Buffy replies, "That's sort of the question before the court" (B4.8). Historically, slaying was thought to be a somewhat solitary activity. Buffy signals a change to this when she includes her friends (her chosen family) and later her mother Joyce and her sister Dawn in her battles against evil. In this scene, Buffy has firmly acknowledged that her chosen family will help her decide how to enforce the law.

But what happens if the monsters are human and the "criminals" are part of the family? Evil human Warren kills Tara and wounds Buffy. A grief-stricken Willow wants revenge and wants to kill Warren. But Buffy is clear on the distinction between human monsters and non-human monsters. She firmly states, "We don't kill humans. That is not the way. The human world has its own rules for dealing with people like Warren" ("Villains," B6.20). Despite Buffy's disagreement with the edicts and authority of the Watchers Council, she firmly believes and respects the laws of man for punishing the crimes of man. However, the conversation in the family changes after Willow kills Warren, a human who murdered Willow's girlfriend and one of their own. The "family" decides he may have deserved it. But this does not seem to be the family applying principles of equity or ethics of care. They change their mind because they love Willow and she is one of them. At the end of the episode, a completely evil Willow tries to destroy the family and the entire world. But the "family" in the form of Giles and Xander stops her and forgives her ("Grave," B6.22). While Giles offers law (not from the Watchers Council but from the gentle Wiccan group who sense a disruption in the natural world), Xander offers pure faith and love. After joining the Wiccan community to learn nondestructive magic, Willow is rehabilitated in the next season. Part of the reason Willow is forgiven is because she truly repents. In the end, Willow is forgiven because she is an integral part of the family, and the family decides not to punish her. Love has supplanted law (Bradney, "It's About Power" 16).

This pattern continues in the season eight and nine comics. In "Anywhere but Here," Buffy and Willow each discover the other has committed transgressions: Buffy is stealing and Willow has been cheating on her girlfriend with a magical tutor. Each forgives the other on the spot, after listening to the explanation. Amy, Andrew, and Angel (to varying extents) betray the team. Amy, the outsider, is treated as an enemy. By contrast, when Andrew throws himself on Buffy's mercy and volunteers to sacrifice himself, Buffy calls him "part of the family" and forgives him (Predators and Prey, B8.5). She judges him on her own, but in this scene, she appears to speak for the family who would clearly rule the same way. In Angel's case, Faith, another member of the family, insists on supervising his rehabilitation, vowing to care for him personally until he can live with himself because he's "the one person who never gave up" on her. Faith considers herself responsible and also as the most practical person for the job since "Buffy can't look at him" and "everyone else wants his head on a pike." Buffy, who stops herself and Xander from executing Angel (presumably because he'll always be an insider and her first love), permits this, and the "family" gives Faith permission. One of the enemies of the season, General Voll, represents the hidebound patriarchy. He decides, based on the evidence, that Buffy and her friends are the enemy, and he orders them destroyed. He, like the Watchers Council, is bound by hierarchy rather than compassion.

In flashback, after teen Giles broke the Council's laws and summoned Eyghon, his grandmother offered him a personal absolution:

> EDNA: You were a young fool who felt immortal, did remarkably ill-advised things, and it cost people their lives, eh? You bloody idiot. That doesn't disqualify you from being a watcher. It makes you perfectly suited to mentor a Slayer. They're young girls granted tremendous power. Who can relate to them better? A man like your father, who's done the right and proper thing his entire life? Or you?
>
> GILES: What I've done goes well beyond a misspent youth.
>
> EDNA: Oh, stop. I know all about Eyghon. Perhaps your soul is damned. Perhaps he'll claim it the moment you die and subject you to an eternity of torment. If you want to be selfish about it, a lifetime of good works may be the one way to save yourself from that fate. The only path to redemption. And if you genuinely want to atone for what you've done, it's your duty. Much as you despise the word. You feel you've done wrong? Then stop crying about it ... and start making amends." (Angel and Faith 4)

While the Edna is literal family not metaphorical, she speaks on behalf of a chosen family – the Watchers Council themselves. She invites young Ripper to join and gives him a personal penance to undergo. She may be a personification of the law, but her speech holds ethics of care, as she insists Ripper seek inner redemption.

Buffy the Vampire Slayer aired from 1997-2003. Marvel's Agents of S.H.I.E.L.D. began its first season in 2013 and is in the middle of the second season as of this writing. But we can already see parallels to Buffy the Vampire Slayer when examining the way Whedon's strong female characters in Marvel's Agents of S.H.I.E.L.D. relate to the law. While Buffy is clearly in charge of her group, Phil Coulson commands the S.H.I.E.L.D. agents. In a sense, he is like Giles in Buffy the Vampire Slayer, but with more power. Is S.H.I.E.L.D the law? S.H.I.E.L.D is similar to the Watchers' Council, but is also a government agency. Coulson and his team report to those in charge at S.H.I.E.L.D, but S.H.I.E.L.D also has legal authority, as least as the series begins.

When we first meet Melinda May, she seems an unlikely candidate to use the ethics of care principle in applying the law. May is a pilot and a fighter whose nickname is "The Cavalry." Wild stories circulate about how she earned the name, which May does not like to discuss ("0-8-4," AS 1.2). Newest member of the team Skye thinks May is "all business" ("Repairs," AS 1.9). This, along with her military background suggests a person who would strictly adhere to neutral principles of law and follow the masculine "ethics of justice" approach. But May is more complicated than that. "May was different. Thought rules were made to be broken," Coulson explains of the old May before a traumatic incident ("Repairs," AS 1.9). In the second episode of the season, Coulson tries to calm his bickering team, as they debate the best course of action after they are attacked in Peru. May responds to the heated discussion by the team about the best way to proceed with a terse, "You guys talk a lot." Despite the fact the she expresses annoyance at their protracted discussion and her "all business" attitude, she wants to strengthen relationships with the team. Later in the series, May plays a prank on the team and laughs ("Repairs," AS 1.9). Her actions show that she is inclined to adopt the ethics of care approach when she must enforce rules.

Later in the first season, Agent Victoria Hand kicks Skye off the team's aircraft home when Skye wants to hack into some financial records in an effort to find a missing Coulson. Agent Hand asks May if Skye will "be of any use to us on this plane?" and May (choosing her words all too carefully) answers, "No." Near the end of the episode we learn that, using ethics of care, May wanted Skye free to find Coulson without the hampering of bureaucracy ("The Magical Place," AS 1. 11). Finding Coulson is more important than following orders from Agent Hand. In the very next episode ("Seeds," AS 1.12), May agrees with Coulson's decision not to turn in a fugitive agent who protected Skye as a baby, a decision that better protects the team. Despite outward appearances, May is not one to follow rules blindly.

While May seems to slowly adopt ethics of care principles, Skye uses them right from the start. Skye doesn't believe one person always has the solution, but that sometimes it takes a group to figure things out ("0-8-4," AS 1.2). Later on, Skye says that she wants to think "outside the box" and break rules to save Fitz and Ward, "two people we care about." She enlists the help of Simmons with the hack. Simmons shoots a guard with a stun gun and Skye breaks into a restricted area. "Are we just numbers?" Skye asks in defense of her decision to go break the rules ("The Hub," AS 1.7). It is clear that her feelings for these two members of the team trump the rules. Even more than that, Skye convinces Agent Simmons to follow suit.

When telekinetic Hannah blames herself for the death of four people, Skye investigates the truth. She realizes that Tobias, a traveler between two worlds, wants Hannah. Coulson explains that Skye helped save Hannah by figuring out what the people around Hannah wanted, saying, "You know what makes people tick. You see the good in them" ("Repairs," AS1.9).

At first, May appears to have no real connections to anyone on the team except for Coulson. Even when she begins a sexual relationship with Ward, the more intimate act for May is revealing it to Coulson ("Seeds," AS 1.12). In the second half of the season, the team suspects that May is a spy. She denies it and reveals that she is taking direct orders from director Nick Fury, on a mission to protect Coulson from the aftereffects of his resurrection, an act she knew she couldn't do alone. May explains, "I assembled this team." In a sense, she chose a family for Coulson that would allow love to determine the way they enforce the law.

Later, May leaves the team because Coulson does not trust her. "I was here for Coulson, but he cannot get past me lying," she explains. May believes that the price of following orders was too high ("The Only Light in the Darkness," AS 1.19). But after May leaves the team, she still contacts Agent Hill to prove herself to Coulson and the team ("Nothing Personal," AS 1.20). A defining moment for both May and Skye comes when H.Y.D.R.A. infiltrates S.H.I.E.L.D. and Coulson and his group go into hiding. They turn from loyal soldiers to outlaws, but they remain intact as a family devoted to protecting the world, even in secret. Near the end of season one, May returns with information that reassures Coulson about her loyalty and his own (as he fears he's been programmed by a H.Y.D.R.A. agent) ("Nothing Personal," AS 1.20). He forgives her and the episode ends with reformed family lounging at a motel pool and awaiting their next assignment.

Skye's path towards the family also begins with Coulson. We learn early in the series that Skye is both an orphan and a loner. She does not know anything about her biological family, and when the series opens, she is a hacker living alone in a van. But then Skye is abducted by S.H.I.E.L.D. and begins to work with them ("Pilot," AS 1.1). Early in the season, Skye crashes a party thrown by evil businessman Ian Quinn, and attempts to gain his trust. When Skye tells Quinn that she has been spending time with S.H.I.E.L.D, Quinn isn't surprised. He says S.H.I.E.L.D. preys on people like her—people with no family ("The Asset," AS 1.3). Skye reveals to Ward that she never fit in with any of the foster parents she was shuffled to as a kid. There was one family in particular that she had hoped to join, but it never happened. Ward assures her they (S.H.I.E.L.D) won't turn their back on her ("The Asset," AS1.3). Like Buffy, Skye will choose her own family, and this family will be S.H.I.E.L.D.

Near the middle of the first season, Coulson tells Skye the truth about her family. Instead of being devastated to learn she was the cause of destruction and S.H.I.E.L.D. agents dying, Skye is relieved. Coulson tells May that what Skye took away from the story was not the family she would never have, but the family she had always had, which was S.H.I.E.L.D protecting her ("Seeds," AS 1.12). After S.H.I.E.L.D. goes into hiding, all members of the team are given a lie detector test. They are all asked the same question by Agent Koenig: Why are they fighting still now that S.H.I.E.L.D. does not exist?" Skye says that S.H.I.E.L.D is the only family she has ever known ("The Only Light in the Darkness," AS 1.19). Her attachment to Coulson has grown to encompass the rest of the team – her chosen family.

The chosen family continues as a law enforcing body and family. While Skye, May and the rest of Coulson's teams are fugitives as Season 2 begins, Ward is imprisoned by S.H.I.E.L.D. after they discover he has been secretly working against them with H.Y.D.R.A.. Skye and May do not forgive him, even when Ward offers to take Skye to her father ("Shadows," AS 2.1). Unlike Willow, who seemed to have a real excuse for turning evil, Ward does not. While Willow was remorseful, Ward is not. Unlike Willow, Ward is rejected by the family, perhaps permanently. While Skye and May seemed so different from each other as the series began, by Season 2 they seem to have reached the same place in their journey through ethics of care and the chosen family as a law enforcing body. Both May and Skye continue to protect Coulson above all others. May tells Coulson she will pull the plug on their mission if she senses things are too much for him, but she refuses Coulson's request to kill him if he becomes dangerous ("Face My Enemy," AS 2.4). Skye protects Coulson from her own father, threatening to shoot him to protect Coulson ("What They Become," AS 2.10). This chosen family is evolving into an entity quite like Buffy's chosen family. They will continue to act as a court of law, using love and family as a guiding principle.

In Buffy the Vampire Slayer, the journey for Buffy and Willow from ethics of care, to equity, to the family and love as law ends when the series ends. Buffy and her chosen family identify all of the females with the potential to be the Slayer ("Potentials," B7.12). These young women train with Buffy and her group and live together in Buffy's house. In the final episode, Buffy and Willow use a spell to activate the Potentials, making all of these women slayers ("Chosen," B7. 22). No longer will there only be one Slayer. A powerful group of women will now fight evil together, and together they save the world. Skye and May discover a similar homecoming, as their team of six (season one) expands to include a mercenary group and other lost characters like Trip. Coulson insists they can rebuild S.H.I.E.L.D. the right way, from the ground up, and transform their little family into a mighty institution. Just like Buffy and her new army of thousands, Skye, May, Coulson and the rest of the group are determined to bring justice and protection to the helpless.

Works Cited

Agents of S.H.I.E.L.D.: Season One. ABC. 2013-2014. Television.

Agents of S.H.I.E.L.D.: Season Two. ABC. 2014-. Television.

Bradney, Anthony. "Choosing Laws, Choosing Families: Images of Law, Love and Authority in "Buffy the Vampire Slayer," *Web Journal of Current Legal* Studies 2. JCLI (2003)..

Bradney, Anthony. "It's About Power: Law in the Fictional Setting of a Quaker Meeting and in the Everyday Reality of Buffy the Vampire Slayer," *Issues in Legal Scholarship* 1.8 (2006): 1-20.

Buffy the Vampire Slayer: The Complete First Season. The WB Television Network. 1997. DVD. Los Angeles: 20th Century Fox, 2002.

Buffy the Vampire Slayer: The Complete Second Season. The WB Television Network. 1997-1998. DVD. Los Angeles: 20th Century Fox, 2002.

Buffy the Vampire Slayer: The Complete Third Season. The WB Television Network. 1998-1999. DVD. Los Angeles: 20th Century Fox, 2006.

Buffy the Vampire Slayer: The Complete Fourth Season. 1999-2000. The WB Television Network. DVD. Los Angeles: 20th Century Fox, 2003.

Buffy the Vampire Slayer: The Complete Fifth Season. The WB Television Network. 2000-2001. DVD. Los Angeles: 20th Century Fox, 2006.

Buffy the Vampire Slayer: The Complete Sixth Season. UPN. 2001-2002. DVD. Los Angeles: 20th Century Fox, 2004.

Buffy the Vampire Slayer: The Complete Seventh Season. UPN. 2002-2003. DVD. Los Angeles: 20th Century Fox, 2008.

Carpi, Daniela. "Failure of the Word: Law, Discretion, Equity in *The Merchant of Venice* and *Measure for Measure.*" *Cardozo Law Review* 26 (2005): 2317-2330

Housel, Rebecca. "Myth, Morality; and the Women of the X-Men." *Superheroes and Philosophy: Truth, Justice, and the Socratic Way.* Ed. Morris, Tom, Matt, Morris, and William Irwin. New York: Open Court, 2001. 80-87.

Posner, R.A. *Law and Literature.* Cambridge, Mass: Harvard University Press; 1998.

Alan Soble

The Love Call of F. Scott Fitzgerald

Hogy túléljünk, imádjuk az
Alliteráció Istenét.
　[Не транслитерация!]

For Philip Milton Roth
il miglior spazzino

I. On the Jewish Question

MATZOH is the driest bread,
baked on the fly, our legend declares.
With the support of Jewish Rye,
I eat strawberry yoghurt topped
with walnut-cinnamon sugar.
Later came a culinary democracy:
Blueberry bagels at Dunkin' Donuts.
In which diaspora did we *fress* as well?
"We built this city" on lox and borscht.

I live on a freshly brewed,
integrated Starbuck Earth,
sprightly sipping esoteric strains
from Guatemala, Rwanda, Timor –
a dark roast, medium Pike, aromatic decaf,
odors that make me cosmopolitan,
turning my buds Arab and Turk.

I often smell, much too near,
a Bukovinan Albert, Allen, or Alvy
adoring my healthy *punim*,
but mostly staring at the deep dish
of seasoned fruit, with glazed-over
graceless starvation understood
better by Pavlov than Plato.
Brutish envy is the sharpest pain.

II. Sexual Revolutions

In plush powder rooms,
the women come and go,
speaking of my cool Angela,
a *tsatske* girl no cuter
than two-day-old shtetl kasha,
adorned by not one poppy,
no onion bit, raisin, garlic, or seed:
the Everything's accessories.
Angela, a plain, unbedazzled Biały.
What the women didn't see
were her smooth brown feet
and familiar warm scent
that kept me aroused, and spent.

The women come and go,
dissing circumcision,
with circumlocutions toned
by the English abhorrence
of Jews, which Tom E.
learned in his counterlife
along with tea at four.
I feel no genital disgrace,
as if Shylock's prick
had no power or right
to be as stiff, and as often,
as Sweeney's erect.

You missed rock-roll bands:
no chance to bard with jumpin'-jack
devils who let it bleed, paint it black.
You missed Dylan, and Clapton's guitar,
"Driver's Seat" and "Stairway" stars.
You missed the lexicon of gangsta rap:
phat shorty's piece – a blasting cap.

You missed the I-net,
where your skill is free,
along with Auden and Klee.
Bloggers hack "Prufrock"
and Facebook befriends
Lou's bored sweet Jane

who clerks the day away,
tokes, gets wasted once again,
drags a brush across her head.

You missed my Portnoy friend.
Like you, T. S. E., he had not
been ready for Larkin's 1963.
Neither was I,
the one lingering naïf
on either stretch of coast
who committed a marriage
before committing a sex.
Call me Pisher.

The Allman Bros. dared
to slurp the juicy peach,
their stage britches tight,
leaving no dry seat in the house.
Stoned freebird roadies
scoured the stained stands.
Daltrey and Plant, too,
had their pick, share, and fill
("Keep your hands offa my stack!")
in the battle of the bands for muff.
The Doors, Fleetwood Mac, Pink Floyd,
all boned the leftover girls ('n' boys)
in Winslow Arizona.
Star fucking,
born voracious in '63,
engendered night moves
of plying leaching hands,
fingers creepy, greedy, sticky, foul,
through marches, protests, sit-ins,
concerts, readings, lectures
from Columbia, D.C., Woodstock,
to the graveyards of disease,
infanticide, and rape.

My envy should not too much complain.
For my second love I, too, had remains.
I groped my Brit Lit teacher's *tuchas*
in a tiny airport motel closet candle-lit.
We couldn't see the floor's filthy bed.

An adulteress became my first "real" love.
Augustine's pulpit rancor groaned.
He charged us "cheat" and "slit"
in a proper Latin that proved him right.

Tommy, we were humbled by your technique.
Neither the Bishop nor I grasp ancient Greek.

High school, the adolescent waste land
where diplomats train as lunchroom killers
aiming higher than cafeteria reform.
I often heard, too loudly,
from the putrid holes of thugs
stuffed with sausage spice,
spewing their considered view
that Jew slits are effin' easy.
I wouldn't know, only foolin' around
with my misinstructing kissing kin.
The goddess *shikse* I craved
dozed off in Psych and Math
wearing a short summer skirt,
her thighs falling unbearably
apart.

"In your wildest dreams,"
the mean girls mocked.

You missed Friedan, Dworkin, Greer,
hooks, Steinem, other mutineers.
Half of humanity, men began to understand,
should not from books and education be banned.
There, next to Shakespeare and Dante
on your shelves, just a kiss or shout away,
should be Wollstonecraft's *Vindication*
and John Stuart Mill's *Subjection*,
both written in prose straightforward,
no forced rhymes, no obscure words,
no allusions or alliteration,
no foreign noise or transliteration.
No edits done by a pal uncouth,
but a nineteen-twenties' truth
that neither F. Scott,
nor you, fully got.

III. Death by Water

Solomon's praise of passion
was doomed by arid winds
that cooked his burning eyes,
two desiccated yellow eggs,
on the dusty road to Dachau.
"Love is as strong as death"?
He was not tanned, as the Bible
says, but burnt.

Why dread a dip in Gatz's pool?
Had we not already been gassed,
gladly we would swim.
Had we not already been gassed,
we would have done it all,
were we not squandered –
for specks of gold and *Lebensraum*.

I forgot (blame my sour soul) –
while fabricating shoddy lines,
constipated polyphilalliterative
strings of obscure miasmal smog –
that in a Southern-hot
August over ten years ago,
instead of fleeing a *Kristallnacht*
I first-hand found that Petty's buoyant
"Refugee" refrain was bogus.
The House of the Rising Sun flailed,
then foundered, in the floods.
Au revoir, szerbusz, מולש, *до свидания, adiós*
I offered to my big-hearted nightingales,
those devout, stoic bodies
bound to my debauched desire.
All were FEMA derooted and rerouted:
Cleveland Baltimore Tampa
Cheyenne Saint Paul Atlanta
Phoenix 'Frisco Miami
Vegas Philly Providence.

GATHER YOUR BAGS LADIES
NEXT STOP PURGATORIO

Shifting, shoving, bouncing,
dancing, flashing, twerking,
shielding their stash
of coke crystal meth crack
roofies pot hash and smack.
Even a charming Dom Perignon,
lifted leisurely looting
a ruptured *gonif*'s Quarter
bodega, would with luck
get to wine's half-heaven.

HURRY UP NOW LADIES
NEXT STOP PURGATORIO

New Orleans, my Bukovina.
Pushed out, flushed out, washed out, flicked out.
("And they put you on the day shift.")
Rotund Nero,
flawless Peter,
whimsical Shade,
boiled-hard Spade,
ghostly Anne Frank,
Machins of many colors,
Hoarded Yverts and Michels,
treasures buried with Gulf oil
in buses-bulging shark bellies,
and a thousand vinyls left behind
in distracting jackets for the troops
during the flight of whores, Jews, and blacks,
street sweepers, bag handlers, dishwashers, busboys,
the whole miserable crew right out of Toole,
stayin' alive, barely, with fungal fever.

I wish I had
a fantasy
while weaving
and shuffling
up I- 55,
running on empty
to Lodi.

I wish I could pretend
that I wasn't running

but was a ramblin' man,
tracing Fonda's map,
crisp clean wind
blowing out, on I-10,
my long brown hair.
In my dream,
there's no shotgun
in a Southern Man's Dodge.
I'd make it all the fuckin' way
with Bogie to the Keys.

IV. Breakdowns

The war and that woman,
poor Tom-Tom, did you in, for a while;
your suffering, the spring of Great Art,
aping de Sade van Gogh
Tchaikovsky Nietzsche
especially J. S. Mill.
My women and my wars,
multiplied beyond yours
and as fruitful as Nature,
still made bananas of me, and crackers.
I should have created greater Great Art,
greater than the Great American Novel
that eludes the gospels
of Herman, Toni, Saul, and Mark:
A Midnight Cowboy Philosopher.

Japan leaks radioactive cream
into garbaged whirlpool seas.
Denver to LA is scorched,
taxing grapes, newts, and gnats.
Christian heads sliced and rolled
on the Damascus-Baghdad road,
like kiddies play kick the can.
Trains, planes, trucks crash galore.
Boston's finish line rages roar.
Exploding cafés in Tel-Aviv,
Paris, Újvidék, Port
Gdańsk, Watts, Harlem,
Newark, Kent State.
Manhattan's "falling towers"

(foreseen by you, Tommy)
clogged our baked throats
with bloody ground muck.

By two thousand fifty:
"Elkúrtuk, nem kicsit, nagyon."
MRSA, *C. Difficile*, and TB
infect a terabyte of mankind
plus the greatest Great Apes.
No shelters trailers huts shacks
beach umbrellas tents lean-tos
outhouses carousels igloos
high-rise balconies gazebos.
Hordes of Texas armadillos,
bony dogs, hippos, snakes sleazy,
snarling rats, lizards, birds eerie,
gargoyles unleashed, coyotes
rummage streets of pipes
and fields of rotting rice
for prime cadaver chunks,
Humans eat their neighbors;
they maim and stomp to drink
thick water slick with jimson weed
and start a *Lion King* stampede.

Swift is now a bad joke
on which second-graders choke.

No more polished granite
engraved with names, dates,
and proverbs of hope.
In a vast blank waste land,
no monuments (no heroes)
pointing to a glorious future.
Celebrations of the Fourth
or for Mothers worldwide
are sarcastic exorcistic
Robot Chicken rituals.
No sanctuary in *Frauenkirche*,
Stephansdom, or St Mark's,
nor in a Riverside church
where Attica is transubstantiated
into a paradise of illusion

that promises safekeeping
from zombies, pirates,
ghoulish gangs of bikes,
other Harry Potter *dreck*,
all manner of dubious
specimens of humanity.

Only in an Absentee Landlord crib,
is no one stupid, evil, or insane,
and only here is Alexander's glib
line, "Whatever is, is right," not arcane.

Prescient, clairvoyant,
you well perceived
a small panorama of waste.
Our waste is boundless,
more than you could see.
When I die,
I would all this shit die with me.
Let it not boast
by having synthetic life
in someone's cloddy verse
marred by tortured glyphs.

Tom, you praised it beyond desert.
Kant knew better; he never reveals
Onan's sin that he condemned,
as a Jew withholds the name of G-d.

V. Mortalities

The prostate is the weakest pulp.
It would have gone first,
smothering slender ducts,
except psoriatic arthritis
had a head start
doing malicious labor
on every innocent
patch of bone and joint.
Deaf-dumb doctors
offer lotions and pills
from fake pharmacopoeia.
So it ascends to reign:

Lord of the Ankle,
Lord of the Knee,
Lord of the Hip,
Lord of the Elbow,
Lord of the Thumb,
Lord of the Neck,
Lord of the Left Big Toe.
Thus we succumb
to Osteoarthritis,
the unmoved mover,
that never meets or knows
any sovereign curb.

I would plead,
"Let us go, then, You and I,"
and engage our few good parts
(eyes that survived Dachau).
But all we'd do
is smoke and fall out,
nodding straight through
広島 *Mon Amour*,
Bergman's *Scenes*,
and Popeye cartoons,
until the screech
of dead and lonely 'rents
wakes us and beckons,
and we, too,
dry out to nothing.

Enough, *already*,
of this wasted
land of old age.
I will not permit a drowning.
I will not suffer dehydration.
I will not lick a poisoned bug.
I must live till
the mother of all bombs,
the Burka Burger,
slams into the slums
of fat, bald, cranky New York,
a city built on lox and borscht.

José A. Tapia

Toward a New Global Recession?
Economic Perspectives for 2016 and Beyond
FOR SWPM, DH, AS, DF, GD & DL

What economists call "macroeconomic variables" are numbers such as the gross domestic product, interest rates, tax revenue, government expenditure, exports, imports, consumption, and the like which are used to describe the economy at large. Variables like these are usually considered the most important ones to describe and understand how our economy works. There are, however, other macroeconomic variables that from an empirical point of view are essential to explain the condition and the workings of the free-market economy, alias capitalism. They are total income received as compensation for labor—i.e., wages and salaries—, total income received from capital ownership—i.e., corporate profits—, and the unemployment rate. The table to the right shows the annual change of these three variables in the United States since 1981. The first two columns show the percentage increase in total labor income (wages and salaries) and capital income (profits) in the corresponding year. Thus in 1981 wages and salaries grew 0.6% compared with 1980, while corporate profits grew 5.8%, both measured in what economists call "real terms," i.e., discounting inflation. As for the unemployment column, it presents the annual increase, measured in percentage points, in the unemployment rate. Thus the 0.5 figure for 1981 indicates that the unemployment rate rose half a percentage point that year (in particular, the unemployment rate was 7.1% in 1980 and 7.6% in 1981).

	W&S	Profits	Unemp		W&S	Profits	Unemp
1981	0.6	5.8	0.5	1991	-0.6	6.4	1.2
1982	-1.0	-14.6	2.1	1992	3.0	4.9	0.7
1983	1.7	19.3	-0.1	1993	1.4	8.1	-0.6
1984	6.2	18.9	-2.1	1994	2.9	19.7	-0.8
1985	4.1	1.8	-0.3	1995	3.4	9.9	-0.5
1986	4.0	-11.7	-0.1	1996	3.9	10.1	-0.2
1987	4.7	9.0	-0.8	1997	5.4	9.0	-0.4
1988	4.4	8.7	-0.7	1998	6.7	-8.5	-0.5
1989	1.9	-6.6	-0.2	1999	5.2	-0.4	-0.3
1990	2.4	-5.2	0.3				

	W&S	Profits	Unemp
2000	5.8	-12.3	-0.2
2001	0.4	-10.1	0.7
2002	-0.7	26.3	1.1
2003	0.8	16.6	0.2
2004	2.7	18.0	-0.5
2005	1.7	11.3	-0.4
2006	3.2	8.9	-0.5
2007	2.8	-17.6	0.0

	W&S	Profits	Unemp
2008	0.2	-26.7	1.2
2009	-5.1	17.4	3.5
2010	0.8	28.4	0.3
2011	1.9	1.1	-0.7
2012	2.6	14.2	-0.8
2013	1.2	3.6	-0.7
2014	3.6	-1.9	-1.2

The table depicts several periods of economic crisis or "recession," in the usual terminology. In these periods unemployment rises (the annual growth is positive) and wages and salaries drop (the annual growth is negative). This is what happens in the early 1980s, the early 1990s, after the turn of the century, and then, again, in 2009. But every crisis is preceded by a drop in the return to capital, which appears as a negative growth of profits. Then in a year or two, sometimes in the same year, wages and salaries start falling at the same time that unemployment rises. For example, in 1989 and 1990 profits decreased by 6.6% and 5.2%, respectively, and in 1991 wages dropped and unemployment, which had been declining in previous years, increased. In 2007 and 2008 profits dropped 17.6% and 26.7%, respectively, and that decline in profits was immediately followed by the slump of 2009 in which wages dropped by 5.1%—the highest wage contraction throughout the period considered—and unemployment increased 3.5 percentage points. In 1998-2001 there were persistent contractions in profits and immediately following them, wages fell and unemployment rose in 2002. Thus, the pattern is one of falling profits (e.g. 2000-2001) followed by falling wages and rising unemployment (2002-2003). Falling wages, rising unemployment and rising profits (2002) lead to a period of expansion with rising wages and falling unemployment (2003-2007), until profits start falling (2007) and the cycle starts again with another recession.

Now, it can be thought that these are phenomena of the so-called U.S. business-cycle that have little to do with the rest of the world. However, it is easy to show that what happens in the U.S. economy has a lot to do with what happens in other countries. The figure on next page shows the annual rate of growth of four national economies in 1960-1985 (top panel) and 1985-2014 (bottom panel). Recessions are apparent as troughs in the growth curve. Focusing in the most recent period (bottom panel) the figure shows clearly the U.S. recessions of the early 1990s, 2001, and then the 2008-2009 slump usually called the "Great Recession." Interestingly, the other countries in the graph also had major declines in economic growth in the early 1990s (somewhat after the US), immediately following the turn of the century, and in the Great Recession of 2008-2009. Comparing the top panel and the bottom panel of the figure it is apparent that the oscillations of the four economies are more synchronized in the most recent period. While in the 1960s and 1970s the four economies oscillated more or less independently, they have oscillated very closely since the 1980s. Indeed, the Japanese recession of the late 1990s is the only discordant note in a quartet playing quite in tune during the past three decades. Of course the crises have not occurred exactly in the same year and with the same intensity in the four countries, but they have a significantly similar timing which has grown more synchronized over time.

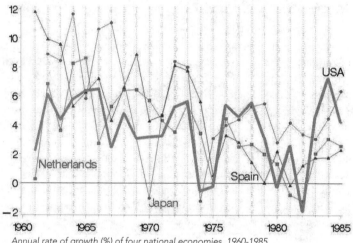

Annual rate of growth (%) of four national economies, 1960-1985

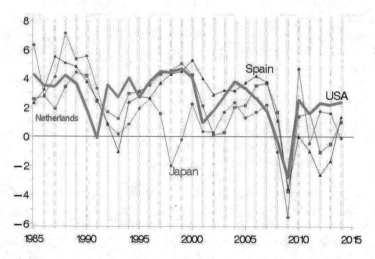

Annual rate of growth (%) of four national economies, 1985-2014

What has been illustrated here with the cases of the United States, Spain, Japan, and the Netherlands could be also illustrated with many other countries. The national economies are increasingly synchronized and there are many reasons to see the slumps around the turn of the century and then in 2008-2009 as crises of the world economy. And the same could be said about recessions in the mid-1970s, the early 1980s, and the early 1990s.

Now, what could explain the increasing synchronization of the national economies? A possible reason would be that the economy of the world at large is becoming increasingly dependent on the U.S. economy. Thus the U.S. economy would be the locomotive pulling the rest of the world and recessions or expansions of the U.S. economy would spread to all the other national economies. This explanation is supported by quite a number of economists and politicians, for instance, in Latin America and Europe. It seems unlikely, however, for several reasons. First, there is general agreement that the weight of the U.S. in the world economy has been declining in recent decades. That would tend to produce less rather than more synchronization if the synchronization were caused by the economy of the rest of the world being dependent on the U.S. Second, the links between the U.S. and economies which have been highly synchronized with the U.S. economy in recent decades are not particularly strong. Thus, for instance, the graphs show that the expansions and recessions of Spain and the U.S. are highly synchronized, even from the 1970s on. However, Spain has much stronger commercial links with the countries of the European Union than with the United States. Third, the timing of the crises does not support the idea that the U.S. is leading and the other economies following. Thus we see, for instance, that the crisis of the early 1980s in the U.S. was in fact preceded by a big decline in economic growth in Spain during the late 1970s, with Spanish GDP growth reaching 0.0% in 1979. Then in the early 1990s the recession occurred earlier in the U.S., when economic growth was -0.1% in 1991, and followed in Spain two years later, when economic growth dropped to -1.0% in 1993. Thus the crisis of the early 1980s started earlier in Spain though it was more intense in the U.S., while in the early 1990s the crisis manifested first in the U.S. but was more intense in Spain.

For these reasons, the view that the U.S. economy is the one that determines the economic conditions of the world is increasingly discredited. With very large rates of growth of so-called emergent economies in the past two decades, while GDP growth has been anemic in the U.S. and the share of U.S. GDP in total world economic output has been shrinking, the idea that the American economy is the engine of the global economy is increasingly unbelievable. It is obvious, however, that the interconnections of the national economies have grown stronger every year, so that expansions and recessions are increasingly synchronized, as it was noted already in 1997 by Allan W Gregory. The opinion of some historians, like Immanuel Wallerstein, is that the world economy was a reality already several centuries ago. That is arguable, but it is unarguable that the world economy has become a very tangible reality in recent decades, when the links binding together national economic spaces—trade, capital flows, flows of people, financial shocks—have become much stronger. Of course, to assert the existence of the global economy does not imply that national economies have no autonomy. In fact, as the figure illustrates, the economies of the U.S., Japan, the Netherlands, and Spain evolved quite differently after the Great Recession of 2008-2009. While the U.S. economy had a weak but real recovery, the Spanish, Japanese, and Dutch economies have been mired in crisis and negative growth throughout the present decade.

Many economists and economic commentators claim that the different evolution of the economies of the U.S., Western Europe, and Japan after the 2009 slump illustrates how different economic policies— austerity or expansionary monetary policy (i.e., quantitative easing)—generate different economic performances. However, the synchronization of national economies actually makes it increasingly hard to believe that economic performance has much to do with the role of national governments. Since national governments have applied different economic policies in past decades, if economic policy had a major influence on economic growth we would expect a broad dis-synchronization of national economies, but we observe precisely the opposite.

But let's leave this controversial issue to return to the economic perspective for the world economy. What has been just said could be taken as suggesting that we have to look at numbers for the world economy to get some insight into the economic perspective for the next years. Numbers for the whole world economy like those in the table accompanying this article would be ideal, but they are not available. However, the figures for the United States can probably be considered good enough to provide insight into what is going on in the world economy. Particularly, as the table shows, in 2014 corporate profits fell in the U.S. by 1.9% and indeed this contraction of profits in the U.S. can very well be taken as an indication that profits probably contracted in 2014 in other national economies and in the world economy at large. (That profits have recently declined in the world economy is also the conclusion of economists like Michael Roberts and Ryan Banerjee.)

Data show that, quite regularly, when profits have declined there has been a recession with rising unemployment and falling wages in the years immediately following. Since profits have dropped in the U.S. economy, and very likely also in the world economy, in 2014, the most likely outlook seems a new general recession of the U.S. and the world economy starting soon, in 2016 or not much later. The pattern of declining profits followed by a recession has very strong statistical support, as it is found not only in data for recent decades but also in earlier times. Wesley Mitchell and Jan Tinbergen found it in statistics covering several decades before World War II. The statistical regularity of declining profits and subsequent recession does not mean, however, that every year of declining profits will necessarily be followed the next year by a recession. As the table shows, in 1986 profits declined and a recession did not occur until several years later. In the early 1990s and the Great Recession the slump was preceded by two years in a row (1989-1990 and 2007-2008) of declining profits, while the recession of the turn of the century was preceded by four years (1998-2001) of declining profits.

For some economists like James Hamilton and Ben Bernanke an important macroeconomic variable is the price of crude oil, the idea being that high oil prices strangle economic activity at large, leading to recession. Since oil prices have indeed increased before each recession of the world economy in recent decades, data appear to give some credence to this view. However, a closer examination of the numbers—as done for instance by Lutz Kilian and Martin Stuermer—strongly reduces the credibility of that interpretation. It happens that oil prices rise when the global economy expands and energy demand increases. So it is the global expansion that raises oil prices. These in turn might contribute to trigger the crisis, but first, the evidence that high oil prices have a direct effect in reducing economic activity is rather weak; second, at any rate, rising oil prices have their cause in the previous expansion. Oil prices have been at quite low levels in recent months and the general agreement is that this is due to the low level of economic activity in most of the world economy.

It is indeed possible that we are right now in a new recession of the world economy, though if that were the case the recession would have begun in an insidious and creeping way, not with financial turmoil like the one that marked the outburst of the Great Recession of 2008 or the recession of the turn of the century, which was very mild in the U.S. but was accompanied by financial debacles in many countries of Latin America and Asia. Another possibility is that we are now in a "rare" period of the global economy in which there is neither a clear expansion nor a clear recession. To decide among these possibilities more perspective is needed. What is certain now is that the reduction of profits in the U.S. in 2014 is likely a manifestation of the decline in capital returns in the world economy. That is the reason why everywhere in the world huge masses of money are idle in safes and bank deposits, waiting for "investment opportunities." Though economists tend to ignore this fact, corporate profits returns on investment are the engine of the capitalist system. Unless some very unexpected factor, like workers deciding to work much more for much less, increases the profitability of capital in the near future, everything suggests that the world economy will go soon into recession if not in 2016, then not much later. But as the joke goes, predictions are always risky, especially when they concern to the future.

Editor's note: This article was received well before early January's stock market turmoil.

Sources:

Growth figures of wages and salaries and corporate profits (domestic industries, before taxes) are taken from the official statistics of the Department of Commerce, NIPA tables. Before calculating annual growth values, nominal dollars were converted into 2009 dollars using the GDP deflator, also from NIPA. Unemployment data are from the Bureau of Labor Statistics. The graph is elaborated with GDP growth rates from the World Development Indicators database of the World Bank.

References

Banerjee, Ryan, Jonathan Kearns, and Marco Lombardi. 2015. (Why) Is investment weak? *BIS Quarterly Review*, March.

Gregory, Allan W., Allen C. Head, and Jacques Raynauld. 1997. Measuring world business cycles. *International Economic Review* 38 (3): 677-701.

Hamilton, James. 2011. Historical oil shocks. *NBER Working Paper* No. 16790.

Kilian, Lutz. 2009. Not all oil price shocks are alike: Disentangling demand and supply shocks in the crude oil market. *American Economic Review* 99 (3): 1053-69.

Mitchell, Wesley C. 1951. *What happens during business cycles: A progress report*, ed. Arthur F. Burns. New York: National Bureau of Economic Research.

Roberts, Michael. Will the world economy enter a new recession next year? Michael Roberts Blog. *https://thenextrecession.wordpress.com/2015/11/21/will-the-world-economy-enter-a-new-recession-next-year/*

Stuermer, Martin. 2014. *150 years of boom and bust: What drives mineral commodity prices.* Presented at the Philadelphia 2014 Meeting of the American Economic Association.

Tinbergen, Jan. 1950. *The dynamics of business cycles: A study in economic fluctuations* (translated from the Dutch and adapted by J. J. Polak). Chicago: University of Chicago Press.

Wallerstein, Immanuel. 1984. *The politics of the world-economy: The states, the movements and the civilizations.* Cambridge University Press.

Kathleen Volk Miller

Thanksgiving Tips For Parents of College Freshmen

Your child is coming home for Thanksgiving, for 3 days or 5 days or a week. You haven't seen him since parents' weekend in late September, and what with all of your time together being in public—the school's organized events, the restaurants, the hotel—that visit barely counts.

I'm a college professor, and your son or daughter has spent more time with me than you the past two months. If I wasn't also a mother, maybe I wouldn't see the fear right beside the bravado, fighting for dominance on the freshmen's faces. I saw her on the first day, looking neither to left or right and fixing squarely on me, fussing with her coffee, because she's allowed coffee in the classroom and so she brings it to class because she can. I've seen your boy start to laugh at something and then catch himself, wonder if he's blown any kind of cool he's built up. None of them realize the others are just as scared, no matter what we, professors or parents, tell them.

I have watched your child establish certain patterns, the coffee, the route to class. But he is nowhere near mastering the best time to do laundry or how to quickly find his ID when he comes back into the building, what pocket he should keep it in. Your freshman is still very fresh.

And now your child is coming home, with everything that home means. You pick her up at the train/bus station/airport and you drive so you have to look at the road and you aren't able to stare at her, which you're both afraid you will. Count to three (in your head) when you hug, or else you will lose track of time; she'll hear you breathing her in; she'll sense you're not going to let go. You chat about simple facts that can be covered—who is at home, when others are arriving, the new butternut squash dish you're making for Thanksgiving.

But then you get home and your son reaches in the back seat for the duffel of dirty laundry and you notice for the first time something different about his face—an angle, a shadow that wasn't there before. You are trying not to stare and your kid is out, up the front steps and shouldering the door before you are fully out of the car, you are just watching like this isn't your driveway anymore. Don't worry; it is yours, it's just different now.

You get in the house and exhale and see that your college kid has moved straight to the kitchen and you are thrilled—this is something you know how to do—you know how to feed your kid, so you practically bound into the kitchen, but try to hide your enthusiasm, your joy at doing something you so often resented. Assume the position you hated to find him in, just a few months ago, look casual while you prop the fridge door open on your hip, and stare inside, looking for something, and ask, "Hungry?"

The turkey sandwich is in front of her now, with salsa and mayo and lettuce, like–you forgive yourself for thinking this–like she has not had for 9 weeks. Sandwiches are always better when someone else makes them, and you are still her mother; yours are still the best.

But everything feels different in this November early dark and now you are staring at her. And you know you shouldn't, that you have to stop, but you cannot help yourself, because look at her: The softness under her chin is gone. You cannot see that blue vein you used to stroke for hours while she nursed. Don't worry, it is still there, it's just under the surface.

Your other daughter finally pulls herself away from her room of devices and joins you in the kitchen. When you say, "We've been home 20 minutes," she says, "I know" and holds up the flat face of her phone. You don't know if they've texted or the returning daughter posted something on some form of social media. It doesn't matter: Know that you have to leave the kitchen very soon. They begin to talk, to say what they can in front of you and you can see so much under this surface talk, waiting to be said: leave the kitchen, like a good mother. Just as much as you are thrilled with the relationship between your daughters you can't help but sting a little, feel a little sore in a band right across your chest, because they don't both want to share it all with you, only you, interrupting each other, sidling against each other trying to step just one millimeter closer to you, to you, to you. Like after-school time when they were at the grade school three blocks away and came in together bubbling with stories, legs, clad in pastels, tangling, pink and blue and yellow papers falling out of their backpacks. They have things to say to only each other now, and as you move up the stairs they are already laughing, a different laugh than grade school, to be sure, but laughing; hold your fist to your heart in both joy and pain and continue up and away from them.

Prepare yourself: by Wednesday night all of the high-school friends are also home, and they pull together like magnets. It's a good thing—of course you want her to continue these friendships, despite what one mother told you about another's daughter, despite what you believe you can predict about any of their futures. They gather at your house, but it cannot contain them all, whoever they are now, and whatever it is that compels them back outside cannot be stopped. They drive around. They text each other from two cars away in the convenience star parking lot—still posing like they did in high school, making decisions of import on whose house to converge on—and leave—next. When you hear them go out, know that they will be back. When they come back, hunker deeper under your covers, revel in the fact the kids are in their rooms, your family is breathing the same air. Rest easy.

By 11:30 a.m. on Thanksgiving morning your college student has not even gotten up to go to the bathroom. You know this because you have been downstairs banging pots and pans around since 8:00 a.m. Do not make more noise then you need to, but now, at 11:20 a.m. you do not need to try to be quiet. When they were little, the day before Thanksgiving meant watching a movie and ordering pizza, which you always joked about since your fridge was barely able to shut, the counters full. You didn't let yourself look at the clock when he got in last night, but it was 2:45 a.m.

Keep cooking. You think you're angry but you're not. It's just that you want him there, at the counter, always. He will be down soon. Yes, somehow your son's voice is deeper. Somehow he did grow two or three inches in nine weeks. Your daughter's face is older in a way you can't explain. She can't already have wrinkles, can she, but yes, something has changed around her eyes. You can hug her again when she comes into the kitchen; she'll allow it if you count to three.

Later, when bottles of hard cider are being distributed don't wonder how you will be judged if you hand her one. Have one yourself. Your sister will engage her in a conversation about immigration that she would never get into with you. Your son will still drink orange juice out of the carton but he will take out the trash without being told for the first time in his life. Allow the pride and pain to battle inside you like her fear and courage, every day. You have both been in training for this since the day she was born.

Marshall Warfield

Grace

Because once I started saying thank you
to the idea of mystery and uncertainty
a kind of gratitude for everything
began knocking on my front door
and I've never lost a lover or a child
so maybe I don't know shit about this
but I still smell the blue crabs
I pulled from the Delaware Bay early
in the morning with the wave slaps
on the dinghy and rising sun skipping
off bay grass just under windswept water
and smell the feast that afternoon
all fire and steam and family smiles
and for a single moment where I deserved
no goodness, it still came and enveloped me
a feeling I wouldn't sense again until
years later when the cold cabin woke me
in the dark morning to light the fire
make the coffee all in a simple slowness
a wool blanket bound at my chest
by my cold fist—all that was grace
but so was the dean of my college
telling me to take a year off but return
when he didn't need to assist me
at all, or the tow from the stranger
that released my car from the icy ditch
with a quick *Cops. Get goin. We're good*
or the girl with a long-distance crush
who showed up in my dorm room just
to fool around with me for a weekend
and now grace is just taking a breath
or my heart skip when someone says
You don't matter so I thank them
sincerely, for being real and reminding me
of my bones and that I can just be
opening the door almost every time
because suddenly I have an old friend
who just holds me close unexpectedly
and my body hums because things happen
and nothing I planned made that happen

it just did—a long thank you, praise
to all that which arrives unexpectedly
unarranged for, but is good just in its isness

Marshall Warfield

Just Drift

Under the canopy of trees
the Mullica River runs cold
even into the shallows where
it gleams like a whiskey
and the armored reptiles
sun themselves on logs
before dripping back into
the water when I pass
at midday in my boat
distant enough from roads
to hear only my paddles
in the water, the song
of a small bird or a dragonfly
at rest on the bow and God
it's quiet. Wonderfully.
I see silence open at the front
of my boat and spread out
to the galaxy to welcome
everything like the bend
where cedar drapes itself
across my sore shoulders
asking me to rest at the bank
where a cluster of wild violets
greets me, these tiny things
five snowflake petals erupt
from a tiny purple fire
to remind me of lavender
honey, mint, the glass water
starboard, the dark mirror
with the trees and heavens
above me, somewhere else.

Scott Warnock

Driving Lesson

In August, the *Inquirer* ran a front-page story titled "A tearful 'How could a father allow this?'" A man gave his 15-year-old daughter the keys to his SUV. She picked up some friends, lost control of the car, and three of the friends were killed. Families were destroyed and people's lives were ruined. A mother of one of the dead children said to the man, "Your decision to be the 'cool dad' devastated our community."

It's a terrible story for everyone, and I don't want to pile on in any way. I froze when I started reading it, because it made me think of a thing I did once.

Not long ago, I gave in to the incessant nagging of my teenage daughter about practicing driving. I adopted a laid back, "it'll be fine" attitude: Aw, let's go! But I didn't take her to a deserted parking lot like any sensible person. Instead, I backed into the "lane" behind our house and put the car in neutral. She took over. This lane is a narrow, one-way alley that runs between the backyards of the homes in my neighborhood. Some garages are within two feet of the asphalt.

My wife and two neighbors saw this occurring and protested vigorously. I rebuffed them, cool guy that I am.

Fortunately, the driving lesson was brief: It lasted about three seconds and about 22 feet. Upon taking her foot off the brake, my daughter immediately panicked, turned the car hard to the right, and cruised into a free-standing basketball hoop, shoving it into our open, two-car garage. The car careened off the hoop's pole and proceeded partially into the open garage before colliding with the inside of the thick garage door jamb. The jamb was pushed about eight inches, and I saw the whole garage wall shift. Then the car paused. I slammed it into park. I thought the whole garage might collapse onto the car.

In response I suppose to my wide-eyed look, my daughter grabbed her phone (of course!), opened the car door, and said with strange calm, "I'm outta here." I jumped into the driver's seat and quickly backed the car out. I got out and surveyed the damage. While we had moved the jamb, the garage was in no danger of collapsing. I looked at the car and saw the bumper was only slightly dented.

My daughter had scampered into the front yard. By coincidence, a friend of hers was driving by. She waved the friend down and they pulled off down the street.

I did what any reasonable, cool guy would do: I walked over to a plastic lawn chair, picked it up, and smashed it against the ground into a million pieces. I followed by bellowing a few stress-release curses.

I looked up and down the empty lane. Then I laid down on the ground in front of the garage and started to cry.

Maybe that part wasn't cool. But I cried because I let my daughter down. I cried because I have a key job, and that is to put my kids in situations in which they'll succeed, and I had failed.

Every day kids run across that lane. Little kids. If she had hit a little kid... If she had accelerated into a building or car... If she had hurt someone, or herself... She wasn't ready to drive in our little, claustrophobic lane.

My phone rang. I wandered over and answered it, and it was my daughter. I told her to come home. She was reluctant: "I heard the cursing!" I said that the cursing and emotion were not directed at her. She was not the one at fault.

The damage was minimal. The car was fine. With the neighborhood crew and a come-a-long, we cranked the garage wall back into place. I took the metal garage door track into the basement, and using a vise, wrenched it back into shape. The door was fine.

Since then, I have told the story in a more or less lighthearted way—the tale of our failed driving lesson. I do that kind of thing, though, taking the rough story, smoothing it out, chuckling about it.

But often when I drive down our lane, I get a sick feeling, especially when I reach the end, where it's overgrown and hard to see onto Fourth Street. I hope that feeling never goes away, because I want to remember the possible cost of idiocy.

The day after our driving lesson, I headed off to work. I reached the end of the lane. A woman with a baby stroller stepped right in front of me.

Contributors

Safa Aman is a computer science student at Drexel. She is an active member of Drexel's Women in Computing Society and also enjoys volunteering in the local community. Her writing interests range from scientific writing to creative young adult pieces. In the future she hopes to continue writing in a scholarly capacity.

Raul Cooke Brossy is a game design major. He has struggled with learning disabilities as a student. He is interested in researching how video games can aid students with learning disabilities.

John Buccieri is a first year computer engineering major. He hopes to receive his M.S. and potentially conduct research on App Design and development. Writing has always been his favorite hobby, and in his free time, he manages his website.

andré m. carrington, Ph.D., is Assistant Professor of African American literature at Drexel University. His first book, *Speculative Blackness: The Future of Race in Science Fiction* (Minnesota, 2016), interrogates the cultural politics of race in the fantastic genres through fanzines, comics, television, and other speculative fiction texts. His writing has also appeared in *Present Tense: A Journal of Rhetoric in Society, African & Black Diaspora, and Callaloo*, as well as the books *A Companion to the Harlem Renaissance, The Blacker the Ink: Constructions of Blackness in Comics & Sequential Art*, and *Black Gay Genius: Answering Joseph Beam's Call*. In 2015, he co-organized the first Queers & Comics international conference in New York.

Julia Casciato is a senior English major with minors in marketing and writing, as well as a certificate in creative writing and publishing. Most days she wishes she could be watching the Phillies at Citizens Bank Park, and other days she wishes she was on a plane traveling someplace new. A former editor-in-chief of *The Triangle*, the Drexel student newspaper, she's written dozens of journalism pieces, but this is her first time publishing fiction.

Valerie Fox's books include *The Rorschach Factory* and *The Glass Book*. Recently she published *Poems for the Writing: Prompts for Poets*, co-authored with Lynn Levin. She's published writing in *Hanging Loose, Ping Pong, Qarrtsiluni, Thrush, Mead, Sentence, West Branch, Apiary*, and other journals. She teaches at Drexel University.

Laurel Gabel is from Rochester, New York and studies Film and Video at Drexel. She enjoys traveling, eating, hanging out with friends, and watching movies when she is not busy creating films of her own. She also enjoys photography as a side hobby, which is why she decided to enter the contest to shoot the cover of this book.

Chloe Hriso is majoring in International Area Studies with a concentration in global health, science and sustainability and a minor in public health. Her interests lie in how certain sociopolitical forces manifest themselves in the health and well-being of individuals, families and their communities. She has always enjoyed writing as a mode of communicating and translating information to a larger audience.

Shalom lkhena is a writer originally from Southern Nigeria but born and raised in Northern Nigeria. She is currently studying Economics at Drexel University. She enjoys exploring the world through the minds and eyes of others. She documents the inspiration drawn from these explorations on her blog: www.mensuwritings.blogspot.com

Henry Israeli's poetry collections include *New Messiahs* (Four Way Books, 2002), *Praying to the Black Cat* (Del Sol, 2010), and *god's breath hovering across the waters*, (Four Way Books, 2016). He is Assistant Teaching Professor of English and Associate Director of the Certificate in Writing & Publishing Program at Drexel University.

Kirsten Kaschock is a poet, a novelist, a critic, and an editor who works in several genres but whose work consistently addresses intersections between language and body. Her most recent book of poetry, *The Dottery*, won the Donald Hall Poetry Prize from the Association of Writers and Writing Programs (AWP). She is currently the editor-in-chief of thINKing dance, an online journal produced by a consortium of dance writers in the Philadelphia Area. Her most recent book *Confessional Science Fiction: A Primer* is forthcoming from Subito Press.

Sean Kirker is a freshman Health Sciences major on the pre-Physician Assistant track from Wilmington, Delaware. In his free time he enjoys listening to Whitney Houston records, going for long walks on the beach, watching *Napoleon Dynamite*, and getting lost while running along the Schuylkill River Trail. This is his first publication.

Scott Knowles' work focuses on risk and disaster, with particular interests in modern cities, technology, and public policy. His most recent book is *The Disaster Experts: Mastering Risk in Modern America* (UPenn Press, 2011), and he is series co-editor of "Critical Studies in Risk and Disaster" (UPenn Press, 2014). Presently, in additional to being Interim Department Head of the Drexel University History Department, he is also a faculty research fellow of the Disaster Research Center at the University of Delaware.

Miriam N. Kotzin teaches creative writing and literature at Drexel University. She is the author of four collections of poetry, most recently, *The Body's Bride* (David Robert Books 2013), a novel, *The Real Deal* (Brick House Press 2012), and a collection of flash fiction, *Just Desserts* (Star Cloud Press 2010). A fifth volume, *Debris Field*, is scheduled for publication by David Robert Books in January 2017. Her poetry appears in *Shenandoah, Boulevard, The Tower Journal, Mezzo Cammin*, and *Valparaiso Poetry Review*, among others. She is founding editor of *Per Contra*, an international journal of the arts, literature and ideas, and a contributing editor of *Boulevard*.

Yih-Chia Lam is a freshman studying Biological Sciences and Criminology and Justice Studies and plans on obtaining a certificate in creative writing while at Drexel University. Yih-Chia is primarily interested in writing poetry. She would like to give a special thanks to Professor Marshall Warfield for his support.

Codi Leager is studying Nursing, lives in Delaware, and enjoys listening to music in her free time.

Lynn Levin, a poet, writer, and translator, is Adjunct Associate Professor of English at Drexel. She is the recipient of twelve Pushcart Prize nominations for poetry. Her most recent book is *Birds on the Kiswar Tree* (2Leaf Press, 2014), a translation from the Spanish of a collection of poems by the Peruvian Andean poet Odi Gonzales. Her poetry collection *Miss Plastique* (Ragged Sky Press, 2013) was named a finalist in poetry in the 2014 Next Generation Indie Book Awards, and *Poems for the Writing: Prompts for Poets* (Texture Press), the craft-of-poetry textbook she co-authored with Valerie Fox, was a finalist in education/academic books in the 2014 Next Generation Indie Book Awards. Lynn Levin's poems, stories, essays, and translations have appeared in *Ploughshare Boulevard, The Hopkins Review, Michigan Quarterly Review, Green Hills Literary Lantern, Per Contra, Painted Bride Quarterly, Verse Daily*, Garrison Keillor has read her work on his radio show *The Writer's Almanac*. Her website is www.lynnlevinpoet.com.

Caitlin McLaughlin is a sophomore English major. She enjoys reading, writing, and participating in feminist discourse. Caitlin spends a majority of her time advocating for LGBT, women's, and mental health issues. She has written web features for *5027mac* and *Loco Mag*.

Lucas McLean is a Screenwriting and Playwriting major who has been writing ever since he learned how. In addition, he enjoys acting, watching movies, and overanalyzing episodes of *Breaking Bad*.

Shawn Mengel is a first-year chemical engineering student at Drexel University. He is an active member of the Pennoni Honors College and the Drexel chapter of AIChE. Shawn plans to participate in the Drexel BS/MS program with a possible focus in materials science and its role in improving renewable energy technologies.

Haley McMenamin co-wrote her piece when she was a first-year student at Drexel.

Harriet Levin Millan is the author of two books of poetry, *The Christmas Show* (Beacon Press), which won the Barnard New Women Poets Prize and the Alice Fay di Castagnola Award from the Poetry Society of America, and *Girl in Cap and Gown* (Mammoth Books), a 2010 National Poetry Series finalist. Her poems and stories appear in *Iowa Review, Kenyon Review, Antioch Review, Smart Set, Ploughshares, Prairie Schooner*–where she is currently blogging on a Drexel University study trip to Haiti–and other journals. She traveled to Kenya and South Sudan on a Summer Literary Seminars and Drexel University International Travel Grant to research "Yalla!" She holds an MFA from the University of Iowa Writers Workshop and is director of the Certificate Program in Writing and Publishing and teaches first-year writing and creative writing in the Department of English and Philosophy.

Ria Mulherkar is a Drexel University student with a major in Biological Sciences. She is an aspiring physician with many hobbies, including music, dancing, cooking, and shopping. Her love for the written word is almost as old as she is, and she hopes to enjoy books and cultivate her writing as long as language remains in fashion.

Gwen Ottinger is an Associate Professor in the Department of Politics and the Center for Science, Technology, and Society. She holds an undergraduate degree in Aerospace Engineering from Georgia Tech and a Ph.D. in Energy and Resources from University of California, Berkeley. She is author of *Refining Expertise: How Responsible Engineers Subvert Grassroots Challenges*, which won the 2015 Rachel Carson Prize from the Society for Social Studies of Science, and is recipient of a CAREER award from the National Science Foundation for her project, "Environmental Justice and the Ethics of Science and Technology."

Don Riggs's first book report was his oral summary of Dr. Seuss's *The Cat in the Hat Comes Back* in the first grade, probably 1959. Since then, he has refined his book report style, writing reviews of both fiction and scholarship for the *Journal of Modern Literature*, the *Journal of the Fantastic in the Arts*, *Extrapolation, Per Contra*, and the online review *magazinefuturefire.net*.

Gail D. Rosen is an Associate Teaching Professor at Drexel University in the Department of English and Philosophy. She teaches in the First-Year Writing Program and various literature classes including Law and Literature and Mythology and the Movies.

Faith Roser is graduating from Drexel with a B. S. in Biological Sciences, a minor in English, and a certificate in medical humanities. She looks forward to attending veterinary school at The University of Pennsylvania.

Denica-Lynyl Santos is currently working towards getting a Bachelors in biology. She owes most of her writing experiences to being in the international baccalaureate program in high school. She enjoys writing in her free time, but no matter what, the first sentence is always the hardest to write.

Christian N. Schill is a biological science major and minors in psychology. His hobbies include writing, reading and watching films.

Chloé Segui majors in biological sciences in hopes of becoming a successful dentist. Some of her interests include marvel movies, fashion, running, and going on adventures with friends. All of her writing experiences stem from school activities and a lab that she had the honor to work in over the course of the summer before senior year of high school. The lab that she interned at published the research that she worked on.

Bhavya Sharma is an English major at Drexel who enjoys reading, running and painting, sometimes all at the same time.

Carly Smith is a Biological Sciences major. She plans on conducting laboratory medical research as her future career. She enjoys reading, swimming, biking and spending time outside. She also has recently become interested in aquaponic planting systems, and their effect on global food production.

Alan Soble has been teaching Philosophy at Drexel since Spring 2007. This piece, one of his few pomes (his preferred spelling), is his second contribution to *The 33rd*.

Russell H. Souders III, joined the Army after he graduated from Springfield Township High School in 2010 and served as a medic for 5 years. Currently, he is a nursing major looking to become a Nurse Practitioner.

Charles B. Strozier is a history professor at John Jay College, CUNY, and a practicing psychoanalyst. He has written or edited 13 books, including "Your Friend Forever, A. Lincoln."

José Tapia studied medicine in Spain and public health and economics in the United States. He is presently an Associate Professor in the Department of Politics, CoAS, Drexel University.

Kiera Townsend is studying Architecture and is passionate about the power of design to effect social change. She has been journaling for years and must thank all of her wonderful teachers, including not only Mr. Sidoli but also Dr. Peckham, who encouraged her to keep writing at Drexel.

Gina Vitale is a sophomore Chemistry major. Her hobbies include reading, writing creatively, writing for the school newspaper, sleeping and watching *The X-Files*.

Kathleen Volk Miller is the Director of the Graduate Program in Publishing and the Drexel Publishing Group. She has written for *Salon*, *NYTimes*, *Family Circle*, *Philadelphia Magazine* and *O, the Oprah magazine*. She is co-editor of the anthology, *Humor: A Reader for Writers* (Oxford University Press, 2014). She has also published in literary magazines, such as *Drunken Boat*, *Opium*, and other venues. She is co-editor of *The Painted Bride Quarterly* and consults on literary magazine start up, working with college students, and getting published in literary magazines.

Sharan Walia is in her 3rd year at Drexel University. In her 21 years of life, she has lived in 3 countries, 5 cities, and speaks 6 languages. Sharan wrote the entirety of "Entre les Lilas (Between the Lilacs)" on a legal pad, it is the first fiction piece she has ever written. Sharan spends her lack of free time ogling Picasso's works, reading classic British literature, and listening to Billy Joel.

Marshall Warfield is a writer who enjoys working collaboratively, including projects with writer Blythe Davenport, sculptor Angela Colasanti, and filmmaker David Kessler. Look for his poems in *Marathon*, *Clover*, *Poems for the Writing: Prompts for Poets*, and an upcoming film *The Pines* (dir. David Kessler) set for release in late 2016. He teaches in Philadelphia.

Scott Warnock is the Director of the University Writing Program. He writes the bi-weekly blog "Virtual Children" for the Website *When Falls the Coliseum*.

Julian Whitehouse is a student at Drexel entering his Sophomore year.